# CHINA'S
# ECONOMIC
# SUPERTRENDS

ISBN 978-0-9879847-1-5

# CHINA'S ECONOMIC SUPERTRENDS

## HOW CHINA IS CHANGING FROM THE INSIDE OUT
## TO BECOME THE WORLD'S NEXT ECONOMIC SUPERPOWER

JASON INCH

2012

*For my mother.*

# Contents

# Table of Figures

# ACKNOWLEDGMENTS

I would like to gratefully acknowledge the kind support of Dr. James Yuann, the co-author of *Supertrends of Future China,* originally published in 2008. The material you are about to read was based on that work, but has been significantly rewritten and updated to reflect the present economic environment.

I thank Dr. Yuann for his permission to reuse portions of the original manuscript, and for the concept of the China Supertrends, which he and I developed together in 2007. I would encourage readers to review the original work to further understand how China has been rapidly changing even in the brief number of years since *Supertrends of Future China* was published.

I would also like to thank the many individuals who have contributed to this work, including my editor, Mike Revzin, and the team at InChina Publishing led by Andrea Liu. A number of colleagues have kindly reviewed this manuscript, and I thank them for their patience, support and ideas.

# PREFACE

ugust 8, 2008, marked the start of the Beijing Olympics and China's bold and confident appearance on the international stage. At the time, China seemed exuberant: the Hong Kong, Shenzhen and Shanghai stock markets were pushing toward historic highs, the economy had hit 14.2 percent GDP growth in 2007—somewhat overheated but running smoothly under cooling measures—and the run-up to the Olympics had proceeded as planned—with billions of dollars spent on the venues and billions more spent on upgrading Beijing's transportation network, environment and infrastructure.

Highlighted by architectural marvels such as the Olympic Stadium—colloquially called the Bird's Nest—or the iconic parallelogram-shaped monolithic CCTV headquarters building, or Beijing's Capital International Airport's massive Terminal 3: all these constructions seemed to say China was, for a developing country, doing the unexpected. That was in August 2008.

By October 2008, and all the way to 2012, the world's economy was in a state of uncertainty. There was the possibility of a double-dip recession in the United States and a fragmenting of the European Union's political solidarity and monetary union. Where investors had fled the dollar and picked up the euro, the global economy again saw a resurgence of the dollar and United States bonds as the world's only remaining perceived safe havens. Stock markets globally showed extremes of fight or flight volatility. If that were not enough, social and political instability in Nigeria, Libya, Iran and other African and Middle Eastern countries resulting from the Arab Spring movements brought a new level of uncertainty to global markets such as oil prices remained high and seemed ready to go higher. In 2012, it is no exaggeration to say the global economy is teetering on a precipice, threatening to fall and end decades of integration and affluence.

In China specifically, the government cautioned 2012 would be a very difficult year for exporters; Shanghai's roller coaster stock market had already lost more than half its value from historical highs set in 2008 and declined more than 20 percent in 2011 alone—making tens of millions of investors who rely on the market for income and their retirement—unhappy; housing prices—a pillar of China's economy and, therefore by extension the world's—are starting to fall; and inflation is averaging about 5 percent since the start of 2011.

The architectural wonders, built just a few years ago, are even showing signs of distress, perhaps symbolic of the Chinese economy as a whole. China's Bird's Nest is home to birds but bereft of people; the CCTV headquarters is all but abandoned following a fireworks accident that gutted one of its sibling towers; and, while the Beijing Capital Airport is one of the busiest in the world, parts of its modern roof superstructure have been known to fly off in high winds—perhaps imitating the nearby airplanes.

Despite all this, China's economy still grew at a greater than 9 percent rate in 2011 and is forecast for at least 8 percent growth in 2012. China has been growing rapidly for the last 30 years, and it is still growing, but the wear and tear is taking its toll.

THE ROARING 2000S?

In some ways, China's confidence as a nation reached its pinnacle in the first decade of this century. It hosted global political meetings, including the APEC Summit in 2001. China established and hosts the annual Boao Forum (China's answer to the Davos World Economic Forum). It held major sports events such as the FIFA Women's World Cup in 2007, the 2008 Beijing Olympics and the 2010 Guangzhou Asian Games. It even hosted the World Expo, a true mega-event, in Shanghai in 2010: more than 70 million people attended the six-month exposition of tourism and industry. The optimism of the Chinese people, both domestic and overseas, is tempered by the fervor with which they express national pride and resilience in the face of any setbacks.

This national confidence and resilience were evident during the decade-long process of China's re-emergence onto the world stage from 2000 to 2010. This period was characterized by both the major accomplishments above and numerous national challenges. The process was started by China's quick recovery following the Asian financial crisis of 1997, continued with its entry into the World Trade Organization in 2001 and capped by the 2008 Beijing Olympic Games. The same period was rocked by social instability in Tibet and Xinjiang, a massive earthquake in Sichuan that killed more than 70,000 people and caused tens of billions of dollars in damage, the SARS respiratory disease epidemic and the 2008 global financial crisis that brought the world to the brink of economic collapse. Throughout, China was, as a nation, undeterred. In the language of China's political elite, its people and government were unwavering in their conviction that this was China's decade and would be, presumably, China's century as well.

CHINA'S OLYMPIC DECADE

In *Supertrends of Future China,* Dr. Yuann and I coined the term *China's Olympic Decade,* to refer to the period between 2008 and 2018. *China's Olympic Decade* started on August 8, 2008 at 8 p.m., to be exact, with the opening ceremony of the Beijing Olympics, when a thousand synchronized drummers ran, shouted and pounded their drums in order to, paraphrasing Napoleon, *shake the world.*[1]

If you are observant and aware of Chinese numerology, you will undoubtedly notice that the Opening Ceremony time involved a lot of 8's: 8/8/2008 8 p.m. (and, depending on where you started the clock of the opening ceremonies, 8 minutes and 8 seconds also came into the realm of significance). Chinese consider the number 8 to be lucky because it shares a similar sound to *"fa"*—"getting rich"—so the date represented a new and auspicious point for China. For the purposes of our original book, the date was to be the start of China's *Olympic Decade,* 10 more years of growth and expansion.

Then, just about a month later, Lehman Brothers made global headlines with its collapse and, with it, the fear grew that the global financial system, China and all, would come crashing down. Droll readers might be tempted to say, *Oops, not such a lucky start after all.*

In fact, the *Olympic Decade* phenomenon was, and remains, the overriding story that is shaping our world in the 2010s. Dr. Yuann's and my predictions for China's rise are, rather than being dashed, happening even faster than we had imagined.

Almost unbelievably China was the only major economy in the world to grow throughout the ensuing crisis and, to the great relief of many executives today, continues to grow even while many Western economies are still struggling to avoid a double-dip recession. For many multinational companies, China is like a beacon on a stormy night. Companies the world over have sought China's apparently recession-proof harbor as a port from which to continue growing. These companies are injecting new capital and effort into their China operations.

For the Chinese government, the effects of the global financial crisis turned out to be the stimulus needed to kick the domestic economy into a new and more sophisticated growth model, as well as a proof that China's national belief in *socialism with Chinese characteristics* was not misplaced. Nobody knows if members of China's Politburo, sitting in their Beijing compound known as *Zhongnanhai,* are enjoying a bit of amusement at the capitalist West's expense, but they could be forgiven for feeling a sense of serendipity at the timing of the East's rise and the West's fall.

Via the sheer spectacle of the Olympics themselves and China's record 51 gold medal haul,[2] the event brought a lot of attention to the host country and was also a public relations coup that was worth every billion spent. The Olympics and the related infrastructure development and environmental cleanup, together, were a face-lift, to improve the country's image to the outside world. China had been longing for this opportunity, for "a thousand years," according to a Chinese saying, to show how far a formerly poor and backward *sick man of Asia* has come to join the ranks of modern prosperous countries. A key public relations message of the Olympics and the *Olympic Decade* is, therefore, *"This is a new China,"* or, perhaps like the sleeping giant Napoleon once imagined, *"We have awakened."*

## 30 GLORIOUS YEARS

The year 2008 fit nicely as a starting point of the *Olympic Decade* as well as an end point, capping 30 years of reform and opening up orchestrated by Deng Xiaoping, starting in 1978. The 30 years of change between 1978 and 2008 were as wrenching as they were wondrous.

Inside China, day after day, year in year out, new regulations have been quickly promulgated with sometimes little warning to the unsuspecting public, creating an environment of disruptive change that has quickly remade China from its post-1949 Communist past. The Deng reforms were characterized by the re-emergence of private enterprise from the shroud of central planning, an openness to trade and new investment from a formerly closed economy, a restructuring of massive state-owned enterprises with hundreds of thousands of employees that had formerly provided *iron rice bowls*—lifetime employment—to their staff, and real estate re-privatization in a land where private property was prohibited and, in the chaos of the Cultural Revolution, even being just an ancestor of a landowner could get you killed.

In the 1990s and the first decade of the 21st century, after Deng receded from power in 1992, reform continued under Jiang Zemin and Hu Jintao. The banking and financial systems were reformed, environmental improvements were made and, at long last and against all odds, better labor regulations were enacted and wages started to be increased, narrowing the wealth gap. China has become the world's second largest economy under their guidance.

The 30 glorious years increased peoples' welfare, but at the same time often caused dramatic social change. Some reforms, especially those concerning social welfare for the country of 1.3 billion people, were undertaken within time spans measured in years or even months. For a Western economy, it might take decades, if not be outright impossible, to achieve just one major change. China, on the other hand, changes continuously. It is this momentum that is carrying China forward in the *Olympic Decade*, setting the stage for new trends that may form the basis for business decisions, career opportunities or retrenchments, and social movements that will change the way the world perceives, and is impacted by, China.

## WHAT IS A SUPERTREND?

This book and the two volumes that follow—*China's Demographic Supertrends* and *China's Political Supertrends*—are about trends, and especially about how to understand and benefit from them. In fact, they are more than just trends, so Dr. Yuann and I refer to them as *supertrends*. The impact of these *supertrends* would supersede other countries' trends and come to define Chinese, or even global, forces. In short, they are the strongest forces for change that the world will see this century, if not ever, as China rises to take its place as the pre-eminent economic superpower.

Some academics can see the trends, perhaps even predict them, but may lack the motivation or resources to act on them. Many businesspeople may have the resources and intent to act, but are often in the unfortunate position of simply following the trends rather than surfing them like a wave. Both, in the end, miss the true power of the trends in one way or another. The Chinese language, on the other hand, has recognized the complexity and power of trends for millennia.

The Chinese character on the inside cover of this book—势— pronounced *shi* like the sound in *shirt*—is used in a number of Chinese words to mean trend. By itself it can be taken to mean a tendency or a force, but it is most commonly seen in modern usage paired with other Chinese characters. For example, *qushi*— 趋势—is a common translation for "trend." The concept of *shi* therefore has a special significance to this book and it is useful to understand how this pictographic representation for this one character can be understood by the two component characters from which it is made.

执

力

On the top half is the pictographic character for *catch, grasp,* or *execute (a plan)* (执) and the bottom half is the character to represent *strength* (力). This could be read to mean cultivating strength, or perhaps strength will master a trend, or executing with force. In *On China,* Henry Kissinger also observes that *shi* is used in Sun Tzu's *Art of War*[3] where its ancient meaning can refer to potential energy, as in "the strategist mastering *shi* is akin to water flowing downhill, automatically finding the swiftest and easiest course. A successful commander waits before charging headlong into battle."[4]

Why should a reader bother to learn about and understand these *supertrends?* An ancient Chinese saying neatly classifies how people react to, and the benefit they derive from, the opportunities that trends represent:

---

不知不觉 *bu zhi bu jue*
后知后觉 *hou zhi hou jue*
先知先觉 *xian zhi xian jue*

---

Read here from left to right, top to bottom, it may be roughly translated to mean, "If you are not aware, you will have no reaction; late awareness, delayed reaction; early awareness, advance reaction." In other words, if you know first, you act first.

The time to learn the trends, understand them, and react with the strength and force of *shi* is now.

## BILLION-DOLLAR OPPORTUNITIES

The trends that shape China's immediate future in 2012, and overall its Olympic Decade from 2008 to 2018, are so large that they can be called *supertrends,* and they will result in many *billion-dollar opportunities,* part of the original sub-title for *Supertrends of Future China.*

China is a country to which the word *billion* is often attached, usually in its relation to population. To put that idea in terms of opportunity, we can paraphrase a comment from one of China's modern leaders, Premier Wen Jiabao: any trend multiplied by 1.3 billion people is bound to have a deep and profound impact on business and society, not only in China but also around the world.[5] *Billion* is the magnitude of dollars the winners stand to gain by being among the first to recognize and operate in the industries that those *supertrends* promote.

The character next to the page numbers—元—is written in *pinyin* alphabetic text and pronounced *yuan.* It is one of the units of Chinese money. The Chinese currency, the *renminbi* (RMB), is also called the *yuan* or Chinese Yuan (CNY) in international markets.[6] This symbol, therefore, represents the growing economy of China, as well as the wealth and success that you can hope to achieve by understanding the *supertrends* and taking action on them to improve your life and business.

# WHO IS THIS BOOK FOR?

This book, *China's Economic Supertrends*, has been written for readers who want to understand China's economy and the opportunities it presents.

Whether you are an investor looking for a growth stock, a corporate executive seeking ideas for a strategic plan, an entrepreneur seeking a business idea, or a person inside or outside China looking for a new career path, by following some of the ideas in this book, or by being inspired by them to find your own, you are opening your own door to future success and wealth via China's *supertrends*.

FOR INVESTORS

China's stock markets are, at present, closed to many types of foreign portfolio investment. There are, however, programs allowing brokerages outside China to run investment funds with a quota of mainland shares. There are also limited options for foreign residents in China to purchase investment products. Yet China is fearful of too much *hot money*—unofficial speculative foreign exchange—entering China, seeking higher returns. Other than the *Qualified Foreign Institutional Investor* funds, another choice for non-Chinese investors involves foreign-listed Chinese companies. Many Chinese stocks are listed in Hong Kong, New York and other markets around the world.

Which of the many funds or companies should investors pick, and how should they avoid the bad apples? American short-sellers, including Carson Block (who co-wrote *Doing Business in China for Dummies*) have highlighted problems with many Chinese companies listed abroad.

The *supertrends* show one investment strategy: by aligning investment decisions with China's overall national goals, in effect investing in the wisdom of the Chinese government, investors may expect stability and growth from such areas that are deemed critical to Chinese interests. China's central government, unlike practically any other government in the world, utilizes fiscal, monetary, and *direct control* of its state-owned banks and large companies to enact national policy.

Most of these state-owned enterprises—many of them in the top 10 in their industries globally and increasingly becoming global multinational companies themselves—are available on Western exchanges, as are many private companies in sectors that will benefit from China's guidance. This book will help investors to identify which Chinese companies stand to grow faster, bigger and more successfully in the *Olympic Decade.*

Deng was the leader responsible for China's opening the door to market economy reforms in 1978 after decades under the Communist doctrines of Mao Zedong. Deng once said, "...To get rich is glorious." This book aims to make investors aware of on-the-ground knowledge from China's burgeoning economy that will help them become rich and glorious.


FOR EXECUTIVES

With the effects of the global financial crisis lingering in many developed economies, China has been seen by multinational company executives as being more essential than ever. Companies that previously had been waiting on the sidelines are making first forays into the market, and those companies that were already in China pre-global financial crisis as manufacturers and sourcing bases, now are seeing China as a consumer market and reorienting their strategies. The question on many executives' minds is, *what will China do next?* The answer is again, the *supertrends.*

China of 2012 is not the China of the immediate post-1978 reform and opening up. It is, in effect, post-modern, developing in new ways that are no longer defined by Western interests. The post-modern development is defined by China's needs. For example, research, innovation and high-value-added industries, services and environmentally clean energy generation. Knowing what China wants is the most important factor in business decision-making in China. This book shows what industries and business models China wants most. The companies that give China these things are going to make billions, while others that insist on running business-as-usual will eventually be superseded by Chinese competitors or kicked out of the market entirely.

## FOR SPECIALISTS

Everyone from engineers to electricians to environmentalists will be affected by China's supply and demand economic forces. Many career choices—inside or outside China—that do not take this into account risk being downsized, right-sized, restructured or redundant before the Olympic Decade is out. How can individuals decide what education to pursue, what job to take, or where to develop their careers? Again, China's *supertrends* provide one answer.

A key criterion for any successful career development today is an internship, a posting, or other business experience in China. More than ever before, people are studying Mandarin, coming to China for job opportunities and looking for ways to integrate China into their career plans. Understanding China's economic development goals is important to making better decisions.

## FOR ENTREPRENEURS

China has, nationally, more than 91 million companies. Many of these are small businesses that would be called entrepreneur-ships and their owners called entrepreneurs in Western countries. Doing business has almost become a national pastime for Chinese, who run side-businesses on *Taobao*—-China's answer to eBay—and constantly seek to achieve wealth and status in China's hyper-competitive market. Even non-Chinese entrepreneurs who do not want to compete in China may still be competing against small Chinese companies going global via the Internet, or require products and services from Chinese suppliers. For those entrepreneurs who do want a Chinese market opportunity, a strategy can be built upon the *supertrends* to give Chinese businesses and consumers what they want.

## FOR EVERYONE ELSE

China is undoubtedly on the minds of people around the world. As China's economy grows, surpassing the United Kingdom, France, Germany and Japan to become the world's number two (and soon to be number one) market, so does interest in what China and its people are doing. Media reports have increased dramatically, from 20 years ago when China was perhaps a controversy, to five years ago when it increasingly became a curiosity, to today where China coverage is an imperative in any international media organization. Everyone wants to know more about China, but the complex nature of its economics, demographics and politics stymies easy understanding. This book, *China's Economic Supertrends*, seeks to unveil China's national strategies and explain what they mean for Western economies, investors, businesses, and individuals.

## WHAT THIS BOOK IS AND IS NOT

This book is not a highly statistical or analytical discussion of Chinese economics, of which there are many useful works from academia. Neither is this book about fearing China's growth, in the tone of the classic *Japan Inc.* from the 1980s, or the question of the various developed Western countries versus China as competitors, as presented in Peter Navarro's and Greg Autry's *Death By China: Confronting the Dragon - A Global Call to Action*. It is not a skeptical examination of the Chinese economic development path as is Minxin Pei's *China's Trapped Transition*, nor a panda-hugging treatise extolling the virtues of the China development model.

Following China's near-miraculous recovery from the global financial crisis, a number of authors and commentators jumped on the China bandwagon, and were being overly optimistic and positive about China's prospects to rule the world. Certainly all such perspectives have a place in the debate, but it is not the purpose of this book to add fuel to any particular fire. As in 2008, this writer remains *cautiously* optimistic about China's role in the world economy and believes that, long-term, China is a positive place to invest and build both companies and careers.

This book is about China's top economic trends and how people from all levels of business and every nationality can profit from them. From multinational corporations to sellers on *Taobao*, China's *supertrends* affect all businesses big and small. They affect you in a positive way if you see them as opportunities and in a negative way if you see them as threats. China is too complex to be treated in black and white. It is, if anything, one big gray area. Thus, while this book is mainly written to reflect a positive viewpoint of China, it will not shy away from many of the arguments raised by proponents of the "China Threat" position.

The controversy over the downsides of China's rapid economic rise is characterized by several key issues, including the detrimental local and global environmental impact of China's carbon-emitting, pollution-discharging factories; the exploitation of workers, many of whom are working in the same polluting factories and suffering poor safety conditions and low wages; China's social problems including wealth distribution, aging and the slow pace of democratic reform; and in the business sector, intellectual property rights protection, protectionism in China, and predatory pricing abroad.

These issues are often presented as either an unfair competitive advantage for China or a reason its rise should be viewed with skepticism. Many of the worst-case scenarios, such as a fight over oil supplies, are often painted as inevitable outcomes in the coming clash of superpowers which only concerted international and Chinese political effort will prevent, if such a clash is even preventable at all.

Like the Malthusian arguments of 19th century Europe (which incorrectly predicted massive shortages and suffering due to lack of food and other limited resources), many of these anti-

China arguments often fail to acknowledge business and markets as potential solutions. Malthus was wrong then, he would still be wrong now: the world didn't run out of food. Instead, productivity increases supported a much larger population than Malthus ever envisioned. Therefore, this book takes a more balanced approach to the environmental, social, and political problems of China. To continue a thought from earlier in this preface, any large problem *divided by* 1.3 billion people may become a very small issue on a per capita level. Thus such paradoxes as China being one of the world's richest countries but its people still being among the poorest, or that its pollution output is the greatest in the world, yet an average Chinese citizen uses far less resources than an average Westerner. These anti-China arguments do not always hold water, and usually do not acknowledge the immense efforts that have been made thus far, such as bringing hundreds of millions out of poverty and urbanizing them with a much higher quality of life.

While negatives do exist, and will be addressed in this book section by section, examples will also show China has a significant capability for positive change at the centralized level. The central government's powers are often, unfortunately, blunt instruments. While China's central government can and does frequently establish strong national laws and reforms—in many cases stricter than the Western economies' equivalents—at the regional or local level the enforcement is not effectively carried out.

This book will refocus the debate about China's paradoxical economic development specifically on China's investment and business attractiveness, in order to appreciate the importance of the key future industries identified by the *supertrends* as *solutions* to the problems Western academics, journalists and politicians have long commented on. Business and markets, productivity improvements and consumer preferences have solved economic problems before and they will do so again in China, especially when accompanied by the determination of its government and a populace striving to improve its quality of life.

The willingness of the Chinese government and the people to improve their living standard through capitalism is powerful, and their approach practical and thus far successful.

## WHY ECONOMIC, DEMOGRAPHIC AND POLITICAL SUPERTRENDS?

*China's Economic Supertrends* is the first volume in a three-volume set to be published in 2012. The other two volumes are *China's Demographic Supertrends* and *China's Political Supertrends,* to be released in the third and fourth quarters of 2012 respectively.

In conducting presentations and consulting related to the original *Supertrends of Future China,* one of the most frequent requests we received was to go deeper into specific trends and ideas. There are two main reasons why this work is now a three-volume set, rather than a single book.

When writing the original *Supertrends of Future China* my co-author and I wanted to produce a guide to the business environment of modern China in a broad overview format with the focus on opportunities, thus its subtitle "Billion-Dollar Business Opportunities for China's Olympic Decade." One of the inherent limitations in writing such a guide was to select the content most relevant only to business readers. As such, a deeper discussion of challenges and ramifications of those opportunities had to be left out.

The second reason for writing this book in three volumes is to capture a more accurate picture of *changing* China, which is now changing especially fast and, in 2012, at a key juncture in economic, demographic, and political transformation. First, 2012 represents the first full year of the 12th Five-Year Plan (which officially began in 2011 but takes some months to pick up speed). The Five-Year Plans, as you will see, have a great influence on China's economic development. Second, in 2010, China completed its once-in-a-decade census, but data from that census only started to become available in 2011 and 2012. These data are still being absorbed, analyzed, and digested by the government, academics and businesspeople. Thus, publishing the second volume, *China's Demographic Supertrends*, in mid-2012 will bring a much fresher perspective on the challenges and opportunities and be more useful to the reader. Finally, 2012 is a significant year for China's *political supertrends* because the Chinese people and the world will see new leadership at the highest levels of the Communist Party of China. President Hu Jintao, Premier Wen Jiabao and other top leaders are set to retire or be reshuffled. The new leaders are officially announced at the National Congress in October 2012, thus making any political analysis prior to that time either outdated or premature.

This first volume, *China's Economic Supertrends*, concerns China's *new manufacturing, urbanization, sustainability* and *affluence supertrends*. All of the data in this 2012 edition have been updated to reflect the full-year 2011 statistics and, wherever possible, early 2012 monthly data. Otherwise, the most-recent data for China's economy are used.

The second volume, *China's Demographic Supertrends*, will cover the social and cultural trends concerning the Chinese people, who are reshaping China and the world by their aspirations, consumption and wealth. It will make extensive use of China's latest census, a once-every-ten-years nationwide collection of data from more than 1.3 billion people.

The final volume, *China's Political Supertrends*, will look at China's changing political landscape, both domestically and globally, as China seeks to keep a tenuous balance of managing its development internally with external imperatives from its neighbors in Asia and the world as a whole.

Only by understanding China's economic and demographic realities can one begin to comprehend China's political challenges and changes that will define what many have already called the "China Century." These volumes do not mean to prognosticate throughout the entire "China Century" or even decades into the future, but rather take 2012 to 2018—the remainder of China's

Olympic Decade—as the prelude to China's ascension into its position as the world's most important, and largest, economy.

## HOW THIS BOOK IS ORGANIZED

This book is intended to help the reader begin to understand the keys to China's rising economy. In terms of the organization and content, the introduction explains, in broad terms, China's economic challenges. The next section describes the Chinese economy's *growth engines, turbochargers* and *roadmap*. The final section covers China's four *economic supertrends*.

The three *growth engines* are China's export-driven manufacturing industry, consumption in the domestic Chinese market, and foreign direct investment (FDI).

Next are the *turbochargers*, the forces in China that push the *growth engines* above and beyond their normal importance to an economy. The *turbochargers* enhance the power of the three *growth engines* in the Olympic Decade from 2008 to 2018. While the *turbochargers* are not unknown elsewhere in the world, their simultaneous emergence in China *is* unique. They are *reverse globalization, people's determination* and *leapfrogging*. Together they will propel the Chinese economy of tomorrow to the position of number one in the world.

Finally there is China's *roadmap*, its GPS so to speak, guiding China to a sustainable development path via China's central government policy and active management of a system it calls socialism with Chinese characteristics. The *roadmap* is best exemplified by the 12th Five-Year Plan, a document that is crafted from the bottom up by tens of thousands of people, and represents the most accurate guide to China's future direction.

Together, the *growth engines,* the *turbochargers,* and the *roadmap* all logically lead to, and furthermore multiply the power of, the *economic supertrends.* The *supertrends* will greatly change the business environment and people's lives, as well as be the targets for the most successful business, investment and career strategies. China has four *economic supertrends*: *new manufactur-*

*ing, urbanization, sustainability* and *affluence*. Each *supertrends* chapter starts with a description of the situation and the challenges China is facing before moving on to discuss the changes and opportunities that are taking place in response. It is these *supertrends* that will move China's Olympic Decade economy forward and change the world.

The reader should start by reading the introduction and the first section of this book—comprised of the *growth engines, turbochargers* and *roadmap*—in order to understand the conceptual model on which the book is structured. Thereafter, the *supertrends* can be read independently of one another and in any order: readers can pick those that are most applicable to their industry, investment portfolio or personal interest.

～

Welcome to the future of China's economy.

*Jason Inch*
*Shanghai,*
*March 2012*

# ABOUT THE AUTHOR

Jason Inch holds an MBA from Canada's Richard Ivey School of Business and also attended one of China's top business schools, China Europe International Business School (CEIBS). He also holds a B.A. in Asian Studies from the University of Victoria (Canada), one of the premier programs for China studies in Canada. He speaks, reads and writes Mandarin and Japanese fluently as a result of his educational and work background.

Since arriving in China in 2003, Jason has worked for some of the world's largest multinational companies as a consultant. At the same time, he has taught courses on China's economy and cross-cultural management at Shanghai Jiaotong University and previously was an adjunct professor for Benedictine College's Shanghai campus, where he taught organizational behavior and international management.

Before coming to China, Jason worked in the United States and Japan. This is his second book.

# CHINA'S
# ECONOMIC
# SUPERTRENDS

# INTRODUCTION

# CHINA, FROM SICK MAN TO SUPERMAN

China has always been thought of as part of the mysterious Orient. When Henry Kissinger arrived in China in 1971 and sat down with Premier Zhou Enlai, for a secret meeting between the People's Republic of China and the United States to lay the groundwork for the first U.S. state visit to China, Kissinger remarked that he had come to a "mysterious land." Premier Zhou was said to have responded that, "When you have become familiar with it, it will not be so mysterious as before."[1] In other words, China might seem mysterious to Western people, but it was hardly mysterious if you took the time to learn something about it. Somewhat exaggerated, this story still gets to the heart of the matter in present day: despite China having been open to the world for more than 30 years, many in the West are still often unsure of or suspicious of what is behind the China curtain.

There are many ideas, beliefs, and stories about China—a country which, to those outside it, may seem mysterious and difficult to understand. To the Chinese themselves, and to Western people who live and do business in China every day, there is no ancient Chinese secret, though there are many things one can learn from China's past. China, among all the civilizations of the world past and present, has the greatest historical memory, yet much of what Western people know of China is limited to *Kung Fu Pandas* and Mao Zedong's *Little Red Books*. Of course, the objective herein is to understand how China went from being the Celestial Kingdom to a sleeping giant, then from a sick man to a superman. The trends and opportunities of today are shaped by the past events, positive and negative, that continuously transformed China.

Before discussing how China's new economy is changing the world order, it is important to understand what has allowed China to rise from being a "sick man of Asia"[2] to being the world's second-largest economy. It is also important to understand what might be keeping China at this penultimate position, forevermore unable to lay claim to the coveted top GDP ranking. The reason for both its rise and its presumed trapped transition—the idea it will never be able to go beyond number two in the world because it will not bridge the wealth divide—is that China, while being one of the largest countries geographically and in terms of population, also has some of the world's largest problems to be solved. To be sure, many of these problems are ones that other countries might even welcome if they could bring the amount of wealth and prosperity that modern China has achieved in the 30-plus years since Deng Xiaoping began the policy of reform and opening up. Other problems would not be desirable under any circumstances, yet are China's lot nonetheless.

## BAMBOO IS ALWAYS GREENER ON THE OTHER SIDE OF THE RIVER

China is dealing with a number of economic and social problems that, by many standards, might actually be considered as advantageous for a developing country's economy. As any large problem divided by 1.3 billion is not such a big problem, any advantage multiplied by 1.3 billion is a huge opportunity:

*High growth rates*: Growth—which can mean opportunities for more business, more money, more expansion, or simply a good time to start a company—is not always a good thing when it comes to a continuously overheated economy with high inflation, environmental protection challenges and conservation of resources.

*Urban affluence*: Often a positive and desirable thing, in China new urban wealth exacerbates the already perilous divide between city and countryside. For businesses, the quickly rising labor and operational costs pose challenges.

*Traveling abroad*: In the past, Chinese often had their tourist visas rejected by the countries they sought to visit, for fear they would work illegally and overstay. But today they are welcomed, and China's wealthy are increasingly going abroad. Looked at one way, this is the growing power of China's moneyed class to tour and have property abroad. Looked at through a different lens, it is China's rich fleeing an economy and society adrift. According to a recent survey by the Hurun Research Institute, producer of one of the lists of China's richest individuals, almost half of the wealthy are thinking about moving abroad. The wealthy Chinese, it seems, prefer to have some or all of their assets abroad and increasingly prefer to live abroad as well. This is another headache for China's leadership (if the officials themselves are not the ones fleeing, which is yet another problem).

*Studying abroad:* A large number of students going abroad to study at top foreign universities is a good thing, if the graduates return with new knowledge and skills. For China, studying abroad has become a brain drain. Hundreds of thousands of students went abroad during the past 30 years, and the number of students going abroad is still increasing. China often has trouble getting its best and brightest scientists and engineers to come back as *haigui,* "sea turtles" (nicknamed because they come back to their birthplace). According to one Chinese study, of approximately 1 million students that went abroad during this period, only 275,000 have returned.[3] If they do return, providing adequate jobs at international compensation levels is a challenge. For younger undergraduates educated abroad, providing the entry-level jobs is also a challenge. Many become *haidai*—seaweed—drifting in the tides of international labor differentials.

How China deals with these issues is of concern to those with an economic perspective on China's development. In some cases, as with the high growth rate and environmental pollution, slowing down the economy for the sake of the environment is not yet a palatable option, with China taking the position that most of the world's pollution problems have been caused by the West. Slowing down might save the environment, but it would create new problems—such as how to employ China's rural migrant workers as they enter the cities. Nevertheless, China is taking steps to both clean up its economy and its pollution.

Balancing the urban and rural incomes is a task that tests China's commitment to market reforms, since the plan was, in fact, for some people to get rich first, as originally envisioned by Deng.[4] The plan, by all accounts, has succeeded too well, returning China to a class-oriented society of landowners, businesspeople, and government officials—all above a huge and increasingly vocal rural and worker majority.

## CHINA IS A BIG GRAY AREA IN MORE WAYS THAN ONE

Stepping out of Shanghai's Pudong International Airport any time between April and October, passengers feel a heat wave, yet they may notice the skies are gray. It looks like it is about to rain, but it is more likely the haze of pollution that settles over one of China's busiest cities during much of the year. To paraphrase William Gibson, who wrote about the science-fiction future of the then-pre-eminent Japan and its capital Tokyo in his 1984 science-fiction novel *Neuromancer,* Shanghai's sky, day or night, is the color of television tuned to a dead channel. Interestingly, Gibson's concept of future Tokyo is nothing like the Tokyo of today, which has blue skies and is immaculate. Rather, it is Shanghai—with its encircling factories and their smog and its skyscrapers that block out the sun—that appears to be the future metropolis Gibson wrote about. While skies are literally gray, China's business environment has many gray areas:

*Laws and regulations:* Laws, now much improved from the 1980s and 1990s—when they often didn't even exist—are still sometimes written without specifics, leaving interpretation in the hands of local officials. With enforcement a subjective decision, connections—known as *guanxi*—come into play among different organizations, different regions and in different situations to avoid prosecution.

*Transparency:* Whether financial or bureaucratic, most businesses and institutions are not transparent, they are at best gray, if not opaque, due to a longstanding practice of working in a kind of black-box environment where the procedures and decision criteria are hidden behind networks of relationships. The Chinese bureaucracy is still this way. Despite a large amount of effort to put up ministry websites, solicit public opinion and so on, the reality is that the workings of the legal system—including the courts and the decision-making processes in the government—are all still difficult to understand, much less influence. Private companies and state-owned enterprises, even if they are listed on the stock markets, provide much less information to the regulators and public than Western firms.

*Environmental pollution:* The high-speed growth and lack of enforcement of environmental regulations quite literally makes the dust-filled air and everything it touches a slightly duller shade, especially in the north and northwest where coal-fired energy is dominant, resulting in pollution both inside and outside China, affecting the quality of life of its citizens and neighbors.

*Workers' rights:* Some workers, such as the floating migrant population of 200 million, exist in a legal gray area, neither allowed to fully integrate with the local communities in which they work, nor receive wages that adequately compensate them for the sacrifices they make in health and income. Much has been done to improve the situation of migrant and rural workers in recent years. Modern challenges include how to ensure a better health and safety environment for factory workers, how to increase their wages so that their spending power in a consumption-oriented economy can increase and how to avoid losing their factories to cheaper domiciles as costs and wages go up. Bridging the wealth divide as well as moving workers up the value chain has been part of the government's 11th and 12th Five-Year Plans. Finally, the issue of human rights—if defined along the lines of the United Nations' Universal Declaration of Human Rights—has much room for improvement in China.

*Aging:* The graying of the working population is also a major concern. Like many other countries, China experienced a baby boom in the post-World War II-era but, *unlike* other countries, it also reduced the size of the subsequent generations artificially with the now-infamous one-child policy (as it is known in the West; in China it is the *Family Planning Policy*).[5] The policy has resulted in nearly 100 million one-child families and prevented the birth of about 400 million additional people, causing a number of unexpected or negative demographic effects. One effect is an increase in the percentage of senior citizens. As fewer babies are born, and as the average person lives longer thanks to improved diet and better health care in modern China, the seniors demographic is growing quickly. Without enough working population to support the pension system, seniors may be left without adequate support in their gray years, and after death may not even have enough offspring to sweep the tomb, a Chinese traditional practice carried out every year to show respect to ancestors.

*Entitlement and moral compass:* Growing materialism, a sense of class superiority, and a lack of societal accountability are starting to exhibit themselves. China's infrastructure may be world-class (with some notable exceptions), but sometimes the behavior of the people is not up to the same standard. For example, Chinese in cars may see the roads as their personal space rather than a shared public area, treating other drivers, cyclists and pedestrians with indifference. In 2011, a toddler in southern China's Guangdong province was stuck by a vehicle and subsequently crushed under its wheels and left for dead but, most shocking, this injured girl was also ignored by 18 pedestrians who passed by for several minutes after the accident, until one woman finally stopped to assist. The girl later died of her injuries. Cases abound of road rage and assault carried out by luxury car-driving youth who are apt to shout out, "My father is so-and-so, I dare you to call the police!"

*Public health:* When it comes to public health, the situation is not much better. Multiple campaigns to eradicate spitting on the street, first after the SARS crisis of 2003, then during the Olympics of 2008 and the World Expo

2010, have all apparently failed, and Chinese tourists traveling abroad are still warned by their own government to tone down their behavior, which sometimes includes shouting, jostling and smoking in public places. Even nearby Hong Kong has seen public opposition to Chinese medical tourism: mainland mothers are delivering their babies in Hong Kong maternity wards (to get automatic residency for the newborn) thereby crowding out local Hong Kong mothers.

*Black market:* China's black market is really more of a gray market since the stores and even malls can be full of counterfeit merchandise and operate in the open, complete with advertising and business cards. The city governments of Shanghai and Beijing have closed the most notorious fake-goods markets, and foreign firms are increasingly winning cases against retailers that sell counterfeit products, but the problem is still rampant in everything from DVDs to clothing to spare parts for just about any machine imaginable, including U.S. military fighter jets.[6]

*Unclear financial and economic data:* China's black market economy above results in massive tax evasion. From companies to consumers, cities to countryside, income-underreporting is rife and difficult to track. Other economic data are often underreported or (only slightly better) retroactively corrected due to the sheer amount and effort involved to collect data for everything from unemployment figures to the floating migrant population (which is, as one would imagine, difficult to pin down when many transient workers are happy to accept cash to avoid taxes). If that were not enough, at times data are exaggerated, for example when provincial governors report their progress on key performance indicators that will make or break their future advancement in the Communist Party. At other times, it is underreported, as in the case of undocumented children born after the one-child policy was implemented: some rural children grow up not knowing they are illegal in their own country until they one day apply to travel or get a job. Data about China is better thought of as gray rather than black and white, though the situation has also improved in recent years with the National Statistics Bureau collecting data independently rather than completely relying on the local governments to self-report, as it had in the past.

The Chinese government is aware of all these problems and has undertaken measures to deal with the largest of them. For example, much of the tax collection at the retail level is now linked electronically and instantaneously to the tax bureau, and there is an automatic reporting method used when companies in major cities issue receipts. Other problems are going to take more time to solve. Fortunately for China, and for businesspeople, many of these problems are not only solvable, they are where the greatest opportunities exist: multi-billion dollar industries that are just waiting for the right companies and entrepreneurs to step in to provide solutions. Environmental business models, senior care and development of Chinese patents and brands are the most obvious.

## CHINA'S MOST SERIOUS CHALLENGES

Finally, there are the problems that are truly devastating to a developing economy's output, social conditions and global reputation:

*Dangerous jobs:* China has occupational injuries and deaths from certain industries, such as coal-mining, that are the highest in the world. China's media now cover these accidents and the acts of negligence that cause them more openly, but the health and safety issues are likely to increase before they get better, with China's high growth and greater cost pressure necessitating shortcuts.

*Dangerous products:* Tainted drugs, food products, personal care products, toys—even baby formula and milk powder that contain dangerous chemicals, sometimes added as a substitute for active ingredients—continue to cause injury or even death when used. In 2007, the Chinese government completed an overhaul of all toy exporters' quality-control processes following the lead paint toy scandals. One year later, it acted not-so-quickly as one might expect to recall contaminated milk and baby formula: for hundreds of thousands of children who drank melamine-laced milk products—causing many children to become sick and some to die—the regulators fell far short. It is not just Chinese products and producers; many foreign products—from Nestle milk powder to Kentucky Fried Chicken chicken wings to Evian water— sold in China have been accused of failing to reach China's food safety standards. Even as late as 2012, products containing carcinogens continued to be found on a regular basis, scaring Chinese and global consumers away from both sold-in-China and made-in-China products. Many Chinese resort to buying imported foods online.

*Worker exploitation:* Despite lessons from the cases of alleged worker abuse at outsourcing factories for Nike and other shoe manufacturers in the 1990s throughout Asia, the practice of worker exploitation is apparently alive and well in China. Extreme exploitation of workers— essentially slave labor—has been found at kilns in remote areas of China. There are also piecework factories with abysmal conditions and low wages. Many such situations are starting to change as company bosses are thrown in jail and the government begins to enforce a new set of labor laws, enacted in January 2008. Foreign companies in China are not above such practices either. As the case of Foxconn—a Taiwanese company acting as a subcontractor to the world's major electronics and computer companies including Apple—showed, even mega-factories that superficially provide good working environments could mask serious psychological pressure: more than a dozen Foxconn workers either fell or jumped to their deaths in 2010.

*Corruption:* Business and government corruption—including land grabs by government officials, price collusion by manufacturers, nepotism, bribes, and kickbacks—are all still present. But these are the target of central government campaigns to prosecute offenders and reduce the distorting effects the crimes have on the economy. So widespread is the problem that more than 200,000 cases have been investigated since 2003, and China's President Hu Jintao made a speech in 2011 to highlight the problem. In 2012, there was further official acknowledgement that, since 2009, more than 31.6 billion *yuan* ($5 billion) had been identified in more than 61,000 hidden slush funds.[7] The threat of the death penalty for many economic crimes is not enough to dissuade government officials, who may receive millions of dollars in bribes and kickbacks, as was the apparent case of the former Minister of Railways, Li Zhijun. He was accused of embezzling more than 800 million *yuan* ($127 million), and was apprehended after investigations into a high-fatality train wreck in 2011.

*Social unrest:* There is social unrest arising from the extreme wealth divide between the cities and countryside and the inevitable accompanying problems, as tens of millions of people relocate to cities, leaving rural lives behind. To provide migrants with affordable housing, the borders of large cities such as Shanghai are expanding quickly with low-income housing projects creating a tiered residential model with the affluent in the center and the poor pushed farther away. In cases where land is grabbed from rural workers at unfair prices in the name of development, more frequent resistance is being reported and covered not only by international media but, increasingly, by Chinese media. The plights of those taken advantage of are even publicized by Chinese *netizens*, the newly vocal online Internet community in China. Mainland Chinese now protest polluting factories with increasing regularity, while exploited workers are showing up *en masse* to collect unpaid wages from construction companies, and entire communities may unite in protest against corruption, such as what happened in 2011 in southern Chinese village of Wukan where residents temporarily kicked out their government and police force. The problem of social unrest is set to increase as long as the wealth divide, pollution, corruption and other problems persist.

*Regional instability:* Territorial disputes between China and virtually all its neighbors are on the increase, creating an environment of regional political instability. Flare-ups in some of these potential hotspots could be prevented by keeping business interests in mind. For example, for those disputes involving sea exploration rights and extension of sea borders around disputed islands, promotion of joint—rather than unilateral—exploration and development of offshore resource could prevent some conflicts. The peaceful reunification of Taiwan with the mainland may yet be achieved via more and more investment linkages but the potential for conflict remains. Other problems, such as China's thirst for oil and access to critical sea routes, could combust unexpectedly and unpredictably as they did when Japan seized a Chinese fishing vessel and crew in disputed waters in 2010, causing a series of retaliatory diplomatic and trade measures.

*Inflation:* China's potential for continued high rates of inflation is a deep concern for China's government. With such a large wealth gap; the poor are disproportionately harmed by high inflation. After successfully controlling the high inflation that was occurring in the run-up to the global financial crisis, when global commodity prices were skyrocketing, including $147/barrel oil, 2011 saw a return to 5 percent and higher inflation rates in China. This persistent problem results from China's trade surplus, its currency exchange rate controls and lack of adequate convertibility of the Chinese *yuan* into other foreign currencies, as well as the booming stock market and land price bubbles. Inflation has the potential to seriously disrupt China's growth trajectory.

These issues have been headline news in the Western media whenever a story on the downsides of China's growth appears, whenever a new trade dispute arises or, in the sadder cases, whenever the circumstances are so truly shocking or sad that foreign media can't help but pay attention.

While examining these deep, mostly structural problems is beyond the scope of this book, it is important to acknowledge that China is still a developing country and, as such, is bound to face growing pains. However, one must be at least aware of China's full situation because several of these problems have the potential to derail the Chinese economic miracle. For example, worker exploitation, social unrest and inflation are particularly pernicious long-term problems. Short-term problems are harder to predict.

In the short-term, so-called *black swan events*, as described by Nassim Nicholas Taleb in his book, *The Black Swan: The Impact of the Highly Improbable,* may occur. The black swan is a metaphor for an unexpected or unknowable occurrence, much like how Europeans once thought all swans were white, until encountering black swans in colonial Australia. A *black swan event*, then, could be anything from a sudden financial crisis to an earthquake (like the one which disrupted Japan's economy and nearly caused a nuclear meltdown in 2011). In a country as large as China, *black swans* could occur anywhere, anytime. They could be especially disastrous given China's emerging economy characteristics.

In China, the *black swans* that have the most potential for devastation are health-related and environmental. From tainted milk affecting hundreds of thousands of children, to sudden chemical spills in rivers affecting the water supply of millions, highly improbable events do have huge impacts in China. Even weather can have a disproportional impact: in 2007 a once-in-a-century blizzard shut down rail transportation for tens of millions during the critical Chinese New Year travel period.

Other, non-*black swan events* that are better defined as long-term problems, such as desertification and a scarce fresh water supply, may reach a tipping point this century, affecting hundreds of millions of Chinese. China's environmental challenges are the greatest to overcome, yet as a developing country it also faces an environment versus development tradeoff that developed countries before it never had to worry about. As China grows at its breakneck pace, the environment suffers. If growth slows, the people suffer. That is why the *problem* of how much growth to aim for is constantly on the minds of China's leadership: Among the world's largest economies, China's is unquestionably the most micromanaged.

## TOO MUCH OF A GOOD THING?

In the coming years, it is possible that the largest creation and accumulation of private wealth ever to occur in the history of the planet will happen in China. In fact, by some projections, China's GDP will soon be bigger than the U.S.'s, as early as 2016. Just a few years ago the best financial institutions in the world predicted that wouldn't happen before 2050. Some of China's own economists predicted China could be as large as 2.5 times the size of the U.S. in terms of GDP as early as 2030.[8] Much of this sounds too good to be true. In fact it is too good, for even as China becomes the world's biggest economy in terms of GDP, its people will remain among the poorest in terms of per capita income. No fortune, no matter how large, remains so when *divided by* 1.3 billion people. Nevertheless, there is an inordinate amount of focus on China's overall GDP growth from both inside and outside China.

China's GDP growth is the first and foremost statistic regularly shown to demonstrate China's rapid rise. In 2011, GDP grew by 9.2 percent for the year, far outpacing all major developed economies. China's growth has been on a tear for more than 30 years. In the years before the global financial crisis, China's National Bureau of Statistics (NBS) announced China's 2007 GDP growth hit an unprecedented 14.2 percent, revised upwards three times from the initial figure of 11.4 percent.

In fact, it has long been suspected that China's GDP statistics—based as they are on an economy where hidden income is so prevalent and collecting data is a time-consuming and error-prone task—hide the true extent of China's rapid growth.

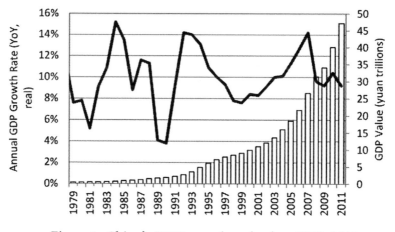

*Figure 1: China's GDP growth and value, 1979–2011*

Goldman Sachs analysts and others had rightly believed the initial GDP growth of 11.4 percent reported in 2007, was higher than first stated given discrepancies when the individual provincial totals and the nationally reported aggregate figures did not match.[9] Either way, even at the initial figure of 11.4 percent, much less the final figure of 14.2 percent, 2007's GDP was far above national targets and straying into overheated growth.

Where most developed countries strive for GDP growth of 3 percent as a respectable figure, 10 percent and higher growth stands out even in China. China's Premier Wen Jiabao said at the 2007 National People's Congress that GDP growth would need to be kept *under* 8 percent in 2007. Perhaps it was meant in jest: China had pledged to keep growth under 7.5 percent during the entire 11th Five-Year Plan (2006–2010), and consistently surpassed the target. Even during the global financial crisis's worst years of 2008 and 2009, growth in China did decrease marginally, to 9.6 percent and 8.7 percent respectively, but by 2010 it was back significantly above the target, at a rate of 10.3 percent.

In 2011, a new five-year plan was initiated and the growth target for the five-year period (2011–2015) was revised downwards to 7 percent, perhaps trying to dampen the expectation that China would continue high growth indefinitely. In fact, GDP growth only decreased slightly in 2011, to 9.2 percent, but this was still more than 2 percent higher than the new national target. Although these targets are subject to year-to-year revision based on current economic conditions, such as in 2012 when China set its yearly GDP target to 7.5 percent (that is, 0.5 percent higher than the five-year plan target would imply), China's persistent inability to slow down growth is causing concern inside and outside China.

One reason for wanting to slow down growth is the fear of overheating in the economy. China's intense focus on increasing GDP since 1978 resulted in a 1998 GDP more than 20 times higher than its 1978 level, a sustained 16 percent annual rate of growth, unprecedented in modern economic history. Not content to rest on its laurels, in 2002 the central government set a new goal of quadrupling the GDP by 2020 from 2000 levels, a goal it seems likely to achieve given the return to 9 percent or greater growth after the financial crisis.

The absolute GDP numbers that are the focus of much international attention are, since the turn of the century, less important to China itself. What is more important to China is balanced growth and fairer wealth distribution. Despite all of the money generated by China's export growth, China's population overall is still very poor by global standards. China's GDP per capita still remains at a mere 10 percent of the U.S.'s levels today. Yet it is this statistic that is often used by the government as a means of energizing the people. At the closing of the 2007 17th National Congress, Communist Party General Secretary and Chinese President Hu Jintao announced a clear mandate to increase per capita GDP to about $4,500 per person by 2020, quadrupling 2000 levels.[10] This shows the determination of the Chinese central government to increase national wealth.

The Chinese government has made it a priority to manage the growth. Among developing countries, such growth rates are not unheard of, but China has maintained high growth for more than 30 years.[11] The first priority then is to keep the economy, awash in money from export trade and investment, from overheating and bring it down to a so-called "soft landing." If the growth cannot be controlled, inflation threatens to wipe out the savings of the already poor rural populace and reduce quality of life for the middle class in the cities.

## CRISIS IS ALSO OPPORTUNITY?

All of the problems mentioned in this *Introduction* certainly exist, are well-known and are reported on in more places every year.

The purpose of the book is not to dwell on them, or to assign blame, or to say what the reader has heard is wrong. These are real issues that concern everyone. Rather, the purpose of this book is to reframe these issues for what they are to enterprising companies, far-sighted investors, and creative entrepreneurs: opportunities.

A popular piece of management-speak holds that the Chinese word for crisis also means opportunity. Any number of linguists will state this is certainly not the case. At most, it is a stretching of the facts. Indeed, the Chinese word for crisis is *weiji*—危机—comprised of two separate characters, the first character meaning *danger* and the second meaning something like *decision-point*. There is no "opportunity" as such to be found: the misnomer comes from the fact that the first character is found in the word *weixian*—危险—meaning danger, and the second character is part of the Chinese word *jihui*—机会—meaning opportunity. So it would be more accurate—though linguistically still wrong—to say that *weiji* equals *weixian* plus *jihui* (meaning crisis equals danger plus opportunity).

Nonetheless, there is a certain seed of market-driven logic that caused this misconception to become so common in the first place. In the same way that Al Gore tells people that *global warming* is one of the greatest threats to the environment and way of life, while at the same time saying it is an opportunity for enterprising energy-saving companies and individuals to shine, each of the above-mentioned challenges in Chinese economic development becomes a chance for somebody to solve a problem and, incidentally, make a lot of money in the process.

Indeed, a graphic from *The Inconvenient Truth* movie shows Shanghai and Tianjin, two of China's most populated cities, being mostly underwater by 2050 if the worst-case climate change predictions are correct. The weight of some of the massive buildings in Shanghai is already causing parts of the city to sink into the ground.[12] This is a problem waiting for a solution—new construction techniques and better materials from the *new manufacturing supertrend*, for example.

Similarly, relocating hundreds of millions of people into cities—the *urbanization supertrend*—is a very tough job, but there will also be plentiful opportunities relating to urban living and growth of new modes of transportation.

When it comes to cleaning up the environment, saving electricity and generating new energy from non-fossil fuels—all part of the *sustainability supertrend*—China needs all three as soon as possible. The resulting opportunities in green businesses, including alternative energy, pollution control, waste reduction and ecotourism are some of the biggest in the world. Red China is becoming *green*.

China's capital markets are immature and unable to support the growth needed to power China's next phase of development. For several decades one of China's *growth engines*, foreign direct investment, has seen foreign companies investing directly in China's economy. The *affluence supertrend* shows how this trend is reversing, with Chinese companies going abroad looking for new opportunities. At the same time, Western investors are participating in China's growth by buying stocks and investing venture capital. One could put ones head in the sand and pretend things have not changed, but for the businesses, investors, and individuals, who can see the change and work with it, Chinese investment is certainly not a crisis, it is an opportunity.

The next section will introduce how these four *supertrends* are influenced by China's *growth engines, turbochargers,* and *roadmap*. By understanding how China's economic *growth engines* are changing, how the pace of that change is magnified by the *turbochargers,* and how one can clearly see China's future direction and destination by looking at its *roadmap,* the *supertrends* become the most powerful predictors of success.

# PART ONE:
## CHINA'S GROWTH ENGINES, TURBOCHARGERS AND ROADMAP

势

# Chapter 1

# CHINA'S THREE GROWTH ENGINES

| 待文王而兴者， | *Dai wen wang er xing zhe,* |
|---|---|
| 凡民也。 | *fan min ye.* |
| 若夫豪杰之士 | *Nuo fu hao jie zhi shi,* |
| 虽无文王犹兴。 | *sui wu wen wang you xing.* |

"The common people wait for Emperor Wen to come and uplift them. But the truly outstanding will uplift themselves, even if Emperor Wen does not appear."—Mencius

W hat are the main forces behind China's growth, now and in the future? There are three engines contributing to the success of China's modern economy—exporting, foreign direct investment (FDI), and domestic market consumption (purchasing by consumers). Of these, exporting and FDI have been the most important to China's development thus far, while the third, consumption, will be the primary growth engine of China's future.

Post-1978 China, under Deng Xiaoping's vision, built its economic growth on exports, much as other "Asian Tigers" and "Asian Dragons" such as South Korea and Singapore did before it. Unlike the others, China relied on its mammoth labor force to make it the low-cost leader and was able to sustain that advantage longer than the economic dragons to establish what has come to be known as the *China price,* the moniker used by sourcing professionals. However, even China's quantity of labor is exhaustible and the end of cheap China is near, though is it more correct to say the end of *cheapest* China, since China still remains an attractive place to do business even with higher labor rates and its labor is still relatively *cheaper* than every other major economy's labor.[1]

China's success through exporting is likely to continue for the remainder of the Olympic Decade, albeit in higher-valued added industries. This also assumes that China's trading partners will not enact trade sanctions over China's export subsidies and under-valued *yuan.* Even if China can avoid a trade war, the country cannot continue to rely on export *growth* as markets globally are already saturated with Chinese goods. There are few, if any markets left to expand to.

What China is doing about this changing trade landscape and why it will not continue to rely on exports for growth are two of the key narratives of China's Olympic Decade. Before 2018, China will seek—and achieve—a shift from the export of low-value-added goods to the export of high-value-added goods, and a shift from export-led growth to consumption-led growth.

## EXPORTS FROM AIGO TO ZTE

AIGO is the English name for one of China's consumer electronics manufacturers, famous for products such as MP3 players. ZTE is China's second-largest mobile phone manufacturer—producing nearly 57 million handsets in 2011—and the world's fifth largest, according to Gartner Group. One day it may rival more famous firms such as Nokia or Samsung for the top spot. AIGO is known outside of China primarily as an OEM, an Original Equipment Manufacturer. ZTE, likewise, is a relatively smaller telecommunications company that produces goods for relatively larger telecommunications companies, on contract, and serves as a hidden link in the supply chain. That is probably why many readers outside of China will have never heard of companies such as AIGO and ZTE. These companies are a key part of China's world-leading $1.9 trillion in product exports in 2011, of which more than half was for the electronic and mechanical goods that AIGO, ZTE, and other Chinese OEMs are best known for.[2]

China exports large amounts of goods to, first and foremost, the United States, but also to the EU, Japan, South Korea, and one of its Special Administrative Regions, Hong Kong. Meanwhile it imports from Japan, South Korea, the United States, Germany and Australia. Australia's place of prominence results from the large amounts of raw materials (metals, oil, gas, and so on) China imports, whereas from the other economies it is importing mostly finished goods.

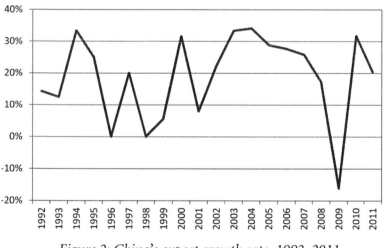

*Figure 2: China's export growth rate, 1992–2011*

The growth of trade, on the other hand, is much faster between China and other emerging markets. Trade with the United States and the European Union grew at 15.9 percent and 18.3 percent respectively, China's trade overall grew at 22.5 percent. The difference came from China's increasing trade with BRICS countries Brazil, Russia, and South Africa, which grew much more quickly at 34.5 percent, 42.7 percent and 76.7 percent respectively.

Even the possibility that developed economies of the West might enter a prolonged L-shaped or double-dip recession in 2008 was not enough to slow China down for more than half a year. In response to growing export dependency on the United States, China has now developed new markets for its goods, should the U.S. become more hostile to Chinese imports.

By 2012, increased bilateral trade agreements, which bypass World Trade Organization mechanisms, with both developed and developing countries, were increasingly common. Furthermore, China's increasing trade with Africa, South America, and Southeast Asia is beginning to buffer a possible trade volume decrease with the large Western economies. Even if China's biggest customer, the United States, enters a prolonged economic correction or recession, it is optimistically thought that this will increase the number of low-priced Chinese exports. This idea could be moot if high oil prices increase transportation costs for low-priced goods.

China's trump card, which becomes stronger every year, is the possibility of *decoupling* from the world economy, which means turning to *internal* demand for Chinese-produced goods. China would, of course, prefer to avoid a radical shift involving shock therapy for its manufacturers. Nor are Chinese consumers ready to take the mantle of world's biggest spenders—Shanghai and Beijing white-collar worker salaries may be quite high but China's overall *per capita* income still ranks among the world's lowest, nowhere near that of developed countries' per capita incomes. Nevertheless, the possibility of decoupling is somewhat more realistic than it was before the 2008 financial crisis.

SHOES OUT, DOLLARS IN

Despite the Chinese *yuan's* appreciation of about 25 percent against the U.S. dollar since 2005, China's export trade has never stopped growing except for a few months of contraction during the peak of the global financial crisis. Annual growth has been around 20 percent. Since the *yuan* peg to the dollar was scrapped in 2005 in favor of an unspecified basket of currencies, a managed float (i.e., a trading band) rather than a fixed rate, the currency has been appreciating slowly but steadily, going from approximately 8.27 to the dollar then to about 6.3 at the start of 2012.

If one notes the growing calls from the U.S. Congress that something should be done about the under-valuation of the *yuan*, with even President Obama of the United States stating that "enough is enough," one might assume that this glacial pace of appreciation is the crux of the trade imbalance between the United States and China. Fast appreciation or revaluation has, however, been ruled out by the central bank of China so that its exporters, one of the linchpin drivers of the economy, have time to adjust to a new high-*yuan* environment, as well as to provide time to prevent rapid inflation that could cause social problems.

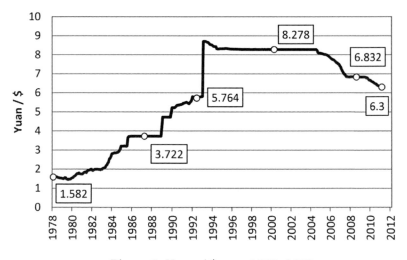

*Figure 3: Yuan / $ rate, 1978–2012*

In response to the higher *yuan*, exporters have upgraded production with more efficient machinery, and many have focused on innovation as the key to remaining competitive. The continued growth of the export sector is both a commendation to the hard work of the Chinese OEMs and a condemnation of the logic that increasing the appreciation rate would somehow make Chinese exports unattractive and bring back jobs to America. However, the renewed strength of the domestic Chinese exporters must also be due to export subsidies by the Chinese government. In order to try to narrow 2007's $253 billion trade gap with the United States and discourage low-value export-oriented industries, export incentives were to be reduced, but by the end of 2009, in response to the global financial crisis, China had restored many of the subsidy programs.[3]

Compared to 1990, when China classified about 7 percent of its exports as high-tech electronic and mechanical goods, that ratio is now above 50 percent and climbing, led by items such as heavy machinery for construction and manufacturing, mobile phones, computer hardware and large ships. Even China's most traditional of industries, silk production, is moving into such non-traditional areas as the production of artificial skin—using silk proteins, costing one-tenth of similar products abroad, thanks to China's low cost of labor and ideal environment for harvesting silk. This is an Adam Smith-style absolute advantage if there ever was one.

An overdependence on exports is a worry for China, and putting all its eggs in one U.S.-based basket is even more troublesome. On a macro level, the Chinese government has felt threatened by its bilateral trade dependence on the United States, so has sought to hedge its bets by increasing trade with the EU and Japan. Trade with the latter has been especially evident in just the last several years as Japan's economy started to recover from its "lost decade" or "lost years," phrases used to describe the period of negative or negligible economic growth in Japan, roughly from 1991 (when Japan's bubble started to burst) up to the present. The EU's trade with China, in aggregate, is technically bigger than even that between the U.S. and China, but it is not homogenous, given the EU's vastly different national markets, so the United States is still the single biggest market for China. One outcome is that China has a large trade surplus and a foreign currency reserve of trillions of dollars. Decreasing that surplus has become a priority for both governments, for different reasons.

From China's perspective, a decrease in United States consumer spending could actually help mitigate hundreds of billions of dollars in trade surplus (or, from the U.S.'s perspective, the trade *deficit*), but no exporter in China wants to see a U.S. slowdown—that would be bad for business. Instead, the Chinese government and exporters alike would prefer to see a diversification of trade, moving beyond dependence on the U.S. market.

Further to the goal of diversifying trade, China was also moving forward with a proposal to join the Organization for Economic Cooperation and Development (OECD), the organization for 30 of the world's market economies, along with the other BRICS countries—Brazil, Russia, and India, and South Africa. It has sought new trade almost everywhere, from Africa to Eastern Europe to Southeast Asia.

China's trade with the other Asian nations has also increased, and it is a supporter of turning ASEAN, the Association of Southeast Asian Nations, into the world's biggest trading bloc if it formally joins. China has already entered a free trade agreement with ASEAN. Disputes in the South China Sea with ASEAN members keep China from formal accession, so a China-led ASEAN is still some time off, but with China now part of the free trade zone, the ASEAN will be a major balancing force against other multilateral trading blocs such as the North American Free Trade Agreement and the EU.[4]

These additional trading partners should insulate China somewhat if its largest trading partner, the United States, reduces imports due to an economic downturn or trade retaliation. Yet the present interconnectedness of U.S.-China trade is also a stabilizing force of global importance because so many countries indirectly rely on that trade. For example, a slowdown in U.S. consumption would lead to less demand for raw materials from China's resource trading partners, including Australia and Russia. Furthermore, it is still important to China's continued development to continue exporting to the United States, a co-dependent relationship that historian Niall Ferguson coined *Chimerica*— China plus America—a "wonderful dual country ... which accounts for just over a tenth of the world's land surface, a quarter of its population, a third of its economic output..."[5]

Thirty years ago, few would have predicted the extraordinary impact that China's economy has today on the global business environment. Japan of the 1980s seemed ready to take the number one spot as top exporter, while at the time the United States and United Kingdom were mired in an economic downturn and ideological war with the Soviet Union, and China was newly opened but uncertain to emerge as a global competitor. Three decades later, China has overtaken Japan *and* the United States, and is now the world's top exporter of merchandise.

From the time of Napoleon, who is thought to have once said that China would make the world tremble when it awoke, people have been aware of China's incredible potential. Yet few would have predicted it could rise so quickly, making the previous rise of Asian economies, including Japan, South Korea, and compatriot Taiwan, seem slow by comparison. Exporting's role in China's modern development cannot be understated, and it is still a pillar on which China derives a great deal of support. But many of these exports would not have been possible if it were not for the foreign multinational companies that invested in China after its opening in 1978, by building factories and transferring technology and skills to China's workers.

### $2 BILLION A WEEK: FOREIGN INVESTMENT IN CHINA

After exports, next in importance of China's *growth engines* during the 30 glorious years of post-1978 reform was foreign direct investment (FDI). FDI in China refers mostly to investment in factories, joint venture companies with Chinese partners and, more recently, establishment of wholly owned foreign enterprises as independent legal corporate entities operating in China as subsidiaries of the global multinational parent. Other types of foreign investment, such as so-called portfolio investment in stocks and bonds, are extremely limited due to China's control over its Capital Account to keep the *yuan* stable and prevent hot money from entering the economy.

## A Brief History of Post-1978 Chinese Economic Policy

In the 1980s, when the country first opened up, every level of government gave a high priority to attracting foreign direct investment. China at the time was lacking foreign currency; it had little to sell other than agricultural goods, and Communist-era products that few other countries wanted. Consequently, every place foreign investors visited, the local government rolled out the red carpet to meet them, to explain how favorable the local policies were, show them the local factories and entertain them with lavish banquets. The officials had good reason to do so: the evaluation of all government leaders was keyed to their ability to attract foreign investment, achieve local GDP growth and export more from their region.

Until 2007, all foreign investments in special economic zones (e.g., export processing zones, designated industrial parks, and even entire regions such as Shenzhen) enjoyed a long tax holiday amounting to 100 percent income tax exemption in the first three profitable years and 50 percent tax reduction in the following two years. The effective rates without subsidies were 24 percent for foreign companies outside the zones, 15 percent inside the zones and 33 percent for Chinese companies. This was a huge factor in attracting many foreign companies to invest. Another factor was the possibility of even greater returns on China investments once *yuan* appreciation was included.

By 2007 then, it had started to become apparent that such tax incentives were no longer necessary. Foreign companies wanted to come to China regardless. They were also increasingly competing in the domestic market, not just exporting, using their tax advantage as a foothold. What was more, the overheating of the economy at the time (14.2 percent GDP growth in 2007) was blamed partially on *hot money*, which some believed many foreign companies contributed to by bringing in as much investment as possible, in expectation of *yuan* appreciation. Besides, the returns were tax free as well. It was a tremendous wealth transfer from Chinese taxpayers to foreign companies, and it was about to end.

In order to level the playing field between domestic and foreign companies, the preferential policy was phased out in 2007 in steps over the next five years in the mostly developed eastern areas, so that Chinese companies and foreign companies would all pay the same 25 percent corporate tax rate by 2012.

For many foreign companies in China, competing on a level playing field would not be easy. They typically paid well for highly skilled multilingual employees, had higher costs in China because of additional regulation levied on foreign enterprises, as well as the global overhead costs, such as maintaining compliance with their head office policies. China started to seem much less attractive, with a growing number of executives saying they would consider relocating China operations. China still had some tools to keep those companies interested.

*Just When You Thought You Were Out...They Pull You Back In*

Despite the harmonization of the corporate tax rate, preferential tax policies have not entirely ended. China is still interested in attracting certain kinds of investments, especially high-tech and developing region investments.

For example, in order to encourage more high-tech investments, companies that locate their facilities in the new high-tech development zones, and meet the definition of a high-tech enterprise or R&D facility, will still receive a preferential two-year tax holiday and 12.5 percent tax rate thereafter, which is possibly why many large MNCs are setting up R&D centers in China at a rapid pace. Also, in an effort to encourage westward migration of foreign investments, a preferential 15 percent rate is available to all foreign investors who go to the central or western regions of China.[6]

In addition, state and local governments, especially those in western China, still have a vast array of incentives to continue to draw foreign investment to their areas. From a steep reduction in value-added tax (VAT), to lower (or even free) land costs, to commercial loan arrangements, the line between government and business is blurry at best. In many places it is virtually indistinguishable where public interests stop and private interests start. On the outskirts of many of China's second-, third- and lower-tiered cities, thousands of acres of farmland have been rezoned to factory and business use, and local bureaucrats have developed industrial parks to attract foreign investments. They often proceed to form mini-cities within the zones, with their own administrators running on-site banks, trade finance and customs services, shops, hospitals and post offices to provide a higher quality of service to their foreign investors.

Along with FDI, export growth was highly encouraged by the Chinese government, so the government often refunded a major portion (up to 75 percent) of the 17 percent VAT to the exporting companies, whether foreign or domestic. Although this heavy subsidization has been gradually reduced since China joined the WTO, various subsidization policies were revived to stimulate the economy in the post-financial crisis period. This time, the subsidies disproportionately helped the Chinese manufacturers to regain market share abroad, to the consternation of other exporting economies.

*Recent Developments for FDI in China*

In 2010, China received more than $105 billion in FDI, a record haul, and was pegged by the United Nations to be the top target for FDI in 2011, which it achieved and then some—$116 billion was sent to China in 2011—underscoring the desire of multinationals to still get into China, or increase their investments, decades after it was first possible.[7]

Interestingly, a well-known relationship in international trade is that FDI to a country usually *follows* a period of exporting to that country. In terms of a single U.S. company as an example, the company would have first begun exporting to China, perhaps through an agent or distributor, later set up its own sales and import office and, finally, via the FDI channel, sought to manufacture locally. Local manufacturing would allow the company to save on transportation costs and possibly receive better tax treatment. According to that trade theory, then, the final step should only occur *after* exports have taken place for some time and *only* once the trade has reached a certain level where marginal costs of exporting prevent additional profits.

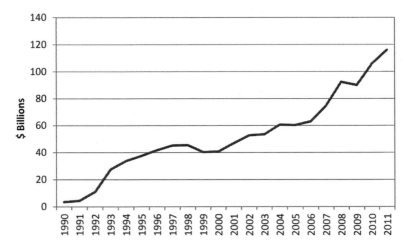

*Figure 4: China's inbound foreign direct investment (actual), 1990–2011*

By this logic, based on the huge amount of FDI coming from the developed countries into China, a lot of products should have been exported to China in the first place, from 1978 onward thanks to the reform and opening up policy of Deng Xiaoping. In reality, this was not the case—because of three characteristics of the Chinese market.[8]

First, the rise of the Chinese OEM companies as a business model, allowing foreign companies to outsource production and avoid the trouble of establishing a factory. This allowed Western companies to gain the benefit of China manufacturing (low costs) without the pain of setting up a factory. Many companies chose this model to increase profits at home.

Second, a general policy that if a foreign company did want to set up its own manufacturing in China (perhaps to ensure better quality or capture more of the profits), it would have to partner with a Chinese company in a joint venture (JV) and invest as well as transfer technology. While there are some key exceptions, in the automotive industry for example, negative stories are legion where Chinese partners have copied technology and established side businesses as competitors or simply found an excuse to eject from the JV, as Chinese food-and-drink manufacturer Wahaha did with France's Danone in 2009 despite a lucrative and apparently mutually beneficial partnership in the China market.

Finally, early on after the reform and opening up policy of 1978, many direct imports into China were highly restricted as import licensing (as well as the foreign currency needed to import foreign products) was strictly controlled by the central government. Many import restrictions remained in place until 2001, when China entered the World Trade Organization (WTO), and for several years after that as industries were phased in gradually. Many industries are still partially or fully protected today to give China's own companies a chance to develop.

Many foreign companies, to be sure, have tried to import their products and compete in the Chinese market directly. However, direct import strategies have not been successful for a number of reasons.

Products created abroad and sold in China without local content or design would probably not be suitable for the Chinese market's tastes. A classic example from the fast-food industry shows how McDonald's—a seller of hamburgers—has been losing out to Kentucky Fried Chicken (KFC) in China, due to a Chinese preference for chicken over beef. Not insignificantly,

KFC also adjusted its menu and even its famous "11 herbs and spices" taste to better suit Chinese consumers' palates.

Another reason is that few Western products cannot be found in China already in some form or another. Many products, even if they have not been formally importer, have been copied and sold in China already. A domestic Chinese product is usually going to be sold at a much lower price than the authentic item, due to much lower labor costs, lack of health, safety and environmental regulations, and ineffective enforcement of intellectual property laws.

A final reason is that prior to China's becoming part of the WTO, many of China's markets were protected by high tariff and non-tariff barriers (NTBs) which a foreign manufacturer had to overcome if it even wanted to get the products into the country for sale. Many did not even bother and simply used the export processing zones to assemble and export. Even after 2001, though the tariffs were often removed, many NTBs remained or were newly created.

One example of a NTB is placing extremely high standards for quality on products. The standards may be imposed on foreign imports when needed and may not be enforced domestically. NTBs can even be used selectively to keep a certain country's products out, or even against a single foreign company when needed. In China, such regulations have caught Evian spring water, which has been cited twice for its supposedly high nitrite levels, as well as Volvic water, both owned, perhaps coincidently, by Danone, the company that was previously in a large dispute with China's Wahaha.[9]

So, as a result of these three factors, a foreign company wanting to sell its products to China would usually be better off setting up a company, factory or assembly facility in China to localize its products, take advantage of low costs and avoid NTBs by becoming, ostensibly, a Chinese-made product.

Such strategies are usually successful but are no guarantee. For example, even though "Buy Local" provisions are supposed to be illegal under WTO trade regulations, many countries—China and the United States included—still use them. In 2012, China's Ministry of Industry and Information Technology mandated that all government vehicles had to be procured from Chinese manufacturers. This regulation would preclude sales from any Sino-foreign joint ventures (since they are not 100 percent local).

Was there another reason that the traditional flow of trade-first, FDI-later reversed when it came to China? The most recent round of globalization, the globalization 2.0 that Thomas Friedman described in *The World is Flat,* had already made clear that companies need no longer worry about where factories were, as long as they were in the lowest-cost location possible. China was already the lowest-cost producer. So it is that most things sold in China are made in China, and if foreign companies wanted to sell there they would have to invest first.

FDI in China had grown to be the biggest in the world in several years of the last decade and is expanding again in the post-global financial crisis environment as multinational companies invest for new growth wherever it can be found.

THE BENEFITS OF FDI FOR CHINA

How important is foreign investment to China? Since 1978, China has received more than $2.5 *trillion* in FDI. In total, nearly 300,000 foreign-funded companies have been set up in China in the past 30 years, with 37,000 companies set up in a single year at the peak of China's stock bubble in 2007. A total of 480 of the world's Fortune 500 companies are doing business inside China.[10] In 2007, China received a then-record-setting $74.7 billion in FDI but this was just the tip of the iceberg.[11] The global financial crisis actually sped up investments into China as if it were a safe harbor, in the same way that cash flees to U.S. dollars and Treasury Bills at times of global uncertainty. This would seem to be a great contradiction for the Communist Party of China: Deng Xiaoping, father of China's modern capitalist rejuvenation, would be proud; Mao Zedong, the Great Helmsman of the rigidly ideological Communist era, would be apoplectic.

Much of the recent FDI in 2011 and 2012 was coming into China to establish centers for research and development (R&D), for which China is granting major tax concessions. For many years post-reform and opening up, tax credits were offered to almost any foreign company. Today, China's tax code has been harmonized but there are still benefits to be had by following China's national objectives. For example, those companies already in the country as a manufacturer, having exhausted the previously offered credits, are suddenly opening up mock labs and hiring token engineers to get the classification of an R&D center (or moving a facility to a less-developed region to get a different tax credit). Consequently, R&D may be coming in merely to get preferential tax treatment or even as hot money, transferring into China as much funds as possible, expectant of further appreciation of the *yuan*. Still more is coming in from new companies that, until now, had taken a wait-and-see attitude toward China, sometimes wisely letting others take the first move (and risk). Whatever the reason, FDI has come a long way since the first tentative investments after Deng opened the country.

In the 1980s, the joint venture was the preferred model for entry into China, in fact often the only model, according to Chinese government regulations designed to ease the economy into capitalism and transfer technology and know-how to Chinese companies. These cooperative partnerships were often anything but mutually beneficial, leading to many problems.

The previously mentioned 2009 case between China's Wahaha and France's Danone involved each suing its joint venture partner over their combined beverages portfolio in China, filing suit in multiple countries where units had been registered and preferential contract terms signed. The entire dispute revolved around whether Wahaha—by developing new beverages outside of the JV while using assets the JV thought it owned, such as the Wahaha brand itself—was not acting in good faith. Wahaha, for its part, made a plea to Chinese law, saying some of the original agreements had not been duly registered with Chinese authorities. Wahaha also claimed that Danone knew of the outside manufacturing, and later Wahaha's president tried to make the dispute about a foreign company using its sophistication to trap a Chinese company in an unfair agreement. Despite Danone having a far stronger legal argument, it lost in the court of public opinion and withdrew from the agreement at a great loss, of both face and finances. To date this is not only the largest and most public spat of its kind, but it is indicative of why joint ventures have become so unpopular with foreign companies in China.

As a result of the decline in popularity and legal necessity for joint ventures, the preferred model today for setting up foreign companies in China is to use a Wholly Owned Foreign Enterprise (WOFE).[12] The WOFE gives total control to the owner of the business and no surprises, such as showing up to work one day to find the joint venture partner has fled with all the equipment and managers. This was a not infrequent occurrence for many early China investors, such as Jack Perkowski who detailed his experiences (and adventures) setting up a now-successful auto parts venture with a motley collection of local partners that came and went, in his 2008 book *Managing the Dragon*.[13]

Back in the 1980s, foreign business in China was, by many accounts, a wild ride. On the half-empty flights to China, most of the passengers were Taiwanese or Hong Kongese. Any Westerners to be seen were most likely their customers traveling with them to visit suppliers or conduct business. In the 1990s, companies started to arrive in China to establish their own factories. Some companies may have even been making money, but repatriation of profits was a problem due to China's currency controls and the legacy idea in China that profits should be reinvested in the state. *Why,* Chinese bureaucrats might have then asked innocently, *would you ever want to take money out of China when the economy is growing so quickly?* For companies involved in joint ventures, FDI was often to China as a roach was to a roach motel: *it went in, it didn't come out.*

Today, WOFEs regularly repatriate up to 90 percent of profits after meeting strict reporting requirements and offsetting any previous losses, but it is hardly as easy as making an international transfer from one account to another. A game of cat and mouse takes place between China's tax authority and foreign companies, which use every trick in the book to get money out—transfer prices, special fees, royalties—while the authorities use every tool they have to keep it in.

China's business environment has matured significantly since China entered the WTO. Today foreign companies come to China for almost every kind of sourcing, outsourcing, manufacturing, or selling—sometimes all four. China has become a regional base of operations for many firms that have relocated their Asia headquarters from places like Singapore and Hong Kong. Shanghai and Beijing are today the most common choices for placing a China or Asia headquarters.

The preferred geographic areas for investment in China, according to a World Bank report in 2006, are the southeast coastal provinces, consisting of the Yangtze River Delta provinces of Jiangsu, Zhejiang and Shanghai; the Pearl River Delta province of Guangdong (near Hong Kong and Macau) whose capital is Guangzhou and which also includes Shenzhen, Dongguan and Zhuhai, all special economic zones (SEZs); and the province of Fujian near Taiwan.[14] The least attractive for investment are the north and northwest—Inner Mongolia and the Xinjiang Autonomous Regions—and the northeast provinces of Heilongjiang and Jilin, which Tsinghua University's Prof. Patrick Chovanec refers to, respectively, as "The Frontier" and "Rust Belt" of China.[15] Not exactly places conservative multinational companies would want to put their money. Lacking investment from both foreign and domestic companies, it is in these same places, unsurprisingly, where worker exploitation, coal-mining disasters, and social unrest often occur. The current hope of the Chinese government is to slow down development in the better-off areas and shift investment to places like Sichuan and Chongqing (the "Refuge" in Prof. Chovanec's regional map of China), and central provinces such as Anhui (the "Crossroads"—which sounds somewhat more optimistic for investment than "Rust Belt"). The influx of FDI creates a need not only for manufacturing facilities, for which the funds are typically applied, but increasingly for services. Relocated multinational headquarters have come to expect certain things of any location where they have significant operations: accounting, legal services, auditing and due diligence, human resources, even consulting and investment banking. All of these point to an urgent need for professional services and therefore, services FDI.

## THE SERVICES FDI SURGE

The next wave of FDI in China, which is beginning to crest now, is related to services, of which China's developing economy needs more, especially in its eastern cities such as Shanghai or Beijing where factories have been moved out of the central city to reduce pollution and improve quality of life, in favor of the higher-value-added service industries.

It is not just professional services, such as finance or accounting, that are growing services-based FDI, it is also entertainment and dining. Restaurant chains, such as Pizza Hut and KFC, now dot the streets of China's metropolises, and parent Yum! Brands is actively looking for acquisition targets which, in 2011, included the Little Sheep Mongolian Hot Pot chain, which Yum! was granted permission by Chinese regulators to acquire in November that year.

As an acquisition, Little Sheep was hardly as diminutive as its name implied; it was one of the first major foreign takeovers of a Chinese domestic brand. Heretofore, this was either thought unnecessary or not allowed. Unnecessary because foreign brands were thought superior by many Chinese consumers, and also many Chinese brands lacked the potential to be global brands because they were too generic: *White Cat* cleaning products, *White Rabbit* candy and so on. Not allowed because the Chinese brand names that tend to have significant recognition are owned by large state-owned enterprises. Purchasing a Chinese brand name is indicative of a paradigm shift. Foreign companies may be expected to acquire more local brands if they want to grow their businesses in China. That Little Sheep is also popular outside of China is an added bonus, part of what this book calls the *reverse globalization turbocharger* described in the following chapter.

In fact, the entire service sector in China, including education, retail, and health care, is growing rapidly. In just the first half of 2007 alone, FDI in the service industry totaled nearly $14 billion, a 58 percent rise over the same period in 2006 and representing more than 43 percent of the total FDI during that time. In 2011, for the first time, services FDI was actually greater than manufacturing FDI, about 47 percent of the total or $55 billion, nearly four times the amount invested just a few years earlier.

Clearly the foreign-invested service industry in China is growing, and the Chinese government is allowing more openness in the sector both as part of its WTO entry commitments (which are now officially completed) as well as accelerating the opening of other industries such as logistics, education, and health care that will bring in foreign know-how that China desperately needs to keep its development apace.

Overall, FDI remains a crucial part of China's development strategy but the preferred investment profile is changing. In terms of the government's preferred FDI targets in 2012, high-tech and service industry investments in the coastal cities, and any investments in the underdeveloped western parts of China, are in. Polluting, energy-intensive, and labor-intensive businesses in the already developed areas of China are out. *In* and *out* being relative terms; China does not often refuse FDI, it is just being more discerning about which projects go in which sectors and areas of China.

While exports and FDI are China's two most important *growth engines* in recent decades, they also point out the strategic weakness that China is depending on outside markets and outside investors to help it grow. That is where the third, and now highest priority, *growth engine* comes in: domestic market consumption.

## HUNGRY HIPPO: CHINA'S 1.3 BILLION CONSUMERS

The dream of 1.3 billion customers has been a draw to China for that last 30 years. The implication of the phrase—and of the myriad anecdotes about selling a pack of gum or an extra length of cotton on the shirts of every Chinese that have always been part of the China dream at one time or another—is that Chinese consumers are homogenous in what they want. For that to be possible, ethnic and cultural homogeneity would be one precondition.

While the vast majority of Chinese are of the *Han* ethnicity, there are geographical, linguistic, and cultural differences that make China's 1.3 billion extraordinarily complex. The 1 billion customer market myth aside, China's domestic market is going to be the biggest in the world, it is just a matter of time before marketers learn to sell to China's majority, who still have very little purchasing power.

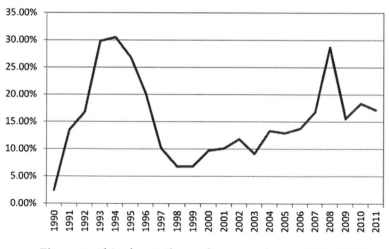

*Figure 5: China's retail spending growth rate, 1990–2011*

In 2007, personal expenditure (i.e., consumption) was just under 40 percent of China's total GDP growth. Disregarding the government's imperative to increase consumption under the 11th Five-Year Plan, consumption actually *decreased* as a portion of total GDP to about 35 percent in 2010. This is just half of the U.S.'s typical consumption expenditure (about 70 percent). It is not that consumption in China was contracting; it was that exports and investment had been growing *faster*. China's export economy and investment (especially after the global financial crisis stimulus program, which included a loosening of monetary policy and fiscal spending) have been hard to slow down. Exports and investments are so large that they actually overwhelm the purchasing power of 1.3 billion consumers. Another reason that China's consumption has been getting relatively small in recent years is that the savings rate of China's consumers' has been going up. Chinese consumers are actually saving more now than they did at the turn of the century, apparently either fearful of the future or unable to spend. There are two reasons why they are not spending more: they are saving more for emergencies and they are being taxed more.

The reason they are saving more will be explored more fully in the next book, *China's Demographic Supertrends*, but simply stated, China's national welfare system is not as good as one might expect for a communist or socialist country: healthcare and pensions are deemed insufficient by many and so they save or invest rather than spend.

In recent years, China stepped up collection of personal income tax. The Forbes Tax Misery & Reform Index in 2009 showed that China's citizens and companies are among the most taxed on Earth—only France was higher. For a country that is struggling to increase consumption, such high taxation—especially of consumers—is at odds with the desired outcome. Added to Chinese consumers' proclivity to save for a rainy day and in spite of retail sales increasing more than 15 percent a year since 2008, consumption in China is actually severely depressed.

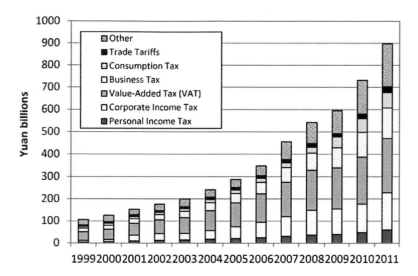

*Figure 6: China's national tax revenues by source, 1999–2011*

Unfortunately, simply cutting personal taxes alone is not likely to have much impact. Much of China's taxation is in the form of value-added tax (17 percent) and social security (23 percent)—which few trust, leading to China's greater-than-50-percent savings rate. With many of China's middle-class and wealthy consumers generating their incomes from entrepreneurship, the 25 percent corporate tax also has an indirect effect on consumption.

To reduce taxes and stimulate consumption, China will likely increase the minimum deductible salary, increase wages (especially in rural and newly developing areas) and give more subsidies or tax cuts to small and medium enterprises. But, for real change to occur, actual relief in the form of lower prices (by allowing the *yuan* to appreciate and buy more in imports, for example), or better social services so that people do not have to save so much, are likely to be the only long-term solutions. A restructuring of the government's tax base is another option, transferring the burden from the low-income and middle-class consumer to the wealthy, allowing China to achieve its goal of decreasing the wealth gap.

With the exception of increasing minimum wages (which China's provincial and local governments have been accelerating in 2011 and 2012), none of the above ideas have actually been implemented. 2012 is likely to see cuts to import taxes on a variety of consumer products, including luxury goods for which the tariff can be above 20 to 30 percent. Despite the lack of concrete measures before 2012, there were, nevertheless, but some small signs of increasing consumption.

Looking at the *growth* in GDP, about 10 percent in 2010, China's Vice Premier Li Keqiang (who will, in all likelihood, be promoted into a top leadership position in 2012, replacing Premier Wen Jiabao) stated that 90 percent of that growth came from consumption. This is almost a complete reversal from 2009 when almost all of China's 8.7 percent GDP growth came from the domestic investment stimulus, and it is assuredly a good thing for China and for the global economy.

Year by year, China steadily marches up in the economic rankings and will, within a decade, challenge the United States for the title of world's biggest market. The importance of Chinese domestic consumption in achieving this cannot be understated, for without strong personal expenditures on the part of the Chinese citizens, China will not be able to reach critical mass and continue developing on its own. Although the possibility of *decoupling*, being able to achieve growth independently of the global environment, still seems to be a challenge and not an entirely desirable outcome, even less likely is the possibility the world will continue to allow China to grow via exporting with an artificially low currency. Thus, while the domestic market consumption *growth engine* has been the third most important until now, it is *the* most important in the future, both to the Chinese economy and to any foreign business venture in China.

This means China *must* find more ways to stimulate consumption either through policy or by changing consumer behavior.

## CHANGING CHINESE CONSUMER ATTITUDES

China has undergone a series of stages in the development of its consumer attitudes and behaviors, which are distinct from the consumption patterns of consumers in many Western countries.

The first generation of consumers, active from around 1958 to 1978, were consuming prior to the opening of China to market reform. Their aspiration was simple: to get the "three rounds and one sound," also called the "old four"—wristwatch, bicycle, sewing machine and radio. At that time, China had strict foreign currency controls, limited imports, and the items in question needed to be paid for not only in cash, but also by having the right to purchase them using a quota ticket system.

The next generation, at the dawn of China's open door policy of the 1980s to about the year 1998, saw the rise of the "new four things"—washing machine, refrigerator, TV and camera. Consumer behavior in this period started to include comparison shopping and bargain hunting as people were freer to spend money and competition was heating up from domestic manufacturers and first forays from foreign manufacturers into the market. Just two decades after opening up, there was no way of stopping the insatiable demand in the cities and, by 2002, it could be said that urban dwellers were fully consumerized, with 126 televisions, 93 washing machines and 87 refrigerators for every 100 households. Their rural equivalents, meanwhile, had 61 televisions, 32 washing machines, and 15 refrigerators per 100 households, indicating a much greater growth potential for rural consumers, hundreds of millions of which have yet to move into cities.[16] Penetration rates for goods such as air conditioners, home computers and mobile phones were even lower at that time for both urban and rural dwellers. These items formed the basis for the next generation of consumers, the post-1980s cohort.

These consumers, born in the 1980s, are very different from those that grew up pre-1978. Many of them are only-children and were doted on by up to six parents and grandparents when growing up. Since becoming adults, they have often focused on a life around work, friends, family, and shopping.

Urban Chinese consumers especially have now entered a period of consumption based on quality of life, and are quickly adopting the same characteristics that motivate Western consumers—aspiration purchasing, emotional purchasing, buying for technical benefits, buying based on quality rather than price, choosing status symbols and brands suitable to their incomes, and so on.

While the past growth in the urban consumer market was largely driven by a need for basic commodities and non-durable goods, the new affluent Chinese consumers are able to buy anything and everything that a global market provides. Many have a new focus on buying durable goods such as cars and houses, in addition to spending on branded clothing, consumer electronics and luxury consumption such as wine, jewelry and overseas travel.

To satisfy these consumers' growing appetites, companies—foreign and domestic—are racing to attract their attention, creating an orgy of brand marketing. While there are growing domestic industries in automotive, construction, and appliances that provide high quality Chinese-made alternatives, usually at a lower price than the foreign-branded imported or domestically produced items, foreign brands still have more prestige and cachet for aspirational consumers.

The difference in prestige is so great that some Chinese manufacturers give themselves a foreign-sounding name to attract these consumers. One company, DaVinci Furniture, was very successful selling high-end furnishings to fill the luxury apartments of China's urban elite. Much of the company's image was a façade. In 2011, it was found that the company went so far as to send products to an export processing zone *still inside China*, and then re-imported its furniture from the zone so it could have a legally obtained import stamp. After the company was caught in the practice by a reporter, the consumer backlash was intense. The store has since closed four outlets in Shanghai and may leave the market permanently after it was fined more than 1.33 million *yuan* ($209,000).

In fact, young urban Chinese consumer attitudes can already be called brand conscious rather than price conscious. A famous and established brand is seen as a guarantee of quality, safety and effectiveness, but in China its esteem value and implied price tag are often more important, creating a flourishing market for counterfeit goods. Customers are increasingly insisting on the real thing, and Chinese quality watchdogs are clamping down more strictly on fake goods. As a result, brand owners are thinking of ways to add value and increase loyalty.

### Sinification and Going West: Two New China Strategies

As increasing standards of living push up the need for more living space, better cars, more fashionable clothes and the newest technology in mobile phones and computing, the companies that want to reach these consumers' wallets must now think about new ways of influencing them to buy. One study about selling in China found that it is no longer enough to simply sell a product designed or manufactured outside China as is. Nor could something be sold in the same way as in another foreign country; it requires a selling approach that takes Chinese consumer attitudes and behaviors into account.

This *Sinification* process means modifying Western products and services to have Chinese characteristics. More generally, this is called localization. Some of the world's largest companies are catching on to this idea and enjoying increased success in China as a result. For example, the global phenomenon that is the *Angry Birds* phone app came out with a Chinese Mid-Autumn Festival edition in 2011 and a Year of the Dragon edition in 2012. China is already its second largest market for Rovio, the maker of *Angry Birds,* and in the future seems poised for even greater growth. The co-founder and current Chief Marketing Officer of Rovio, Peter Vesterbacka, says, "China has great potential for growth but, just as exciting is the opportunity to build a creative franchise, a marriage of virtual and real life, that is special for China and exciting for our Chinese fans." The company is planning a retail strategy of official merchandise to combat the rampant piracy of its products, already popular in China.[17]

Another sea change is in the way Chinese consumers are being seen by multinational corporations—as heterogeneous. Frankly speaking, the Chinese consumers always were so but, as described earlier, for many years after China's initial opening post-1978, the "Chinese Market" idea of a homogenous consumer prevailed—with only minor attempts at segmentation, such as targeting the "Little Emperor" children of one-child families. Furthermore, attention then was focused on the so-called first-tier cities, such as Shanghai, Guangzhou and Beijing, where purchasing power was highest. In the last five years, tier-two cities have been increasingly targeted. With many of these cities being located inland, away from the East coast, this selling in these lower-tied cities is a kind of *Going West* strategic approach.

Now, with China's new rich being found all over, and the first- and second-tier markets being saturated with marketing, the next frontier in the Olympic Decade is the third-, fourth-, fifth-tier cities and beyond into the rural areas. While these lower-tiered cities are more numerous and geographically fragmented, the third- to fifth-tier cities have more than double the population of the first two tiers, approximately 234 million people versus about 118 million, and represent 43 percent of GDP versus 34 percent. Furthermore, those consumers' annual salaries are only about half of those in the upper tiered cities.[18] Consumption is growing quickly in these tiers, as these millions of newly affluent people see the better lives and better products in the first- and second-tiers and want the same.

The new China marketing strategies that will be most successful for multinational companies will be *Sinification* and *Going West* to the lower-tiered cities. In addition, these strategies are not mutually exclusive. Multinationals that want to be successful in these new markets have to follow *Sinification* strategies for every part of their China business operations—localize management, processes, products and services to produce items more suitable for Chinese consumers' tastes. In regard to these lower-tier cities in particular, the MNCs must also improve their distribution and supply chains in order to more effectively compete against local Chinese competitors already in the hearts and back-pockets of retailers. For many manufacturers, this may mean strategies that they have not used in other markets, such as television-shopping, manufacturer-owned stores, creating low-price versions of their product suitable for the local market, and so on.

## SUMMARY: CHINA'S GROWTH ENGINES

China's three growth engines are exports, foreign direct investment and the developing consumer market. Of these, exports and FDI have historically been most important, while in the future the growth of the consumer market is critical to China's continued development:

> *Exports:* Exporting from China is still a viable business opportunity. China's exports are growing, albeit at a slower pace. This shows there are still opportunities to operate export-oriented businesses in China. This includes sourcing, contract manufacturing (OEM), assembly or even full production as a JV or WOFE company inside China.
>
> *FDI:* The trends within FDI are toward cleaner capital-intensive high-tech manufacturing in the cities, low-tech labor-intensive manufacturing in the western parts of China and service industry investments just about anywhere.
>
> *Consumption:* China's domestic market is growing very quickly, and consumers are buying quality goods for their social esteem value. Especially in the big cities, brand-conscious consumers look at quality and brand, while rural and lower-tiered cities hold most of China's latest purchasing power. Consumers should be properly segmented according to localized marketing characteristics for the best results when selling in China's domestic markets.

All three of China's *growth engines* continue to operate, driving the country into the future.

## Chapter 2

# THE TURBOCHARGERS

识天下实势者，     *shi tian xia shi shi zhe,*
为俊杰           *wei jun jie*

"The person who knows the current trends is a person of outstanding talent."

The Chinese economic growth engines are exports, FDI, and domestic consumption, as described in the previous chapter. They are central to continued China's growth. China is trying to move beyond dependence on exports and FDI, and move to consumption as its primary growth engine.

However, China cannot simply turn off the other *growth engines*; they are still crucial to balanced growth and prevention of an economic hard-landing that might result from a sudden deceleration of the export sector or a crash in investment.

And then there are the *turbochargers*. Like turbochargers on vehicles, the *turbochargers* of China's economic growth engines propel the economy forward with a burst of energy.

The turbochargers are: *reverse globalization, Chinese determination,* and *leapfrogging*.

## THE RIGHT TIME, RIGHT PLACE, AND RIGHT PEOPLE

To understand why the *turbochargers* have appeared now, and have such a large influence on China's economic growth, ancient wisdom can provide a clue:

| 天时地利人和　*tian shi, di li, ren he* |
| --- |

The Right Timing, the Right Place, the Right People

This phrase describes, in characteristic Chinese poetic conciseness, how, with *time provided by the heavens, favorable geographic position,* and *unity and order of the people working toward a common good,* China is now enjoying opportunities that are among the greatest in the history of the world.

### The Right Time

The current era of globalization has brought prosperity to China. The world seems to be in an age of unbridled global trade. This is not, however, unprecedented. As the phases of globalization that Thomas Friedman described in *The World Is Flat* show, pre-World War I was similarly characterized by economic expansion, trade and prosperity. Heretofore, global expansion could often, if not always, be characterized as flowing from *the West* to *the rest.*

Early colonial power was often Western European countries extending their reach into Africa, South America and Asia. The only Asian colonial power, Japan, may be an exception, but only once it had adopted many Western practices in the Meiji Restoration period of the late 1860s.

In the mid-20th century, global institutions such as the United Nations, International Monetary Fund (IMF), World Bank, and the General Agreement on Tariffs and Trade (GATT, the precursor to the World Trade Organization (WTO)) were defined by Western power led by the United States, as well as the World War

II victors, including China and the Soviet Union. Until the present day, the majority shares and power in these organizations are still controlled by the predominantly Western powers that formed them in the first place.

In more recent decades, even modern approaches to open markets, trade, and investment have continued to be defined by Western ideals, such as the so-called Washington Consensus, and implemented under the aegis of the IMF and World Bank. These institutions and ideas were sometimes forced upon, other times welcomed, by the *rest* of the world.

If there was a turning point, a defining year in which the philosophy of *the West* to *the rest* ceased to be a legitimate and accepted ideal, in was undoubtedly 2008. That year, more than any other, would define the *right time* for China to appear on the world stage. It was both the start of China's Olympic Decade and the end of Western preeminence and moral superiority, as a result of the global financial crisis.

## The Right Place

China is arguably both the country most affected by globalization as well as one of the greatest beneficiaries of it. No other country has welcomed foreign manufacturers so willingly, nor has another country benefited as much, given China's extraordinary progress in just over 30 years since Deng Xiaoping's reforms began.

It is worth remembering that, prior to 1978, China was an isolated and undeveloped country compared with many of its Asian peers. The earlier Asian wave of globalization, from the 1960s to the 1980s, saw the rise of Japan as an export powerhouse and then Four Tigers—South Korea, Singapore, Hong Kong and Taiwan. China became the *right place* to outsource manufacturing, not only as a result of Deng's policies, but also because, starting in the 1980s, developed Western economies such as the United States and Western European nations, along with Japan and the Four Tigers, began looking for a low-cost labor zone as their own costs began to rise. China, with its massive quantities of cheap labor, its geographic location in the middle of Asia and its coastal region newly opened to investment and export processing, fit the bill nicely to become the next *world's factory*.

## The Right People

Finally, the *right people* refers not to the people themselves, who are of course no different than any other people, but to the characteristics of Chinese society and culture that make the Chinese population a significant factor in China's rise since 1978. These factors include the large absolute number of people that were available to work in the manufacturing jobs that drove the export economy; the willingness of many of them to migrate long distances to work and live, speeding up China's urbanization; and the determination and optimism of those who would become rich first and then take up roles as China's consumers.

What motivates the Chinese people to worker harder, farther from home, and achieve business success and personal wealth ahead of others? And is there anything unique to Chinese culture that is not present in other cultures? While such an assertion would be difficult if not impossible to prove, an answer might be found in a combination of traditional Confucian values, plus the recent historical events of the tumultuous 1950s and 1960s under Communism, the Cultural Revolution of the 1960s and 1970s, and the reforms of the 1980s. Each period brought enormous change to China and required the Chinese people to adapt continuously. Now, in a relatively open economy, China's people desire to reach their place among the ranks of the world's top consumers. This drives an enormous race to prosperity with Chinese characteristics. Relationships, mutual support, and entrepreneurial spirit all come into play.

～

The *right time, right place* and *right people* are the foundations that allowed for the emergence of the *turbochargers*—the accelerators of China's *growth engines* and the *economic supertrends*.

## THE THREE *TURBOCHARGERS*

The idea of a turbocharger of China's *growth engines*, already some of the most powerful engines in the world economy, may seem like overkill. In fact, there are three such *turbochargers*, each one amplifying the effect of not only the *growth engines* but the *supertrends* as well. They are *reverse globalization, Chinese determination* and *leapfrogging*.

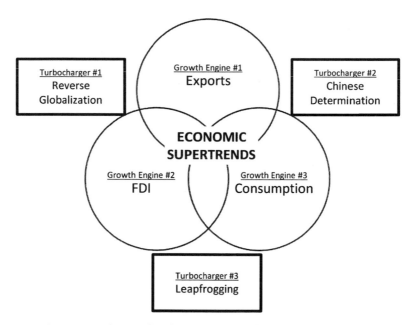

*Figure 7: Relationship between growth engines, turbochargers and supertrends*

REVERSE GLOBALIZATION FROM CHINA

*Reverse globalization* is the first *turbocharger*. It refers to the new direction of expansion of China's economy and interests, and underlies several of the *growth engines* covered in the first chapter, as well as the *supertrends* later in the book. Inasmuch as globalization affected China from the outside-in, with many so-called Western ideas being brought into China, *reverse globalization* will be an inward-out force.

The original outward-in globalization was led by Western countries and refers to the opening of markets and expansion of foreign trade. The first era of globalization occurred in the 19th and early 20th centuries until the time of World War II. Following World War II, a new American-led *free world* formed, but this was not globalization as it is defined today because *free world* did not mean *open markets*. The notable opponents to the *free world*, the USSR and China, had formed their own bloc of nations affiliated with Communism and traded little with the West. Globalization was only again practiced after the opening of China in 1978 and the collapse of the USSR in 1991, two events which allowed trade to occur almost anywhere, enabled by inter-connected markets for capital, manufacturing, and technology.

The first globalization of the 19th century was defined by the colonial powers. As the second large-scale process of globalization began in the 1980s, it was again largely defined by the Western countries, organizations and agreements, including the Group of Seven (G7) economic cooperative, the OECD, and of course the GATT and its later incarnation, the WTO. This second phase of globalization had the U.S. market as the prize that every emerging economy wanted access to.

The next stage of globalization, which started in 2008 with the financial crisis and the concurrent start of China's Olympic Decade, will be defined by China. To paraphrase a line from the movie *Casablanca,* maybe not today, maybe not tomorrow, but soon and for the rest of our lives, China is the market that every other economy will want access to. Thanks to its size and growing power, China will be able to define new rules of the game. More than just an expansion of globalization, *reverse globalization* changes the direction from a Western-led model to a China-led model.

## What Will the China Reverse Globalization Model Look Like?

When China has attained sufficient market power—and it will do so within the Olympic Decade—globalization will fundamentally change. Everything from trade, to markets, to the flow of people and culture, will reverse, from *West-to-East*, to *East-to-West*.

Among other characteristics of the *reverse globalization turbocharger*, China will become a net importer of many products as its currency becomes stronger and globally exchangeable, it will become an exporter of culture, language, and ideas to a curious world eager to embrace the Chinese way. China's role in global organizations will change from that of follower to that of leader. To be sure, it will not be alone, and power will be contested; the United States will *not go gentle into that good night*. Furthermore the *reverse globalization turbocharger* is not likely to be a harbinger of geopolitical conflict, but merely a broadening of competition among cultural or societal norms. It will likely change the way trade is conducted, not just the directional flow. After the perceived failure of the Doha Development Round of trade talks to address the concerns of developing nations, China appears to be both more sophisticated in using the mechanisms of the WTO to protect its interests and more selective in applying the principles that define the WTO, such as avoiding the use of bilateral agreements that the WTO was in part designed to eliminate.

China has already demonstrated that it does not need the WTO except for access to the largest markets (primarily the United States and the EU). For many other markets, China is pursuing bilateral trade agreements. In the case of ASEAN—the Association of Southeast Asian Nations—it will likely be part of a multilateral trading bloc. These bilateral and multilateral trade agreements improve China's market power at the same time they make the WTO agreement obsolete.

Will China still need the U.S. market of 300+ million consumers when China itself has a population that is bigger than the United States, the European Union and Japan combined? China's consumption, as mentioned in *China's Growth Engines*, is still far below the level of a developed economy and will likely never be high enough to decouple completely from the global economy, but it will be less dependent on it all the same. To be sure, this will not be an overnight change in trade direction, but it will happen over the *Olympic Decade* and beyond as China matures and becomes more affluent.

### From FDI to CDI: Chinese Direct Investment

Another of the *growth engines* that will be changing direction under the *reverse globalization turbocharger* is *foreign direct investment* (FDI). China today is the world's largest recipient of FDI, but in the future it will become the world's greatest exporter of capital as *overseas direct investment* (ODI). As China's companies grow and prosper in a market of 1.3 billion, their equity will grow and they will become a much greater percentage of the world's Fortune 500 or Global 1,000 companies by valuation. As China's *yuan* appreciates, this effect will be multiplied. Based on the strength and size of their home market and a climbing stock market, their investment power will increase, much as it did for Japanese companies during the 1980s Bubble Economy years. China's $3.2 trillion currency reserves are already being used to purchase assets abroad through its sovereign wealth fund; it won't be long before private companies are more successfully doing the same. Before the global financial crisis, many investments by Chinese companies were rejected by the governments of many countries for national security reasons (since the acquiring companies were often Chinese state-owned enterprises). In 2012, the climate has changed. Although national security still trumps all other rationale in the United States, many other countries now welcome investments from China that provide financial relief from lingering effects of the crisis and declining national competitiveness. By the end of the Olympic Decade, Chinese investments will be eagerly sought and competed for by countries that once rejected them, making *reverse globalization* one of the most important *turbochargers* of the *affluence supertrend.*

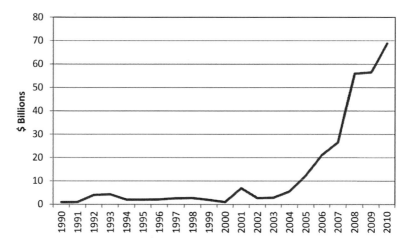

*Figure 8: China's overseas direct investment, 1990–2010*

### Flow of People and Culture from China

Global tourism will see its own *reverse globalization* impact. In 2008, at the start of the Olympic Decade, *Supertrends of Future China* stated that businesses that wanted to profit from the coming boom in Chinese tourism should start investing in marketing and customer service for Chinese travelers. Chinese tourists in 2011 were already the most desirable luxury shoppers when abroad, spending the most per person in many overseas destinations including Australia, France and the United Kingdom. Tomorrow it is the middle-class Chinese tourists going abroad that will be a major economic force. Again helped by a rising *yuan*, these tourists will be cash-rich and numerous.

In the recent past, developed countries feared that Chinese people only wanted to visit their countries in order to attempt illegal immigration, dropping out of the official tours at the first chance they got, to run off and take jobs as dishwashers and garment workers. That image has been turned on its head: people from all over the world now come to China to work illegally on tourist visas while Chinese travelers buy out the stock of one luxury boutique after another when they travel to Hong Kong, London or New York.

Smart countries will begin courting Chinese travelers, attracting them with new direct air routes. In January 2012, President Barack Obama announced a streamlining of visa procedures to help boost the tourism economy and spur job creation. To give some idea of the scale, Gary Locke, the U.S. ambassador to China, said that visa processing increasing by 34 percent in 2011 to more than 1 million processed and 900,000 issued.

Also in 2011, Chinese travelers were courted by Japan and were being credited with saving the ski season near post-meltdown Fukushima. That is not to say the Chinese are chasing bargains; Japan travel is still expensive for almost everyone, but the Chinese have money in their pockets and a lack of places to spend it at home. This topic will be returned to in the next book in this series, *China's Demographic Supertrends*.

Another aspect of Chinese culture that is migrating abroad is traditional Chinese medicine (TCM). Although the scientific proof, quality and efficacy of TCM is debated outside China, inside China TCM is part of China's culture and exists side-by-side with Western medical practices and medicines. China is actively trying to expand TCM awareness outside of China via the Confucius Institutes. It is also welcoming increasing numbers of foreign students who want to study at China's TCM colleges. Finally it is encouraging the export of TCM products around the world as the holistic medicine approach gains acceptance by Western practitioners and their patients. In 2011, China exported approximately $2.3 billion of TCM products, up more than 36 percent from the previous year, according to the China Chamber of Commerce for Import & Export of Medicines and Health Products. The United States was China's largest export market by far in recent years but other large economies, such as the United Kingdom, Russia and Brazil, are growing at rates of about 50 percent annually.

TCM will not be China's only major cultural export, there will eventually be hundreds—everything from *feng shui* to foot juggling. Viewers of the 2012 Academy Awards witnessed an entertaining performance from a Chinese acrobatic troop, bringing a dose of Chinese flavor to the proceedings. Chinese acrobats have long been a part of Westernized circus troops, such as *Cirque du Soleil*, but this performance was special for Chinese culture since it was identified as a performance by the Shandong Acrobatic Troop. Chinese cultural influences will soon be everywhere; they are already being seen in television and movies.

*Cultural Ambassadors Po and Kato*

One final example of *reverse globalization* is media and popular culture. Western culture and English media are still dominant, and will remain so for some time, but signs are increasingly appearing that Chinese cultural "soft power" is broadening China's appeal.

As Western children were once studying Japanese, now they are studying Mandarin. The same children might have watched Japanese animation such as *Pokemon* in the past, now they are watching made-in-China *Pleasant Goat and Big Big Wolf.*

At the movies, Jackie Chan and Jet Li once dominated as distinctive Chinese faces in kung fu fighting roles. Today, Western audiences may be watching a more sophisticated and multi-talented Chinese performer without even realizing it. Examples, such as Taiwanese singer and actor Jay Chou, most recently co-starring in *The Green Hornet* movie franchise, or Maggie Q in *Mission Impossible III* and the second TV remake of *La Femme Nikita,* are the most recent examples of Chinese cross-over stars. Maggie Q, herself an American of Asian/Western mixed ethnicity, parlayed her Eastern fame in Hong Kong movies and media into Western culture, rather than the other way around. Mainland Chinese actors are also appearing more often in foreign-release movies. While Zhang Ziyi and Gong Li have featured in numerous Chinese-produced films by Zhang Yimou, Gong Li also co-starred in the American-made movie *Miami Vice* and played a Japanese courtesan in the movie adaptation of *Memoirs of a Geisha*. Popular Chinese actress Li Bingbing will appear in *Resident Evil: Retribution*, the latest installment in the megahit *Resident Evil* movie and videogame franchise. Chinese faces in Western movies are on the rise; so are Chinese-culture-influenced plotlines, another indication of China's media spreading from China *outward*.

American movies, once culturally insular, are now making attempts, obvious ones bordering on pandering at times, to connect with Chinese audiences, recognizing that China's 1.3 billion will drive a great deal of future ticket sales. Examples abound since 2008, when Hollywood keyed into the trend after noticing the blockbuster success of DreamWorks' *Kung Fu Panda* in both Western and the China markets. Thereafter, the tide turned, with productions including the 2010 remake of *The Karate Kid*, now set in China and co-starring Jackie Chan (and, significantly, casting off Mr. Miyagi's Japanese karate for Chan's Chinese kung fu), a sequel to *Kung Fu Panda* and numerous globally released Chinese movies such as director Zhang Yimou's *Hero* or more recent *Flowers of War*, starring Christian Bale.

It is not just China-themed or Chinese-produced movies that are influencing audiences, Chinese advertising has made its first forays into global media. While Lenovo's global sponsorship of the Beijing Olympics was something of a given, more recently viewers have even seen egregious product placements of Chinese milk in *Transformers 3* and *The Big Bang Theory*. While it is doubtful that consumers will be clamoring to buy the Inner Mongolia-produced *Shuhua* milk from China's Yili Industrial Group—given the reputation some Chinese dairies have for poor quality control—the domestic Chinese audience for both *Trans-*

*formers 3* and *The Big Bang Theory* is in the millions, which is why these channels are being used for product placement. Western and Chinese consumers alike might be more attracted by the Lenovo computers, Meters/bowne clothing and TCL televisions, which also appeared in *Transformers 3*.

The list of exported Chinese movies, music, television and other culture is only expected to increase as China announced a new initiative in early 2012 to make culture a pillar industry, ahead of regional cultural leaders such as Japan. A pillar industry is defined by China as 5 percent or more of the nation's GDP, which, at 2011 levels, would mean cultural industries could contribute 2.4 trillion *yuan* ($373 billion) as early as 2015.[1]

The list of *reverse globalization* factors is extensive; they will be covered chapter by chapter as the *supertrends* are discussed.

CHINESE DETERMINED TO BE RICH *AND* GLORIOUS

The second *turbocharger* is *Chinese determination* or, more evocatively, the *determination of the Chinese people to succeed.* The most abstract of the *turbochargers,* it is nonetheless extremely potent, since it goes right to the heart of the belief system of many of China's citizens.

Certainly, when it comes to success and making money, there is not a magic formula and this feeling is far from exclusive to the Chinese. But, in China today, there is at least a strong national determination, among virtually everyone, from the Communist government down to the millions of housekeepers, to get wealthy. This atmosphere predates Deng's famously paraphrased words, "To get rich is glorious." And it also certainly pre-dates Mao's Communist experiment from 1949 to 1978. In fact, it has been a characteristic of China far back into antiquity.

*The Origins of Chinese Determination*

During the pre-industrial era and dating back about 2,000 years, Chinese traders are known to have plied the Silk Road, bringing tea, porcelain, firearms and other products to Europe. In the relatively modern times of the past 600 years, Chinese were active sea traders throughout the South China Sea and beyond on the voyages of Admiral *Zheng He*. It would seem that, in China, the determination to become rich and successful is stronger than ever, with modern Chinese success being in part due to the strength of Chinese bonds at home *and* abroad.

## *The Bamboo Network*

Historically, Chinese spread to all corners of the world, forming an unrivaled network of overseas Chinese people who often keep their ethnicity and cultural identity alive, sometimes in the so-called *Chinatowns* that can be found in almost any large city around the world.

Indeed, these émigrés created overseas enclaves that not only were a platform for trade among themselves, but also served as support networks by supplying favors, loans and cooperation. Many overseas Chinese communities display numerous examples of Chinese entrepreneurial zeal. Many are Chinese businesspeople who fled the mainland post-1949 when Mao's Communists captured and remade China into the People's Republic of China.

Some of these businesspeople that ended up in nearby Hong Kong, or further afield in Malaysia, Indonesia and Thailand, became successful entrepreneurs and, post-1978, brought back capital and know-how to their original homeland. Murray Weidenbaum and Samuel Hughes described the phenomenon in their book, *The Bamboo Network: How Expatriate Chinese Entrepreneurs Are Creating a New Economic Superpower in Asia*. Those overseas Chinese were often in the best position to gain from renewed business ties with mainland China because of their long-standing family bonds, shared language and common cultural background.

There is a word in Mandarin describing those who moved abroad: *huaqiao* (华侨), made up of the characters representing China and to live abroad. In other words, Chinese may be abroad, but they are still Chinese, keeping their essential *Chineseness* while living outside the Middle Kingdom.

The Bamboo Network and concept of *overseas Chinese* retaining their original ties of ethnicity means that, for example, a Malaysian-Chinese might have better luck doing business in nearby Fujian or Guangdong provinces than would, say, a Caucasian American, all other things being equal. The ethnic connection is further enhanced if some form of Chinese dialect is still spoken, no matter how thickly accented it may have become from years or decades overseas. The desire to keep Chinese ethnicity alive is one defining aspect of the *Chinese determination turbocharger,* a desire for success for oneself and one's children is another.

As the recent book *Battle Hymn of the Tiger Mother,* by Yale professor and ethnic Chinese Amy Chua shows, the Chinese cultural driver of determination and success is not location dependent. Research indicates that children of Asian ethnicity in the American school system score marginally higher than those of Caucasian ethnicity and significantly higher than African-Americans. Without opening a debate into nature versus nurture, the fact that, in China, many parents are similarly obsessed with their children's grades and test scores still says much about the determination of Chinese parents everywhere to see better lives for their children. Where did these values come from?

### Confucian Values in Modern China

Born more than 2,500 years ago, the philosopher Confucius still has a strong influence on modern Chinese society. This is especially true when it comes to so-called Confucian family values as a possible underpinning of China's determination to sacrifice for the sake of prosperity for the next generation.

The philosophy emphasizes concepts of benevolence and goodness, the importance of a structured society, respect for family and elders, and attainment of knowledge and wisdom as a form of strength. Confucian values undoubtedly helped the traditional family to remain strong against hardships, such as the yearly risk of flood, drought and starvation that plagued the Yellow River basin, thought to be the cradle of Chinese civilization. The frequent disasters forced its inhabitants into a process of continual adaptation and rejuvenation: following the precepts of Confucianism meant facing problems with acceptance and stoicism, even in tragic circumstances.

It could be said that Mother Nature played a trick on the Chinese by placing all of the major energy sources away from the most-easily populated areas, or giving the country the third-largest landmass (virtually tied with the United States in terms of area) yet making it deficient in arable land. Thus, China may be called a resource-poor nation whose people in ancient times were always in a state of uncertainty over where the next meal would come from. Rivers flooded, droughts parched. Historically, the country has had warlords and civil wars that created a cultural pragmatism in the people, adaptability to changing circumstances and, perhaps most importantly, roots in family values as the only stable unit in time of change: the family members stick together and support one another. This applies at the family level but, under Confucianism, the state is another level where the first of five important relationships is between ruler and subject.

Throughout the early years of Chinese civilization, characterized by war, natural disasters, and bureaucratic corruption, the Chinese learned that monetary wealth is transitory, so the only true wealth a person or family can hold on to is education. Education is the best way to change the outcome for a family over a single generation. This principle continues today to define much of Chinese thinking about success and determination.

Despite Mao's attempts to remove influences of Confucianism as part of the "four olds,"[2] the philosophy has re-emerged in modern China in everything from lively discussions and reinterpretations on popular television shows and best-selling books, to corporate training extolling the virtues of "Confucian management." CEOs pay big money to business schools to attend workshops on Confucian theory for the workplace (*"Be kind but stern to your workers, you are a father figure…"*).

## Education First

Family values are also deeply embedded in Confucianism which, when strictly followed, involves filial piety and ancestor worship. More practically speaking, this also helps to explain the emphasis Chinese parents place on education as the path for their children to succeed: only investing in the education of the next generation will ensure descendants to sweep your tomb.

Children are taught to value study as a means to prosperity, to live simply and frugally by saving money to grow wealthy but, above all, to not value material possessions over the bonds of family. The parents save every penny from their hard labor by working from early morning to late at night, while their savings are generously used on their children to educate them.

Chinese families today may spend much of their savings to send their children to the best schools they could afford, even borrowing money from others in order to pay for education abroad. Such Chinese parents have set goals for their children early in the children's' lives to attend Yale or Oxford, even when they have just started kindergarten.

## Working Together in Social Harmony

One could say that the Confucian cultural commonality of the majority of the Chinese people is one thing that gives them the inner strength and direction to work together to achieve a common goal of their country's development, what the Chinese government calls the development of a *harmonious society*. Other countries' populations may lack this sense of social cohesion, perhaps because they are more individualistic rather than relationship-oriented, as described in theories by Geert Hofstede or Fons Trompenaars' cross-cultural comparative studies.[3]

It is worth examining in more detail the effect of Confucian cultural values on China's multi-millennial history as a civilization and whether Western people might not learn something from it instead of automatically assuming China's lagging development versus the West confirms the flawed nature of Confucian philosophy as a basis for life in a society.

The Chinese government itself indicated the return of Confucius to a place of public reverence by erecting a statue of the scholar-philosopher prominently in Tiananmen Square, near the mausoleum for Mao, who once sought to depose his influence by becoming, in effect, the supreme father-figure to the People's Republic of China.

Confucius, while forming the core of the *Chinese Determination turbocharger,* also can be found within the *reverse globalization turbocharger,* as part of China's soft power forays abroad. The Confucius name is now used for the Confucius Institutes, cultural exchange and education centers opened around the world to spread Chinese language education and cultural awareness. The institutes are not free, that would be too *Communist* for most peoples' tastes, but they are highly subsidized by China and operate as non-profit organizations. So far, there are several hundred of the Institutes established in more than 100 countries around the world, with 350 Confucius Institutes in the United States alone. [4]

The use of the Confucius name does not end there. Unashamedly, there is also a newly established Confucius Prize—meant to rival the Nobel Peace Prize. The Confucius Prize was most recently awarded in 2011 to Vladimir Putin, after the Nobel Peace Prize went to Liu Xiaobo, an imprisoned Chinese dissident, in 2010.

Clearly, the Chinese social determination and political will are aligned to a degree that some countries might envy for their positive benefits of having the majority of the population focused on growth of the country, the society, the company, the family and the individual, in that order. Other countries might fear such a system, believing it to be merely a sign of too-effective propaganda and repressed individual freedoms. Yet, for China, the system has yet to face a destabilization-level event of the sort that many China-doom prognosticators see in China's near future. Perennial China doomsayer Gordon Chang, author of *The Coming Collapse of China,* predicted modern China would fall in 2012. China is increasingly open about the problems inherent in its political and social systems and will avoid a dramatic collapse, though it can no longer pretend the problems do not exist.

### *The Negative Side of Getting Rich*

The high pressure to succeed, to become gloriously rich, also creates a number of social problems, the largest of them the wealth divide. There are also lesser but still significant social problems associated with extra-legal and illegal activities (i.e., getting rich no matter what it takes); lack of transparency (i.e., hiding true success and wealth, thus avoiding social contribution such as taxes, for fear it might be taken away); government collusion in overly ambitious projects (i.e., more growth or bust); and exploitation of workers (i.e., a shift from Communitarian self-sacrifice to individual greed). How well China addresses these problems associated with the societal determination to be successful will be the difference between sustainable success and short-term success.

Therefore the fast growth of China's economy and lure of easy money can cause damage to society, but there is still no shortage in sight of Chinese people willing to *jump in the sea,* a Chinese euphemism for taking a risk by starting your own venture.

High speed, however, can wear out the tires on the car. In China, the entrepreneurs and the common workers are most certainly the tires: they absorb the wear and tear as the economy surges forward, and are also the first to feel the burn when the economy hits the skids.

Although *Chinese determination* may lead to some negative social effects, the Chinese government has recognized those effects and has even made balanced development a core theme of its two most-recent national development plans. Modern *Chinese determination* is largely responsible for the resiliency of the people and the strength of new Chinese companies in global competition.

### Characteristics of Modern Chinese Determination

China today, from its global-scale events such as the Olympics and the World Expo, from its world's largest companies, and from its newly rich entrepreneurs, has a consistent feeling of success and optimism about the future.

While China cannot be treated as having a homogenous culture, with its 56 ethnicities and hundreds of languages and dialects, there is nevertheless a shared determination, an entrepreneurial drive, an emphasis on education and helping the next generation to achieve more than their parents, that, when put together, creates a common cultural will to succeed no matter what hardships are required.

As in *Battle Hymn of the Tiger Mother*, Chinese parents would almost never allow their child to take valuable time away from studies on aimless play or to make a few extra *yuan* doing a part-time job with no future. Rather, the parents work doubly hard themselves, making that few extra *yuan*, to make sure their children have every need looked after and create the opportunities, which they never had, for their children. Chinese parents, and even grandparents, will go so far as letting the child take their seat on a bus or train in order to give them extra rest for their studies. Unfortunately, this *determination* of the parents may lead to spoiled children who, later in life, find it difficult to work or live independently.

The thirst for education and knowledge is apparent throughout Chinese society. Aside from the nearly 7 million new college graduates each year, Chinese master's and doctoral programs are overflowing, and hundreds of thousands more Chinese students go abroad to study. In the job market, Chinese *curriculum vitae* are often a laundry list of certifications achieved, and millions study for popular tests in every imaginable skill to get that one marginal difference over another applicant that might result in a better job opportunity. As the saying goes, if you are one in a million in China, there are 1,300 others just like you.

China's bookstores are full of people on any day of the week, filling aisles and sitting on benches, against walls, anywhere that will allow them to read, literally spending hours at a time in a noisy retail environment acquiring knowledge. The Chinese government has long used the bookstores as a place to disseminate information. The largest chain, *Xinhua,* is a government-controlled media conglomerate that also publishes much of the official news in the country, but newer chains are sprouting all the time. In Shanghai's largest, the *Shanghai Book City*, the aisles are filled not with young Communist Party cadres absorbing Mao Zedong Thought—they are the youth of today seeking information that will give them a leg up in school or in the workforce.

This means that books, blogs, and other information media are some of China's fastest growing sectors. The *determination turbocharger* is a driving force behind the *urbanization* and *affluence supertrends* described later in this book, as well as an important theme in the third volume of this series, *China's Political Supertrends.*

### Recent Tests of China's National Determination

When the Chinese state—the nation—is threatened in some way, the Chinese people come together in a strong bond of nationalism, sometimes with negative hostility directed outward but also with inward strength.

In May 2008, China's Sichuan region was struck by a magnitude 8.0 earthquake that killed more than 70,000 people and left millions homeless. It was the largest natural disaster to hit China since the 1976 Tangshan earthquake that killed more than 240,000 people. Following the Sichuan earthquake, the Chinese people came together like never before in modern times in an unprecedented show of support and assistance for the region.

Billions of *yuan* were raised in donation campaigns that were often conducted door-to-door, with donated amounts being posted in prominent locations around the community. This perhaps increased the feeling of solidarity in sharing the burden or, more cynically, served to pressure others into giving more or face being shamed in front of their neighbors.

For China, the people's national spirit was especially strong in 2008 because of hosting the Olympics. After enduring protests in foreign countries, including the United Kingdom and France, against the Torch Relay (which many interpreted as protests against China's harsh response to the Tibetan unrest in March 2008), the Chinese people came together to retaliate against foreign firms, including France's Carrefour, support the Olympic spirit, and protect the runners as the Torch Relay continued on to other countries.

At one point, millions of Chinese simultaneously changed their MSN Messenger screen names to include "I Love China," and have never stopped posting the heart icon to this day, a memento perhaps of the Olympics or a reminder to never forget the pride, or shame, China felt during the height of the protests against China.

Other countries have difficulty duplicating this national pride. For example, in Greece, average people imagine the government as corrupt and would protest against it, whereas most Chinese *know* the government is corrupt but would never think of protesting as long as it is still perceived to be acting in the people's interest overall.

China's national consciousness is not to be trifled with, and *hurting the feelings of the Chinese people* is a diplomatic admonishment that China's Foreign Ministry often levels toward actions by foreign governments and organizations felt to have impinged on China's pride. The Communist Party has used nationalism and supposed persecution of China by non-Chinese nations, companies and individuals (especially from Western developed economies) as a way to consolidate its support and justify its mandate to govern.[5]

When directed toward China's economy, this feeling of Chinese solidarity and nationalism will certainly drive continued growth and development in the future. If the other two *turbochargers* are rational, this one is certainly *emotional*, making it a powerfully motivating *turbocharger*.

LEAPING AHEAD

The third and final *turbocharger* is *leapfrogging*, the ability to skip over old ideas, old rules, old technology, and old infrastructure, due to China's unique position as both a developing country and an extraordinarily rich country in absolute terms.

*Bypassing Old Technology and Infrastructure*

Being able to skip over old technology and infrastructure is not a new phenomenon for China. As mentioned previously in the discussion on *China's determination*, in the past China has had to rebuild, restructure, and reorient itself almost continuously after numerous natural disasters, invading conquerors and changing dynasties. In more modern times, it had to deal with colonialism, civil war, and dramatic changes in political and economic ideology. This has created a historical norm of disruptive transformation.

It is, therefore, no coincidence that China was a global leader—although isolated from the rest of the world—up until the 1800s: it had innovated its way out of problems for millennia with technological evolution, it had created engineering wonders such as the Grand Canal and the Great Wall, and it was even the first region to use centrally issued fiat currency—paper money—instead of actual gold or other valuable metals, making it economically stronger as well.

After the 1949 establishment of the People's Republic of China, China's technology and infrastructure were somewhat hamstrung by the country's reliance on Soviet Communist-era technology and methods. China's only advantage was that, after nearly 30 years of civil war, occupation by the Japanese, and World War II, it was nearly a blank slate, an agrarian society ready to be modernized.

## The Failure of Mao's Modernization

In 1949, China was an agrarian society and economy, meaning the scale of the needed modernization was large and unprecedented. The closest example, the Soviet Union's formation in 1922 after the October Revolution and civil war, was still far from China's situation: Russia had modernized and industrialized much earlier, and its population was nowhere near the size of China's at the time. Despite China's blank slate, a number of mistakes—some disastrous—in central planning were made—the failed Great Leap Forward and Cultural Revolution among them.[6]

Consequently, much of the modernization that was supposed to occur in the Communist era happened in fits and starts, and was limited by information asymmetries—the central government did not know exactly what every province and local town was doing, and vice versa—and resource allocation inefficiencies—planning for an economy the size of China turned out to be more complex than anyone had imagined. In other words, the central government may have received data—if they were available at all—that had been purposely exaggerated or delayed by weeks or months. The centrally managed system of how to allocate resources for such a large and complex economy was even harder for China than it was for the USSR.

In September 1976, during the final tumultuous year of the decade-long Cultural Revolution, China plunged into uncertainty with the death of Mao. The much more moderate premier, Zhou Enlai, who had planted the first seeds of reform, had died eight months earlier. Upon Mao's death, Mao's chief lieutenants and widow—together known as the Gang of Four—briefly seized control. Had they stayed in power, China would have taken another step backward—but they were soon deposed by military loyalists supporting Mao's chosen successor, Hua Guofeng. The new leadership brought Deng back from exile, with China's economy still in disarray. After a power struggle with Hua, the more-senior Deng consolidated his power and began the fateful economic reforms and modernization in 1978. This time, reforms would not fail.

The *turbocharger* of *leapfrogging* has meant that China could build completely new infrastructure without public debate, and its central government stability meant it would be easier to implement long-term projects—such as the Three Gorges Dam—faster and at scales previously unimagined. China's development has proceeded in leaps, bypassing older, less-sophisticated and expensive ways of doing things for newer, better ways.

For example, China has built new transportation infrastructure, including trains, roads, ports, and airports that are now among the newest and most expansive in the world. China has embarked on several projects in the last 10 years that are similar in size and scale to the U.S. interstate highway network project championed by President Dwight Eisenhower in 1956, except China is building both interstate highways and high-speed rail networks simultaneously.

One of the biggest and most important additions to China's modern economy is its telecommunication infrastructure. Here too, the *leapfrogging turbocharger* has given China a significant advantage: foregoing large-scale investments in fixed-line telecommunications, today's China is a country of mobile phones and mobile Internet. China's people are using hundreds of millions of mobile phones, on three national 3G networks, with coverage literally to the ends of the Earth—even Mount Everest has a mobile phone base station. China also largely skipped over dial-up Internet access and has invested heavily in ADSL, cable, and fiber optic Internet delivery, in addition to the metropolitan wireless networks.

Several chapters feature the *leapfrogging turbocharger* in relation to technology and infrastructure, but it is also an important contributor to the changing of ideas.

*Skipping Old Ideas, Rules and Culture*

*Leapfrogging* can also apply in the sense of leaping over old ideas, rules and culture. This harkens back to Mao's failed attempt to eliminate the *four olds* of culture, customs, ideas and habits. He thought that letting go of the past would be the only way to thoroughly and irreversibly modernize China. Nowhere is the leapfrogging of ideas more apparent than in the thinking of China's leadership.

In today's China, dramatic differences in ideology can be seen throughout China's ruling class:

> *Environment:* China's is adopting some of the world's most challenging clean technologies at a scale that makes China not only the world leader in usage but also in production. From their position on global warming and pollution to their national investment in electric cars and high-speed rail, China's leaders—many of them engineers—have quickly adopted the most aggressive environmental strategies today. They ought to, for China is currently one of the most polluted large economies on the planet.

> *Currency policy:* China's *yuan* is going from being a controversial one that cannot be used abroad to one of the world's most desirable reserve currencies via swap agreements. As countries line up to get access to a cache of Chinese currency, they increase the *yuan's* respectability and usefulness.

> *Investment:* After keeping a limit on overseas direct investment by Chinese firms for decades, China has recently changed directions and opened the floodgates to become one of the world's biggest investors through its $400 billion sovereign wealth fund. It has also allowed Chinese companies (especially state-owned enterprises) to make more foreign acquisitions in natural resources

such as oil and natural gas, as well as technology crucial to China's continued development.

*Lending:* China has also used its foreign currency reserves to lend money back to others in the form of bond purchases, notably of U.S. Treasuries, whereas in the not-distant past it frequently received aid. The shift from debtor to creditor has happened extraordinarily quickly.

*Trade:* China is shifting from a global trade policy to a regional multilateral or bilateral policy, dealing with countries on a case by case basis now that China's market is so desirable.

The *leapfrogging turbocharger* gives China the opportunity to not only catch up to the West, but to leap ahead of many developed countries saddled with older systems and ways of doing things.

## SUMMARY: THE TURBOCHARGERS

This chapter introduced the three *turbochargers* of the new Chinese economy. These *turbochargers* act in the same way on the Chinese economic *growth engines* as a turbocharger does on a car, by generating more power from the same engine. China's *turbochargers* in effect increase the power of China's *growth engines*:

*Reverse globalization:* China's economy will begin to expand from the inside outward, as Chinese culture, people and investments increasingly seek to move outside of its borders, influencing the rest of the world and reversing the previous globalization trend.

*Chinese determination:* This *turbocharger* counts for a lot in driving Chinese companies to global aspirations, so do not underestimate Chinese competitors, or consumers, who are apt to protest against brands and companies that do not support China.

*Leapfrogging:* China has the ability to leapfrog over old technologies, old infrastructure, and old ways of doing things, being able to adopt the best solutions to surpass slower countries, institutions, and companies that may be unable, or unwilling, to respond.

These *turbochargers* will have a multiplying effect on the *supertrends* as well.

## Chapter 3

# CHINA'S ROADMAP

## 中国五年计划
### *ZHONGGUO WUNIAN JIHUA*
### CHINA'S FIVE-YEAR PLAN

Most drivers would not think about a long trip without some kind of roadmap, lest they end up lost or going in the wrong direction. China, with the 1949 establishment of its new Communist government, borrowed a roadmap from the Soviet Union. But, once the Great Helmsman, Mao Zedong, came into his own, he was loath to use the maps of others, and turned against his Soviet advisers when their idea of where China should be going diverged from his. In today's global economy, China has been adamant in refusing to join the world's freely floating currencies and has, indeed, rejected many of the other precepts of free market capitalism. China has, since the time of Mao, been following its own path.

The model of supreme leadership in China dates back thousands of years. China may have left behind the dynastic system of emperors with its 1911 Xinhai Revolution, but it soon found a new patriarch in Sun Yat-sen and, later, his protégé Chiang Kai-shek (who unified post-Qing Dynasty China after it fragmented, and fought against Mao in its last civil war before fleeing to Taiwan). Post-1949, China had Mao as its patriarch but, after critical errors in judgment that led to the tragedy of the Great Leap Forward, the government would thereafter fear putting its trust entirely in the hands of a single person, though Mao remained the final authority on most matters one way or another until his death.

Clearly, in the case of the Great Leap Forward and Cultural Revolution, Mao's guidance was fallible. To the surprise of many outside of China, much introspection over Mao's policies does occur, and the Chinese government has opted to treat his quarter century rule as, on balance, more worthy of praise than of sanction. It is thought that Mao formed his policies with the best interests of China in mind and, unfortunately, some did not work well, others were disasters, yet modern China could not have risen without the dramatic changes he brought about.

Deng Xiaoping, another patriarchal leader, sought to avoid the appearance of a Mao-like personality cult, so he never officially took the title of chairman or premier, but led the country into a governance model more focused on the separation of planning and implementation, a civil service, and consensus-building political processes rather than autocracy. The Communist Party of China (CPC) would form the policies, the bureaucracy would implement them. While this was just an ideal at the start, when party members *were* the bureaucrats, today China's civil service, as well as its think tanks and other advisers, is increasingly diverse.

Thus, the formation of China's roadmap, its Five-Year Plan, has, since the time of Deng, been an increasingly vetted and collaborative process of government policymaking. The overwhelming focus is, however, on increasing China's wealth through capitalist and socialist, not communist, policies.

## PRO-BUSINESS GOVERNMENT POLICY

In fact, the role of government policy in China cannot be understated nor fully understood by outsiders: the highest levels of the Communist Party of China Central Committee (CPCCC) bodies, such as the Politburo and its Standing Committee, are non-transparent, with meetings held behind the walls of the *Zhongnanhai* compound—China's equivalent to the White House, except for the entire leadership rather than just for one leader—in central Beijing. China's press is mostly an organ of the state, publishing what the government wants known, including to foreign readership through China's English newspapers such as the *China Daily* and websites such as the *People's Daily Online*. To be sure, investigative reporting does occur, but central government matters and the inner workings of the CPC are generally off-limits, and how exactly the CPC arrives at certain policy decisions remains clouded in mystery.

As Francis Fukuyama describes in *The Origins of Political Order*, China's strongest characteristic of political organization is its element of statehood. The People's Republic of China carries on a millennia-old institutional tradition of centralized control, formerly by its emperors under the various dynasties, sometimes lasting hundreds of years. Now China is in the midst of what may be called the newest dynasty, for more than six uninterrupted decades, under the aegis of the CPC. As such, it is an extraordinarily stable country with an unparalleled ability—among large economies—to enact change.

### CHINA'S POLITICAL AND MARKET IDEOLOGY

After the time of 1949 when Mao's followers—down-trodden peasants and die-hard Communist revolutionaries—defeated the Nationalist forces of Chiang Kai-shek, the Chinese political ideology was called Communist. To this day, China describes its own economic ideology as a planned market economy, bypassing the inherent contradiction between *control* and *free market* by dropping the "free."

Complicating matters, in more recent times, China has ceased to be anything similar to a true Communist system of government, and instead describes itself as pursuing "Socialism with Chinese characteristics."

Whatever it is called, its chosen path of development has been successful by most international measures: GDP and incomes, literacy and life expectancy are all up; child mortality is down. At the same time, problems, including the worsening pollution, the expansion of the wealth divide and relative lack of development in the western provinces of China, have vexed the central government. So, its pursuit of socialist policies is anything but perfect, but where China's policy effectiveness really shines is in one area in particular: the economy.

## Black Cat, White Cat: Deng's Reforms

In 1978 Deng decided to reform the Chinese economy by wiping out poverty and reversing other damage to the country from the time of Mao and his extreme fundamentalists who had led throughout the destructive Cultural Revolution. Deng, once high among the associates of Mao before being purged in a power struggle, built up his power carefully within the CPC and built up opposition against the remaining fundamentalists in the couple of years after Mao's 1976 death.

The Cultural Revolution had recently ended. Many intellectuals who were forced to the countryside for labor reeducation returned to the cities and were hand-picked by Deng to the leadership of a new CPC, which would undertake the nationwide reforms Deng was envisioning. To Deng, who had always been pragmatic and reform-minded, the goal was more important than the method, an ideal he expressed by saying "it does not matter if the cat is black or white as long as it catches mice."

First, the government started to liberate the agricultural economy by allowing farmers to give up the farming collectives;

manage their own land leased from the local governments; and sell some of their produce freely in markets. While a vast majority of China's hundreds of millions of farmers continued what had been done for millennia, others quickly abandoned the life of agriculture by establishing small factories producing daily necessities such as toothbrushes, simple clothes, tools and utensils, and selling them at small booths or on simple blankets laid out along the streets. Some of the farmers even collected their savings together to start producing larger-scale products, selling them first to their native villages and later to others.

It was not long before China's first free market producers began acting like free market consumers. When they had saved enough money, they bought black-and-white TVs and electric fans, and even built larger houses.

Many Chinese workers in the state-owned enterprises also decided to go into business for themselves: seeing the quick returns on investment and more exciting business life, tens of thousands of state employees who left their jobs voluntarily, or who were forced to by restructuring, decided to join the growing ranks of entrepreneurs. Instead of controlling the people's output as it had for the previous 30 years, the government accommodated and encouraged this move into private enterprise because it would help to drive economic reform and would release some of the pressure on laid-off workers to find another state-owned enterprise job.

Chinese are, despite the aberration of 30 years of hard-line Communism during the Mao years, diehard entrepreneurs. As one saying goes, "Of 1 billion Chinese, 99 percent are in business and the remaining 1 percent are waiting for a new opportunity."

THIS IS NOT YOUR FATHER'S COMMUNIST PARTY

Often non-Chinese, especially Westerners, have a viewpoint on China that is somewhat dated. The image is reinforced, thanks in part to recent movies that sometimes inadvertently portray China as backward, such as 2006's *Mission Impossible III* in which one minute Tom Cruise was swinging from modern skyscrapers and a few scenes later running through chicken-infested streets complete with canals and stone bridges. Such perceived offenses to the dignity of China are even edited out in the domestic movie release, but common stereotypes about China persist abroad. When it comes to envisioning China's government, many still picture Mao Zedong himself and imagine a totalitarian state. Those who have a more open-minded view of China now know this is almost exactly opposite to the current situation.

Today's CPC is probably best described as Communist in name only, as the Chinese state has not had true Communist policies for more than 30 years. Instead, CPC could just as well mean the Capitalist Party of China, a more accurate moniker for what its policies are doing to the economy right now.

No nationwide voting for top leadership? This is true, but China's politicians and bureaucrats today, with the CPC as the pre-eminent political group holding all key positions, are not *Little Red Book*-toting automatons trained in Mao's image. Rather, new CPC members may be the best and the brightest of China's university-educated youth, sometimes recruited directly from China's top universities such as *Tsinghua* or *Bei Da* (Beijing University also known as Peking University). Once in the CPC, people are rewarded for their ability to work hard and get results; the best leaders rise in the party by being promoted to higher levels of responsibility. In this sense, the CPC may be thought of as a meritocracy rather than a democracy and, for now, this system is suiting China well. At the lowest levels of government, small townships and so on, the local representatives of the party may actually be voted on, but anything higher is usually handled through assignments and promotions within the party's Central Organization Department, which monitors, grades and promotes party members.

In the CPC today, the main ideology is not Marxism, or even socialism: it is wealth-building. China's development depends, in the short term, on an efficient (rather than equitable, as Communist or socialist principles would suppose) distribution of wealth, much as what Deng famously said more than 25 years ago, "Some must get rich first." Those prospering earlier were meant to be examples for others to aspire to, primers of the economic pump, and consumers. Many of them, however, were party members or related to them, taking advantage of official positions to skim some of the cream, what economists might call rent-seeking behavior. China's economy during the reform period was, in many ways, up for grabs: privatization of state-owned enterprises and property, business licenses and insider information were all frequently tied to corruption, and this has led to social stratification and expansion of the wealth divide. Was this still *some getting rich first?* Or had generation of wealth gone too far?

The way that the party's changing attitudes about this and other societal issues can best be understood is an examination and comparison of the Five-Year Plans.

## CHINA'S METAPHORICAL GPS: THE FIVE-YEAR PLAN

No document better exemplifies China's desire to create a roadmap for the future than its Five-Year Plan. Since 1953, China has used a Five-Year Plan (FYP) as both a forward looking document for the next phase of development as well as an introspective check to see whether it had attained the goals it had set out in the previous plan. A great deal of thought, research, and discussion goes into each plan, with work starting on the next plan almost as soon as the current one is enacted and in use. The most recent plan, the 12th FYP, from 2011 to 2015, is one of the most reliable documents published globally on how a country's economic, social, political and technological progress will occur.

The FYP's association with Communism and its relationship to the failed model of centrally planned economies notwithstanding, China's success in employing such plans under its brand of socialism with Chinese characteristics has been borne out by its economic performance during the last 30 years.

Not necessarily linked to the policies of any one leader, the plans are more reflective of a gestalt of decision-making within the CPC all the way down to the citizen-delegates of the People's Congress and, in theory, the average people those delegates are supposed to represent. In practice, the People's Congress rubber-stamps whatever is put before it, but the drafts of the FYP are more widely discussed. Since 1953, the plans have had themes and content which were strong predictors of the Chinese economy, because any given FYP is meant to be a sacred document, only to be changed in the case of significant failure of the Chinese economy or disruption in society.

One such case where a plan was abandoned was the second FYP from 1958 to 1962. Unsatisfied by the pace of change, Mao wanted to revolutionize China's agricultural productivity and speed up industrialization: the period from 1958 to 1960 has become known as the Great Leap Forward, during and after which tens of millions died from starvation. So disastrous were the policies that the plan was abandoned midway and an adjustment period from 1961 to 1965 focused on back-to-basics agricultural practices.

The third FYP was another agricultural plan, with the additional focus on building up China's national defense capability and infrastructure for the possibility of conflict. The fourth (1971–1975) and the fifth FYP (1976–1980) plans' focus was centrally planned production targets with frequent over- and under-achievements necessitating adjustments midway.

It was only with the first post-reform and opening up plan, the sixth FYP (1981–1985), and onward, that the plans have become more comprehensive in terms of a greater number of economic, societal, and technological development measures rather than targets for specific agricultural and industrial production, as was the norm during the centrally planned Communist government of Mao. This meant that more aspects of the Chinese economy and society could be managed, including controversial issues, such as population growth. On balance, they are useful to understand China's economic focus and can be relied upon to plan corporate and individual growth strategies.

## THE 11TH FIVE-YEAR PLAN: BUILDING A HARMONIOUS SOCIETY

The period of the 10th FYP (2001–2005) marked a significant transition for the Chinese economy. After recovering from the effects of economic contraction in the United States and other markets post-9/11, and the SARS epidemic within its own borders in 2003, China saw its growth speed up dramatically. The economy was characterized by annual GDP growth of 10 percent or more from 2003 onward, especially in the coastal regions that hosted the Special Economic Zones, where regional growth was often much higher than the national figure.

This concerned policymakers, to the extent that the direction of the 11th FYP (2006–2010) was a radical departure from any previous plan. Its overall theme was restructuring the economy by encouraging more rural development and a "Go West" drive for investment and manufacturing away from the more-developed coast. It was also the first indication of understanding the need to transition to a consumption-based economy. Finally, this FYP was also renamed a "guideline" rather than a "plan" to emphasize the broad nature of the policy goals and to allow other organizational bodies and planning documents (such as the preferred investments list mentioned in the next section) to take higher precedence.

### The River Crab Society

One of the main catchphrases of the 11th FYP was "Harmonious Society," verbiage that was part of the main overview of the plan and became an oft-repeated phrase by China's leadership. This phrase was also relentlessly lampooned by China's netizens, who mocked the proponents of the government's position on a given issue as "River Crabs"—a pun on the Chinese pronunciation of "harmonious" (*hexie*) as well as "to be harmonized"—as in for a person or behavior to be brought back to official standards.

Another catch-phrase, also oft-repeated, was the leadership's desire to build a "moderately prosperous" society, backing away from the previous ideal of getting rich, which had created the wealth gap dilemma.

These ideas encompassed just two of the main themes. Other parts of the plan laid out China's vision for a high-tech and innovative business sector.

Surprising many people was the strong focus on rural development (to the detriment of the eastern coastal areas, which had received most of the attention and investments in the 1980s and 1990s). Rural development was included in several major themes, such as improvement of agriculture and social security.

A second, and perhaps bigger, surprise for the world was the prominence of green issues and targets in the plan. Not only were specific problems acknowledged directly, aggressive targets were attached to them—sometimes much more forthcoming and emphatic than those in the greenest of countries. Environmental issues were best exemplified by China's goal to reduce energy usage per unit of GDP by 20 percent over the term of the plan. This goal would require everything from new methods of high-tech manufacturing to better usage of resources, and reduction of waste. But it was the emphasis on reducing waste and pollution that made other countries take notice, because China set stricter goals and standards than many developed countries did.

To be fair, China was starting from a rather low base. For example, it was one of the most *in*efficient countries in terms of energy used per unit of GDP; among major economies only Russia was less efficient, and that was mostly because it was so resource rich. China didn't have such an excuse. Nevertheless, China achieved many of its objectives, for example by shuttering old coal-powered generators and banning free plastic bags at stores, and nearly reached its goal of 20 percent reduction in energy intensity per unit of GDP.

Before the 11th FYP, government officials were ranked and graded on broad measures, such as GDP growth, FDI growth and improvements in the standard of living. While this was adequate for China's needs in the 1980s and 1990s, it was clearly at the cost of quantity over quality, growth rather than sustainability and, above all else, investment in practically anything that would push China's development as an industrial superpower forward, no matter how much damage might occur to the society or the environment. The Three Gorges Dam project was symbolic of that trend. It involved massive investment of tens of billions of dollars, relocation of millions of people and, it is now becoming apparent, significant environmental damage.

After examining the results of this grading system, new measures were created, to also judge local officials on their ability to hit the energy-savings targets, sustainably develop what was left of the environment and create socially beneficial harmonious development.

Finally, the 11th FYP laid out industry and investment strategies that would almost all come to fruition during the time of the plan. For foreign businesses, following the plan was the easiest and most accurate way to forecast of China's national strategies and policies. For example, China's ambitions in wind and solar energy were clearly laid out in its environmental plan and resulted in China's clean technology industry growing from basically zero to a position rivaling those of the United States, Japan and Germany, the three international leaders. China now has top companies in wind and solar and, not only that, is also leading the world in new implementation projects both inside and outside of China.

This is why a detailed study of the 12th FYP is also highly recommended for any investor, executive or individual who wants to understand China's strategic direction from 2011 to 2015.

## THE 12TH FIVE-YEAR PLAN

The 12th FYP (also technically a guideline rather than a plan) came into effect in mid-2011. It has maintained some of the themes of the 11th plan, while breaking new ground in others.

First, the country will have a 7 percent target for average GDP growth throughout the term, a rate that is thought sufficient to keep job growth and new workforce entrants in balance. The country consistently exceeded the GDP target in previous plans, and the Chinese government remains committed to using whatever measures are needed to not go below the target: increasing export subsidies to prop up trade, encouraging new construction and investment by having state-owned lenders increase new loans, and increasing minimum wage levels to improve consumption. The government has used all of these levers in the past and has in fact already used them all again during the first two years of the 12th FYP.

Second, the country will continue on the path of urbanization. With a current level of 49.7 percent, according to China's 2010 national census, the plan calls for slightly more than 50 percent of the Chinese population to be in urban areas by the end of the period. While it is only a small increase percentagewise, it still represents tens of millions of people moving into cities. They will require new public infrastructure, housing and business hubs to be built from scratch in some places, expanded in others. A significant expansion of the rail network is to continue, despite several rail accidents and a corruption scandal in 2011. The expansion will enable more efficient transportation, commerce and migration between rural and urban locations and city to city. New roads, highways and airports are also to be built. *Urbanization* is the most far-reaching of China's *economic supertrends*.

Third, the restructuring of the Chinese economy will continue, changing China from an export- and investment-driven economy to one that is more consumption- and investment-driven.

Fourth, environmental themes are also highly prominent in the plan, with everything from continued pursuit of energy efficiency and reduction of waste to encouragement of investment in clean technology industries. China has acknowledged the problem of global warming and will take additional steps to reduce its greenhouse gas emissions by further reducing energy intensity and decreasing reliance on coal and oil by promoting hydropower, nuclear, wind, solar and other clean energy sources.

The 12th FYP breaks new ground in some areas, such as acknowledging some specific problems and aiming to fix them. The goals include closing the wealth gap, especially between rural and urban workers, lowering the price of housing for low- and middle-income citizens, and moving away from mass-production and polluting industries, especially in the coastal regions, to higher-value-added and high-tech industries. For example, China also plans to become a world leader in R&D, by spending up to 2.2 percent of its GDP on research by 2015, which would put it in the same league as the United States, Japan and Germany. This will likely make China the second largest investor globally in research and development.

While the new plan is somewhat similar to the 11th FYP, the 12th FYP has a different emphasis. One of the main differences is how it treats exports (the traditional *growth engine* of the Chinese economy), consumption (the new most-favored *growth engine*) and investment (also an important driver of the economy).

Whereas in previous plans, increasing manufacturing capability was the general goal, now it is restructuring the format and location of manufacturing, and importance to the Chinese economy. For example, following its green theme (which it also shares with the 11th FYP), electric cars are designated as a strategic emerging industry. In 2011 China took a step to encourage green vehicles by having one of its state-owned electricity companies begin to establish charging stations that could support electric buses.

At the same time, manufacturing is being shifted geographically, by pushing polluting manufacturers and low-value-added industries out of the cities and farther inland, to ensure China does not lose its spot as the world's factory. This is *not* the "end of cheap China" as a series of article titles and the name of a book seem to imply. China has hundreds of millions of rural workers that are moving into new towns in inland provinces as manufacturing jobs shift away from the traditional eastern coastal locations. Many of the migrant workers at those formerly coastal manufacturers will simply move back inland with the factories, enjoying a job closer to home. Wages inland will remain lower than on the coast during the Olympic Decade, maintaining a "cheap China" trend, but the wage growth inland is going to be faster. Since China's government needs these manufacturers to provide jobs for the workers being displaced by agricultural productivity increases and aggregated in new inland cities via the *urbanization supertrend*, the local and central governments will offer additional subsidies and incentives, thereby preserving a *cheap*—if not the *cheapest*—business environment for years to come.

The second major point of difference of the 12th FYP is its additional emphasis on consumption, which must be increased if China is to reduce its dependence on exports. As urbanization policies bring people into the cities, and higher minimum wages encourage development of the service sector, consumption must increase in order for the new economic engine to run smoothly. While China's 11th FYP also mentioned encouraging consumption, the 12th FYP is far more direct and emphatic, meaning that new policies will surely follow in the next four years to help achieve the goal.

When it comes to investment, China is sending mixed signals. On the one hand, China is afraid that too much investment will overheat the economy, leading to a Japanese-style real estate bubble that could usher in a "lost decade." On the other hand, China relies on investment to bridge the gap between actual and necessary GDP growth. As a result, many of its new policies seem to be encouraging some types of investment and discouraging others.

The government is starting to allow incoming flows of *yuan* from abroad via investment funds and swap agreements, while continuing to fear foreign hot money and inflation. It now encourages Chinese companies to pursue overseas direct investment (ODI) as part of a "Going Out" strategy of acquiring foreign competitors and greater access to markets abroad, while at the same time discouraging additional inbound foreign direct investment (except for high-tech, R&D, environmental or other encouraged industries). And it supports the development of a domestic finance industry centered in Shanghai, encouraging foreign companies to raise capital on Chinese stock markets, while limiting foreign participation in the Chinese finance sector.

The 12th FYP's influences and impact will be made clearer in the three chapters on China's *manufacturing, urbanization, sustainability* and *affluence supertrends* in this volume, and in the additional *supertrends* found in the final two volumes, *China's Demographic Supertrends* and *China's Political Supertrends.*

As a predictor, the 12th FYP is very broad so, as with the 11th FYP, it is the sub-plans and derivative documents that will fill out the details to show, for example, which industries, products, and services are going to be the top sectors for growth for stock investments, corporate strategies or careers.

THE SUB-PLANS AND OTHER DOCUMENTS

The Five-Year Plan is far from being the only defining document but its themes and priorities form the basis for many other planning documents. During the five-year period of the official plan, many other documents are created, as well as more detailed sub-plans, such as an Environmental Five-Year Plan; a Space Five-Year Plan; and regional and city-level plans that cascade down from the national plan. Several are profiled herein, but these are not the only documents that should be considered. Yet a definitive list is also impossible as they are published throughout the period of the FYP and, in many cases, without a fixed schedule; some updated every year, others once in 10 years.

*Space Plan*

China caught the world's attention at the end of 2011 by announcing its newest Five-Year Space plan, the third after the ones in 2000 and 2006.

The main themes are upgraded and new rocket designs to carry different payloads, new orbital satellites and further experiments with manned space flight, space stations and studies for the planned lunar landing—the third stage in China's moon exploration plan. China has made clear its intention to put people on the moon.

The first stage in the moon exploration plan was accomplished previously, via moon probes twice in the last decade. As a result, China now has a complete high-resolution map of the moon's surface and reconnaissance of the likely landing zone. The second stage, expected under the current plan, is an unmanned probe landing on the moon, which is to happen in 2013. The third stage, for which no deadline was set, was the manned moon mission and landing.

While this is the kind of announcement that nations make as a grand gesture, similar to President Kennedy's public challenge to the United States of putting a man on the moon by the end of the 1960s, China's space plan also had aspirations closer to Earth.

This section's title, "China's Metaphorical GPS: The Five-Year Plan," comparing China's FYP to a roadmap or GPS, is more than just an analogy: China now has an *actual* GPS system of its own. At the end of 2011 China went public with plans for its latest major infrastructure project, its own satellite network to establish a global positioning system, both for China's own use as well as an alternative for other countries to use.

China's new network is called *Beidou*—the Big Dipper in Mandarin—and will be a potential competitor to the American Global Positioning System (GPS), the Russian GLONASS, and European Galileo satellite networks to provide geolocation data to any device that can receive the information.

China had been testing the system on a smaller scale for more than a decade, with experiments on government car fleets, emergency assistance during the Sichuan earthquake in 2008 and other tests. In 2011, a popular Internet sensation was the existence of unexplained symmetrical grids etched into vast swathes of China's Gobi Desert, visible on Google Earth. Arranged with what appeared to be hundreds of laser-straight roads on a scale of tens of kilometers each, it is thought the grids were made for either testing satellite-based weapons or GPS, perhaps both.

With an accuracy reported in 2011 of 25 meters—much less than the accuracy of GPS's 10 meters—and coverage only available in China and parts of Southeast Asia, the network has a long way to go before being a true competitor to GPS, but it does establish China as an alternative to the other two global systems. By the end of the 2012, the *Beidou* system will be increased to a total of 16 satellites from the current 10 and have accuracy comparable to the U.S. GPS. It does provide two other major benefits for China: information security and economic development.

Much as with food self-sufficiency, China desires to have its own satellite network to avoid dependence on the American-controlled GPS network (which could, in theory, be turned off to China in a time of conflict). Also, trying to *leapfrog* over the current standard, China's system would enable more options for data transmission. In theory, this would make it more useful than the U.S. system. *Beido* can send and receive bursts of 120 characters, a kind of Twitter-for-satellite communication. This would, among other things, allow a device to broadcast not only its location but also its status (such as a distress signal), which could be sent to others on the network. This would be a very useful feature for logistics, fisheries, search and rescue and telecommunications services. It is hoped that the system will allow China to develop new business models for economic advantage, though China has promised to keep the use of the system free of charge—another element of China's soft-power strategy.

In addition to announcing the newest competitor to the U.S. GPS system, China also plans to launch a total of 100 satellites using some of its new or upgraded designs from the *Long March* rocket series. At present, the *Long March's* largest payloads include the *Long March-5* with 25 tons into near-Earth orbit and 14 tons into geostationary orbit, while the new *Long March-7* would carry payloads of up to 5.5 tons to near-Earth orbits cheaply and efficiently. This is a key component of China's goal of having its own manned space station, which requires frequent and economical payload deliveries for construction and maintenance.

The goal of a space station is realistic for China. It has already proven its manned spaceflight capability through the *Shenzhou* series of spacecraft, with which it has already sent manned missions into orbit. Its first manned spaceflight was in 2003, and has since launched two other manned *Shenzhou* rockets and a total of six astronauts—or *taikonauts,* as they are sometimes called, in reference to the Mandarin word *taikong,* "outer space." With its first spacewalk already completed in 2008, China will attempt manned docking maneuvers with its *Tiangong-1* orbiting module for the first time in 2012.

China has made its space ambitions very clear. It wants to rival and then surpass the United States and Russia, the world's current dominant space powers. The next time the world sees a man on the moon, it may be someone with a Chinese face.

### The Preferred Industries, Sectors, Products and Services List

This list is produced for domestic use, and is based on the priorities of the current FYP. The latest revision of this document was released in April 2011 and contains more than 100 pages, in specific detail, on which businesses the government encourages via preferential policies, tax breaks and so on. It also lists which businesses will not be subject to preferential policies but are not yet discouraged, which ones are in the process of being eliminated (e.g., low-value-added industries that China is trying to reduce investment in) and which ones are actually prohibited (certain polluting industries or dated technology). This constitutes as clear a picture as any businessperson or investor should need to tell where the government will focus its industrial policies in the remaining years of the 12th FYP.

The 12th FYP encourages businesses related to agricultural productivity, environmentally friendly products and clean energy. This includes everything from cloud seeding and genetic modification of food crops, to advanced materials used in thin film solar cells, and battery recharging technology needed to support an infrastructure of electric vehicles. The emphasis on environmentally friendly production methods was also part of this latest version of the document, meaning that certain kinds of chemical- or materials-production were still encouraged, but should now be less energy-intensive and cleaner in their production. For example, production technologies involving better methods of producing steel that use less energy, or energy generation using clean coal methods such as coal liquefaction and gasification, would still be encouraged even while steel and coal in general will no longer be preferred.

In addition to clean technology, China encourages investment in almost every high-tech industry from gene sequencing and other biotech to space and aeronautics technology, up to and including the development of passenger jets.

At the same time, China is not letting go of its key manufacturing industries, including textiles and electronics assembly, but rather moving them farther inland to receive subsidies and support. They do not receive any preferential treatment if they choose to remain in the coastal areas.

Unsurprisingly, China is putting a stop to certain polluting industries and production of dangerous chemicals, as well as eliminating production methods that are archaic or wasteful. Nor are those industries being encouraged to move inland, rather they are being shut down or forced to move outside of China.

*Foreign Direct Investment Guideline*

Related to the above document on preferred industries, the FDI Guideline is familiar to many foreign businesspeople as the investment list that tells which sectors are encouraged, permitted, restricted and prohibited for foreign enterprises. A derivative document, the 29-page FDI Guideline is published by China's National Development and Reform Commission (which has overall responsibility for the above preferred industries list) and the Ministry of Commerce (responsible for foreign investment). It clearly outlines what foreign companies are allowed to invest in.

The last update to the guide was in 2007. At that time, China opted to align the list with the new 12th FYP goals in national energy policy, high-tech innovation and clean technology business development. It has also opened up a few new sectors that might be attractive to foreign companies, but the main emphasis, it must be remembered, is on what is attractive to China. If those interests overlap with foreign investment, that is a plus, and if they do not, the foreign company needs to be more careful.

While many analysts were underwhelmed by the number of new sectors opened up, some significant additions were in the service sector, with investments now encouraged in hospitals and leasing businesses, areas where foreign know-how and capital could be helpful. Health care is a prime sector for lucrative returns from China's growing number of affluent consumers and aging population seeking a better option than the state-provided medical services. Leasing companies, on the other hand, will likely be an uphill challenge, with many state-owned Chinese companies being cash buyers for everything from company-owned cars to heavy equipment, factories and office space or even entire buildings. Nor do Chinese buyers balk at second-hand equipment rather than leasing new; many manufacturing companies in China got their start by buying old factory equipment from Western manufacturers that had upgraded or gone out of business. Domestic aircraft leasing, for example, was just beginning to take off at the start of China's Olympic Decade.

Certain sectors have been partially closed to foreign investment. For example, under the new FDI guidelines, China moved to further protect its oil and gas sectors by restricting foreign investment in smaller refining facilities, but it still welcomed complex, large-scale refinery investments that would require significant technology transfer—technology that China is eager to obtain. China appears to be protecting two of its most valuable state-owned enterprises, namely PetroChina and Sinopec, while at the same time still encouraging foreign companies to transfer technology into China that would be used to strengthen China's future energy capability. It remains to be seen which Western companies will take the bait.

Also, despite China's emphasis on establishing a strategic emerging industry in clean technology, China does not want more foreign investment in polysilicon (for solar cell and integrated circuit chip industries), which is suffering from overcapacity. The same reason, over-capacity, is given for discouraging foreign investment in the auto industry. This must be heartbreaking to foreign auto companies, such as GM and Volkswagen, that have invested in China for decades and helped build China's auto industry into the biggest in the world by vehicle sales, only now to be told, quoting *Hitchhiker's Guide to the Galaxy*, "So long, and thanks for all the fish." The automotive industry investments have apparently run their course. Instead, China hopes foreign automotive *parts* manufacturers, especially those specializing in electric cars, will be encouraged to move their R&D and facilities to China.

What will happen to all the existing automotive manufacturers who have invested billions of dollars into joint ventures with Chinese companies, now that their additional investments are no longer encouraged? It may not be long before minor disputes— such as the one that eventually caused a long-standing and profitable venture between France's Danone and China's Wahaha to be dismantled—suddenly start causing major headaches for foreign partners. Again, FDI in China is welcome only so long as it is providing true development and support of Chinese industry.

*Environmental Five-Year Plan*

Originally introduced during the 11th FYP, the Environmental FYP is another derivative document that follows the overall themes and targets of the full FYP while adding more details. Some of the measures that are covered in the main body of the FYP could also be considered environmental, inasmuch as they involve things like saving energy (such as reducing energy used per unit of GDP).

The need for a separate environmental plan was based on mounting evidence of environmental damage through incidents such as the 2005 toxic chemical spill in the Songhua River, which affected the water supply of millions. As well, China's government realized many of its environmental dilemmas and pledged to become a greener economy. Foremost would be the guidance of the 11th FYP to begin environmentally sustainable development and reduce energy inefficiency. China's government officials would thereafter be judged on their ability to govern sustainably, not just in terms of basic GDP growth, but now also including energy efficiency, pollution reduction and economic restructuring targets.

Under the 11th FYP, the goal of decreasing power consumption by 20 percent meant an average 4 percent reduction a year, a huge amount considering the size of China's economy. Much of it was achieved by upgrading technology and closing older, less-efficient power plants. Certain inefficient industries, such as steel and iron production, had their capacities cut by 42 million tons and 49 million tons respectively by 2010.[1] In 2007, China closed about 9,000 megawatts of inefficient coal-powered generators, saving about 13.5 million tons of coal a year and reducing carbon dioxide emissions by about 27 million tons—but this is actually just a drop in the bucket.[2] China completely missed its energy reduction targets in 2006 and 2007, due to the overheated economic growth, but it still made a significant effort to reach the 11th FYP goal of a 20 percent reduction in energy intensity, coming up just 0.9 percent short of the goal.

In the 12th FYP and 12th Environmental Five-Year Plan, China will maintain emphasis on reducing energy use per unit of GDP and reducing many kinds of air, water and land (e.g., landfills and other solid waste) pollution through such actions as adding two new metrics targeting reduction in ammonia and nitrogen oxides. It is also encouraging industries, such as electric cars, under the main plan, while the environmental plan encourages environmental services such as pollution monitoring.

Also in the 12th FYP is a switch to more emphasis on solar energy for domestic power generation, with nuclear power falling into temporary disfavor after the Japanese Fukushima nuclear disaster. Measures under the plan will act to reduce China's dependence on exporting solar photovoltaic modules (currently about 90 percent of production is exported) by stimulating domestic installation, thereby producing more renewable energy. China will target more than a tenfold increase in installed solar generation capacity, from 800,000 kilowatts (kW) in 2010 to 10 million kilowatts by 2015. It will further provide investment loans and subsidies to the industry, from basic materials such as polysilicon all the way up to complete solar installations, to encourage more use of the preferential purchase rate onto the grid set at 1 to 1.15 *yuan* per kWh. China is following the German model of preferential feed-in tariffs for solar energy, which helped Germany become a world leader. China's solar energy purchase rate is twice the amount allocated for purchase of either wind power or standard thermal energy generated from coal and other means, giving solar energy providers a strong incentive and showing the degree that China wants more solar power. Wind power has been possibly overbuilt in the country, which is why it has no longer has preferential feed-in tariff versus coal, China's main energy source.[3]

Interestingly, during the 11th FYP period, China had previously favored wind and already became the world's number one user of wind turbines. It will be interesting to see if the same impact will be seen in solar energy as well.

If anything, this is the greenest plan to date for China and probably the strongest statement by a large economy on how it is imperative to address growth sustainably.

### THE FIVE-YEAR PLAN AS A TRADE BARRIER?

While government policy can sometimes work against foreign companies that find their business model deprecated by China's new national interests, China is not creating these policies to hobble foreign competition only. Many of the policies also affect Chinese companies negatively.

For example, in 2011, China's securities regulator announced that the practice of using *variable interest entities* and *reverse mergers* to go public on U.S. stock markets was no longer looked upon favorably. These two models were frequently used by Chinese firms to go public in the United States. Arguably, losing these channels hurt Chinese domestic companies far more than it did foreign venture capitalists, investment banks and accounting firms. The goal of China's policymakers is to have more of these companies raising capital in China so that China's own financial markets can mature.

The opportunity, then, should come from the resulting increase in the number of foreign and domestic IPOs that will occur in China's markets during the Olympic Decade. In theory, there are new opportunities for those foreign investment banks and accounting firms in China but, in reality, they face substantial barriers: foreign investment banks, including Goldman Sachs and J.P. Morgan, cannot have a wholly owned investment banking operation and are not allowed majority ownership in a joint venture.

That is what the roadmap is for: knowing which industries will be deregulated (or regulated), when that will happen and how it affects a business model, an investment or a career.

## SUMMARY: CHINA'S ROADMAP

The answer to where China is going in the next five years is in the Five-Year Plan and its related documents. For investors, the plans tell where the best growth will come from in the Chinese economy. For public policy planners, the FYP and industry guidelines could be a model to emulate. For executives, the FYP shows where to allocate resources in a China strategy, and for individuals the FYP can tell you where to develop a promising career.

*History:* Understanding how China's post-1949 economic policy influences the present is important, and explains why China uses Five-Year Plans.

*The Communist Party of China:* The Party is the ultimate guardian of the plan, but inputs come from all levels of Chinese society and the information is studied and vetted by numerous think tanks and policymaking institutions within China. Knowing that the CPC ideology is no longer entirely about growth at any cost helps understand why the last two FYPs have been more balanced in terms of rural versus urban, growth versus sustainability.

*11th FYP:* The harmonious society plan started in 2006 as China's path to restructure the economy, redistribute wealth, and develop sustainably.

*12th FYP:* China's current plan (2011–2015) is the key document to understanding how China will grow its economy and is the best resource for planning a China strategy of any kind. It also has a number of related documents, such as China's Environmental FYP, which should be read for a deeper understanding of key areas.

Now that the *growth engines, turbochargers,* and *roadmap* have been established, the *economic supertrends* can be understood in context.

# CHINA SUPERTRENDS PHOTOGRAPHY PROJECT

Visit the website for this series of books at www.ChinaSupertrends.com to see more images from the China Supertrends Photography Project. The Project aims to capture images of a changing China, in terms of its economic, demographic and political trends. On the following pages are some samples from the project's Shanghai-based photographers.

*Image 1: Meizu Electronics Shop, as discussed in Chapter 5 –
The New Manufacturing Supertrend: "Knockoffs, Clones and
Copies, oh my!" (Photo by DK Wong)*

*Image 2: A house waiting to be demolished, as discussed in Chapter 6 – The Urbanization Supertrend. (Photo by DK Wong)*

*Image 3: The skyscrapers of Shanghai's financial district.
(Photo by DK Wong)*

*Image 4: Sinification - Shikumen houses with modern hotel in the background. (Photo by Han Yi)*

*Image 5: Rural living just an hour from Shanghai, on Chongming Island, from Chapter 7 – The Sustainability Super-trend. (Photo by Han Yi)*

*Image 6: China's fresh water challenge, as seen in a typical urban river, highly polluted, as discussed in Chapter 7 – The Sustainability Supertrend – Feng Shui: Wind and Water. (Photo by Sun Lei)*

*Image 7: Apple built one of its biggest Apple Stores in the world in Shanghai, taking advantage of the Consumption Growth Engine. (Photo by Han Yi)*

*Image 8: A branch of the world's largest bank—Industrial and Commercial Bank of China—as profiled in Chapter 8 – The Affluence Supertrend. (Photo by Hu Yinqiao)*

*Image 9: Some typical Wahaha drinks, as discussed in the Wahaha-Danone dispute of Chapter 1 – China's Three Growth Engines – The Benefits of FDI for China. (Photo by DK Wong)*

*Image 10: A very expensive "lucky" license plate, as described in Chapter 6 – The Urbanization Supertrend – The world's most profitable DMV. (Photo by DK Wong)*

# PART TWO:
# CHINA'S ECONOMIC SUPERTRENDS

中国经济大趋势

## Chapter 4

# AN INTRODUCTION TO
# CHINA'S ECONOMIC SUPERTRENDS

| 春江水暖, | *Chun jiang shui nuan,* |
| 鸭先知。 | *ya xian zhi.* |

"When the spring river warms, the duck is first to know."—Su Shi, famous Chinese poet

Where are the greatest opportunities to be found in the Chinese economy? They can be found using the four *economic supertrends.* These *supertrends,* based on the *growth engines* and *turbochargers* previously discussed, are the most important to understand during China's Olympic Decade from 2008 to 2018.

What is a *supertrend?*[1] A *supertrend* is a confluence of the three *growth engines* of the Chinese economy meeting one or more of the three *turbochargers* and an economic, demographic or political force, thereby being compounded into a much bigger trend.

Another way to think about the relationship is that any of the three *growth engines,* three *turbochargers* and four *supertrends* may be found in any economy in the world, but only China has them all.

The *growth engines* provide the underlying force present across all industries and sectors of the Chinese economy. For example, China exports just about anything and everything other than raw materials, from products to outsourced services. Therefore exports can be said to *drive* the economy forward like an engine. Similarly FDI can touch a subset of industries and brings foreign capital and know-how. The most important *growth engine* of the future development of China is the *consumption growth engine*: Chinese consumers must begin to purchase more, save less and increase their quality of life. Each of these forces is present everywhere in the Chinese economy and will not go away.

The *turbochargers* act on the three *growth engines* to send certain sectors and industries into overdrive.

The *reverse globalization turbocharger* will expand Chinese creative industries—such as film, music and media—as global demand for Chinese culture increases. As China and its people become wealthier, China's companies will invest more abroad, and its people will start to travel more.

The *determination turbocharger,* which has to do with the optimism and perseverance of the Chinese people, will impact, for example, Chinese companies' ability to maintain exports in a stronger *yuan* market by becoming more innovative. A changing China requires more *determination* from the workers, as productivity in agriculture and manufacturing must go up, a willingness to once again *eat bitterness*—a Chinese phrase meaning to endure hardship—as the Chinese economy increases the pressure to maintain growth in the face of a global slowdown.

Finally, the *leapfrogging turbocharger* is allowing the Chinese government—with its unique political and economic mix of socialism and capitalism that it calls the planned market economy—to skip over old ways of doing things and even, to the consternation of many, disregard what are thought of as the rules of the economic game: liberalization of currency, trade and regulation. For example, as will be discussed in *China's Demographic Supertrends,* Chinese tourists will have an increased ability to travel abroad through visa waiver programs as Western governments rush to let in affluent Chinese travelers, notwithstanding those same governments' opposition to China's trade practices or human rights record. Dealing with China is becoming increasingly complex.

The *economic supertrends* are thus formed at the intersection where the *growth engines, turbochargers* and economic forces overlap:

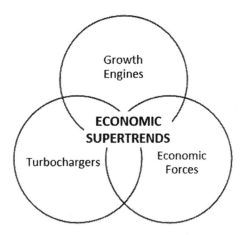

*Figure 9: How the Supertrends are formed*

There are four *economic supertrends*: *new manufacturing, urbanization, sustainability,* and *affluence*. Some are industry focused; others are macroeconomic and broadly influence all sectors (in different ways). It is within these *supertrends* that one can find the greatest business opportunities of the Olympic Decade.

These *supertrends* are sometimes taken for granted within China since they permeate the social consciousness and business environment to such an extent that one may forget they are there. One such example is the degree to which government and private enterprise may be cooperating, which results in an extremely fast pace of change in all aspects of modern China other than, of course, the political system itself.

*The Fast Pace of Change*

One of the things that can surprise people living in China is the speed of change in everything from business law, to demolition and reconstruction, to consumer attitudes and behaviors. All of them can, and do, change quickly and regularly. Much of this change is only possible with the close cooperation between government, its state-owned enterprises and the private sector.

The close cooperation between government and private business has advantages, one of which is the ability to react quickly. During the global financial crisis of 2008, China was able to create a stimulus plan *and* implement it through the government's control of the largest banks and state-owned enterprises, more quickly than any other large economy. While many countries, including the United States, were still debating the appropriate response, China was already spending money through the state-owned companies and banks by flooding the market with liquidity. This must have worked, because China's economy barely skipped a beat, and overall GDP growth remained strong (though fueled almost exclusively by investment).

This cooperation is possible because boards of governors of banks and top directors of the state-owned enterprises, as well most of the top executives in larger private enterprises, are members of the CPC. As such, they do not need much convincing to carry out government directives. So, unlike in the United States where officials had to practically beg banks to take money and use it, in China the bankers unleashed a wave of liquidity that inflated the economy out of the crisis faster than any other large economy.

Of course, government–business cooperation has many downsides as well. When done in a selfish way, the potential to enrich the few at the expense of the many is great, and there has been a history of what Western critics of big government would call *feeding at the trough,* if not outright *stealing* the trough. As recently as 2007, China had major graft and influence-peddling scandals that actually resulted in death penalties for those involved. In 2008, Chen Liangyu, the Shanghai CPC chief and former mayor of Shanghai, was sentenced to 18 years in prison for his role in a pension fund scandal.

Clearly, the problem of business and government corruption will take more time to stamp out, especially in the less-developed regions. While China has already proven in some ways the effectiveness of a government-led business revolution, it still needs more time to add checks and balances.

### The New China Normal

In a sense, the *fast pace* in the last 30 years has blinded people to the *magnitude* and *frequency* of the changes occurring. Until 2008, the situation heretofore had been *China normal*.

Here, *China normal* refers to the *"normal–new normal"* conceptual model defined by Mohamed El-Erian, CEO of bond fund and asset management firm PIMCO. After the effects of the global financial crisis, he referred to the pre-crisis *normal* state of affairs as well as a *new normal* outlook post-crisis for the United States and global economy. This book will use *China normal* to refer to pre-2008 pre-Olympic Decade China, and *new China normal* for China's economic environment after the start of Olympic Decade. *New China normal* means, among other things, that the world must adjust to China's greater financial and economic influence post-crisis.

China reached a transition point in 2008 with the global financial crisis. This point defines where China launched onto a new trajectory as not only the future world's largest economy but also the most important economic superpower. Previous predictions had been as late as 2050 for China's GDP to overtake the U.S.'s, and the notion that China's currency could with ten years rival that of the U.S. dollar was thought absurd before 2008. *New China normal* thinking is that China's GDP will grow much more quickly to become the world's largest, and its currency will challenge the U.S. dollar supremacy as a reserve currency. As recent calls by the Chinese government actions to end global dependence on the dollar have shown, China is already exercising influence that could only be wielded by an economic superpower.

The *supertrends* are, then, part of the *new China normal,* as China powers through the Olympic Decade to become the pre-eminent economic superpower by 2018.

Outside of China, these *economic supertrends* are often actually misunderstood or misconstrued as problems that China is facing or that will negatively influence Western interests. In fact, they are not problems at all, but rather opportunities that some-body—the government, private enterprise or individuals—are sure to solve. Though China will undoubtedly go through growing pains—the economic cycle of boom and bust, of collapse and renewal—it has had 5,000 years of practice dealing with disasters, wars, corruption and societal change. The last 30 years of China's rapid and steady growth were actually a rare period of respite from the turmoil that has shaped China through millennia. China, in fact, has not yet begun its mature growth phase—growing at a slower, more manageable rate of 4–7 percent for several more decades. The 30 glorious years of growth until 2008 were merely the promising stage of germination as a seed. In 2008 the seedling was ready to grow into an oak.

*China's economic supertrends,* then, can and will be seen as immense challenges and impossible missions for China, but China—the state and its people—will not let any problem derail the country's now almost certain rise. Where non-Chinese businesses, investors and individuals can benefit is from the plethora of related opportunities. By being involved in China's growth, one may feel the *ice thawing on the river first.*

Each of the *economic supertrends* will be introduced briefly below, with important background and context on how they came about, before going into detail in the following chapters.

## NEW MANUFACTURING SUPERTREND

If you were to divide the Chinese economy into three indus-trial components—primary representing agriculture, secondary for manufacturing and tertiary for service—by *value,* the two biggest components of the Chinese economy are secondary (i.e., manufacturing) and tertiary (i.e., services). That said, the primary industry—agriculture—including food production as well as forestry, fishing and related industries—actually employs far more people that either the secondary or tertiary industries, yet produces a relatively small part of total national output value as measured by GDP. This indicates how inefficient China's main employment sector actually is.

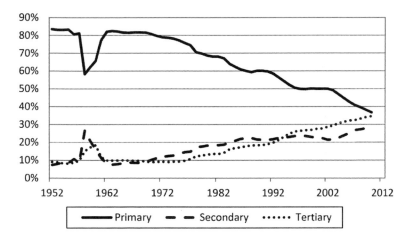

*Figure 10: China's employment by industry type, 1952–2012*

China's level of agricultural productivity is at a developing country level—labor-intensive and inefficient—and is mostly for domestic food security, a legacy of Mao's policy of self-sufficiency. The primary industry is also needed to keep employment high: literally hundreds of millions of people still work in the sector.

The largest component of China's GDP by value is manufacturing. In the past, *China normal* was manufacturing characterized by mass production, low-value-added, and lack of innovation. The *new China normal* means adding value, increasing productivity, upgrading and modernizing equipment and production processes, and innovating.

JIAZHI HUA: VALUE-ADDING

China is known as the world's factory in many quarters. U.S. politicians are fond of saying that a large number of jobs are lost to China's manufacturing sector due to the too-low exchange rate.

The smarter politicians are aware now that the low-cost-labor is only part of the picture; it also has to do with China's low health, safety and environmental standards in factories, government subsidies, intellectual property theft, and lack of competitiveness of some United States companies for a variety of reasons. It is, in other words, a multi-dimensional problem, even though politicians tend to focus on hot-button issues like the exchange rate as the main cause.

The reality is that many of the jobs supposedly lost to China were low-end, low-value manufacturing, and would have been lost to another country if not China. Furthermore, by value, the United States still produces 21 percent of the world's products while China produces only 8 percent, showing that China is still not as significant as the U.S. when it comes to value.

To exemplify how little of the value chain China actually captured before 2008, in a study of an older-model iPod value chain, it was found that of the $300 retail price in the United States, Apple and domestic retailers captured more than half of the total, while more than 50 percent of the remainder was captured by major parts suppliers, most of them not from mainland China, such as Japan's Toshiba, which produced the hard drive. When other costs, such as shipping, were taken out, Chinese companies that actually assembled the device but added very little value got, at most, a few dollars (and the workers were paid a tiny fraction per unit).[2]

Moving forward, it is that value figure that China has its eye on: China wants to restructure its manufacturing sector from mass-produced goods in high volume to high-value goods with better quality in lower volume. A case in point, China now manufactures many of the world's most advanced smartphones and tablets, such as the iPhone and iPad, whereas in pre-2008 China was mostly producing low-tech models with no touchscreen and countries such as South Korea and Japan produced the advanced models. Today, China produces both the simple *and* the complex models.

Many of these high-tech high-value products are also directly or indirectly targeted at Chinese users, who have become the biggest consumers in the world for almost every kind of electronic product. Before 2008, it was often the case—perceived or actual—that foreign companies thought Chinese consumers only wanted or only could afford simpler, cheaper models. Today, Chinese consumers want the best the world has to offer, meaning foreign manufacturers are having to offer—and build—the most complex and expensive models in China.

This is happening not just in high-tech electronics manufacturing, it is happening in almost every industry, from metalworking to chemicals to textiles. For example, the massive Chinese coal industry, led by world number two Shenhua Energy, is investing heavily in R&D for coal chemistry, liquefaction, gasification and cleaner-burning technologies—as well as eyeing overseas acquisitions to secure more coal. It has increased its output to 28,000 tons per worker per year, compared with the 10,000 tons per worker industry average in the United States. But the huge productivity output has not been at the cost of lives as some China skeptics might suspect: Shenhua has accomplished it by using the most modern mining equipment available and keeping a safety record that is 0.027 fatalities per 1 million tons of coal, compared with more than two fatalities per ton for the Chinese industry in general. This gives Shenhua the best safety rate in China's mining industry and puts it on a par with global mining firms' averages.

Clearly, Chinese manufacturing is becoming cost-efficient and disciplined, but it can also benefit from more innovation and modernization.

GEXIN HUA: INNOVATION IN CHINA

In 2011, China received more than 938,000 domestic patent applications, compared with about 92,600 applications from abroad. Just a few short years ago in 2007, pre-Olympic Decade, China received only 300,000 domestic patent applications and about 50,000 patent applications from abroad. This shows two things. First, Chinese companies, research institutes and individuals have tripled their patent applications in China while foreign companies have less than doubled theirs. The *new China normal* has also reversed a trend from the 1990s, where foreign patent applications outnumbered domestic applications. In 2011, Chinese invention patents (distinct from the more generic design patents which cover improvements rather than inventions) finally exceed foreign-registered invention patents.

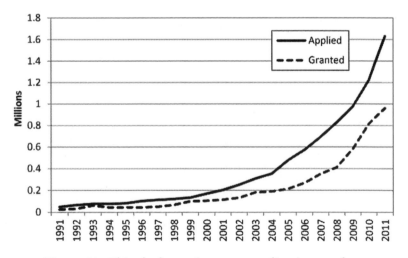

*Figure 11: China's domestic patent applications and grants*

As of 2011, China has nearly 3 million patents—invention and improvement together—on file, with almost one-third of this coming from 2010, when China granted more than 800,000 patents in a single year. This is up from typical figures not exceeding 250,000 in previous years.

Regionally, most invention patents in China are registered in the eastern coastal areas, such as Guangdong and Jiangsu provinces, and cities such as Shenzhen, the first special economic zone created in the early 1980s and home to aforementioned ZTE and telecom hardware manufacturer Huawei, one of the world's patent leaders among Toshiba and Philips. Less than 25 percent of China's invention patents come from the less-developed western regions, showing both the positive effects of technology transfer in the east and lack of development in the west.

This recent surge in patent registrations is not spontaneous: the Chinese government has put pressure on research institutes and companies to register as many patents as possible inside China. China has recognized that patents can represent a non-tariff barrier against foreign firms doing business in China. Expecting such patent applications to grow in future, China has also hired more patent inspectors to cope with the expected demand as China becomes a global patent leader.[3]

Although it is true that foreign companies are often protected in their domestic markets and under global patents with the World Intellectual Property Office, the *reverse globalization* of this *supertrend* is apparent: Chinese inventors are innovating more, or at least seeking more intellectual property rights protection offered by patents than ever before. This will become a major force for Chinese economic power in the future.

Far from being the birthplace of all patent infringement that China is made out to be, China actually has the third most active patent office in the world after Japan and the United States, ahead of high-tech countries such as South Korea and Germany. On a per capita basis, however, China is much lower than virtually all of the OECD industrialized countries, but still ahead of developed countries such as Belgium and Spain.

Enforcing protection of patents and other forms of intellectual property rights (IPR) such as trademarks in Chinese courts is also more common since 2008. Apple faced a trademark dispute over the iPad brand in China in 2012 that saw its iPads yanked from store shelves and threatened to disrupt Apple's global supply chain. Until this major case, it had been mostly foreign companies suing Chinese companies that were using their trademarks in China.

Legal defenses for infringing companies include trademarks had not been registered in China, marks not being registered for all product line, and Chinese translations of the trademark were informal or not famous enough to warrant protection. For example, luxury brand Hermès, basketball player Michael Jordon and whiskey brand Chivas Regal all lost suits in 2012 because either their original brands or their Chinese translations were not famous enough in China before a Chinese entrepreneur registered them. Such cases do not always go badly for foreign brands, and Chinese courts have, in fact, often found in favor of foreign IPR holders.

The first decade of the 21st century saw a series of landmark court cases, such as Starbucks successfully suing a copycat coffee shop called *Xing ba ke*, which sounds nearly identical to Starbucks' Chinese-translated name. However, there is no punitive damage award under Chinese IPR law, only compensatory damages for actual losses incurred, so the deterrent effect is not great and the victories are often symbolic.[4]

Trademarks and all other types of IPR infringement—including copyrights, patents and trade secrets—are increasingly heard by Chinese courts. The number of such cases increased to 66,000 in 2011, more than doubling in number since 2008, when about 28,000 cases were heard.

In order to maintain its place as the world's factory while still continuing its ascent up the value chain, China is doing several things to improve the amount of innovation.

First, as described above, China is providing a faster patenting process and stronger protection for IPR through the courts. This not only should encourage more multinationals to produce higher-value products in China but also will help its own manufacturers protect their own investments in innovation. Chinese

IPR violations will still exist throughout the Olympic Decade, but there will be an increasing number of Chinese companies suing other Chinese companies, and Chinese firms suing foreign firms inside—and outside—China.

Second, China is directing the production of more capital-intensive goods rather than labor-intensive goods. This is done via the FYP's focus on strategic emerging industries (in China) such as clean technology, health care and energy, and its general objective of being more innovative. China does not want to lose low-tech jobs; however, it is trying to move the low-value-added jobs into the western regions of China to help satisfy the yearly thirst for 10–20 million new jobs needed for new graduates and newly urbanizing rural workers.[5]

In China' government planning, this strategy is known as *Go West* or *Going West*. "West" refers to China's western regions. There, growing consumption power means companies can open new markets, as mentioned in Chapter 1—*China's Growth Engines*. In the *new manufacturing supertrend, Going West* means the process of moving all kinds of manufacturing facilities to the less-developed, western regions of China where costs can be cheaper. A new trend since the start of the Olympic Decade has been to move or locate even high-tech enterprises and R&D to those regions because of greater government incentives.

It is value-adding and innovation that China desperately wants to increase, and the government has made it a mission to do so. China's *new manufacturing supertrend* has far-reaching effects on foreign manufacturers and consumers as well.

## URBANIZATION SUPERTREND

As of January 2012, China had already officially urbanized more than 49.7 percent of its population. If migrant workers (those in a city but not possessing an official residency permit called a *hukou*) are not included, the urbanization rate is just over 40 percent, according to China's National Bureau of Statistics. This means about 650 million people have already been urbanized in some way. The majority of those people were transformed from rural to urban status in just over three decades since the start of the reform period in 1978. During the remaining four years of the 12th FYP, tens of millions more will move into cities.

The overall task of urbanization is so large that, by 2030, the total urbanization rate will still only be between 70–75 percent, when about one billion people will be living in China's cities. This also means several hundred million people will still be classified as rural. Urbanization will therefore be one of the constants of Chinese development in at least the first half of the China Century and the *urban supertrend* is one of the surest bets.

XIN CHENGSHI: NEW CITIES FOR A "BETTER CITY, BETTER LIFE"

The theme of the 2010 World's Expo, which was hosted in Shanghai, was *Better City, Better Life,* an ideal that neatly encapsulates the current urbanization drive in China.

China is building new cities, relocating millions of people for infrastructure projects, and—year-in, year-out—sees the largest temporary migration of people in the world as they return to their hometowns from their adopted cities and back again during the Chinese New Year holiday season. The holiday migration puts enormous pressure on the central government to build transportation infrastructure since planes, trains and automobiles (and buses, trucks and scooters) are all running over-capacity. The *chunyun* (the Chinese New Year rush) is at the same time an impetus to developing better transportation networks, such as high-speed rail, and also a symptom of China's too-fast pace of urbanization: people are not willing or able to break ties to their hometowns and must live a kind of double life, their city life and their hometown life.

For China's migrant workforce, straining to cross the wealth divide, this is an enormous expense and effort equivalent to a tax on migration that leaves many people unhappy as they deal with scalpers to buy train tickets, slog through overcrowded stations and airports, or sit in endless traffic jams on the highways. The government hopes, however, that by urbanizing quickly, China can avoid a confrontation between the haves and the have-nots by bringing hundreds of millions more out of poverty and centralizing and standardizing social services for all through the urban centers.

The early adopters of the urbanization model are the so-called migrant workers, the *liudong renkou* (the floating population) of China's formerly rural population seeking work in bigger cities. They may leave their hometowns for up to several years at a time while retaining ties to people left behind, including parents, spouses and children. Increasingly many of them are settling down in the new cities, but this is not always easy since there may be discrimination against becoming official residents.

While China's percentage of migrant workers, the proportion as a part of the total population, is about 15 percent, the absolute number surely is the highest in the world. Migrant workers in just 10 of China's provinces account for a total of almost 100 million moving around the country for jobs. Cities such as Shanghai, Guangzhou, Beijing, and developing second-tier cities such as Nanjing or Dalian may see their official population numbers inflated by as many as several *million* because of the floating population.

Shanghai, for example, grew its migrant workers from 1.3 million in 1985, to 2.7 million in 1997, to 5.8 million in 2005 and 6.3 million in 2007 plus nearly 380,000 migrant children. In 2010, according to the most recent census, Shanghai's migrant population was topping 8 million. In 2006, Shenzhen, the built-to-order city envisioned by Deng Xiaoping as mainland China's answer to Hong Kong, estimated that an amazing 9.4 million people were classified as non- migrant workers—nearly doubling the city's population. Shenzhen, in fact, could be thought of as an entire city of migrants, since virtually all of its population has moved there since the early 1980s when it was designated a Special Economic Zone. The capital, Beijing, is estimated to have 5.1 million migrant workers, a figure that is one third of the official population.[6]

With the latest census, migrant workers were included for the first time, but many migrants are working under the radar without any official legal status and may never divulge their presence in an adopted city. Even when they disclose their presence to authorities, they may be denied rights that a permanent resident (i.e., a *hukou*-permit holder) has, such as the right to send children to public schools, health care, or other city services. Migrant children, if they are educated at all, are often put into segregated, migrant-only schools.

While difficult to pin down the true total number of migrant workers in any given year, China's own best estimates are around 242 million. The migrants generally travel from the rural, inland provinces, to the industrial coastal provinces with manufacturing hubs, such as Guangdong province, where many of China's "workshops" are located. When the reverse migration occurs, during longer national holidays such as Chinese New Year or the National Day holiday season, tens of millions of migrant workers ride the rails back to their hometowns. Alarmingly for the regional governments where they work, starting in 2008 many migrants were staying home as they found better opportunities, better living conditions, increasing salaries, or closer cities to work in. This has created the contradiction of the world's most populated country being short of workers in some places where they are most needed.

The migrant worker urbanization is not without controversy. Unscrupulous urban employers take advantage of the fact the newly arrived workers have unclear—or simply lack—local residency rights, then use fear to keep them on the job for long hours without breaks or holidays. Other cases of poor treatment of workers are common, such as not providing proper medical care and insurance in the case of accidents, housing them in unheated or non-air-conditioned barracks, and withholding their pay for months at a time. It is not uncommon to hear of worker riots because of pay being withheld for a year or more and then the company going bankrupt with the owners fleeing the scene. Other problems may include worker suicide, worker beatings and threats of violence against workers. The problems are starting to be addressed.

For example, the government is more often stepping in to clean up a bankruptcy where workers are left holding the bag, and the new labor law of 2008 is now beginning to protect workers' rights and forcing employers to provide consistent benefits to all employees. These actions begin to acknowledge that much of China's hardest labor, such as construction work in cities, is done by these workers and that they deserve to be treated better—even if it will be many years before they can actually afford to live in one of the buildings they construct.

In a further effort to clean up the practice of migrant worker exploitation, progressive cities, such as Shanghai, have moved to legitimize the migrant workers' status and have granted them social benefits and rights, such as access to education and health care. But, at the same time, the city faces an existential crisis when migrants start to outnumber residents in certain demographics. The local Shanghainese are grappling with problems, such as how to communicate with new migrants (who may not speak the local dialect), or how to keep them from overwhelming social services.

With more than 33 percent of the births in Shanghai from migrants in 2005, the city established 18,000 free condom distribution points in locations, including the shantytowns surrounding major construction developments, as if to say, "Hey folks, stop having so many babies in our city."[7] Ironically, this policy may come back to haunt Shanghai—which has a larger percentage of older people than other cities—when there are not enough young workers for the service industries that an aging population will require.

The process of urbanization is a huge and complicated issue, but within it also can be found some of the biggest opportunities of China's Olympic Decade. During the 1990s and in the first decade of the new century, this might have been in real estate and construction to house the millions of new residents. In 2012 onwards, it is more to do with how to make life more enjoyable in the city and build integrated communities rather than developed cores surrounded by shantytowns. To bridge the gap, a more robust service industry must be developed in each newly urbanizing city to provide a higher quality of life with better jobs and higher incomes.

### JICHU FAZHAN: ESTABLISHING NEW INFRASTRUCTURE

One half of the *urbanization supertrend* is convincing people to move into the cities, the other half is getting them there in the first place.

China's several attempts at modernizations failed under the Communist policies of Mao, but one of his successful legacies is China's love of rail travel. The country has used rail to move people to and fro for decades. For this reason, the cultural mindset is favorable towards rail. As it happens, rail is one of the most efficient ways to move people over long distances other than by boat. This makes China's vast geography and large population nearly an ideal match for large-scale rail travel.

During the Olympic Decade, rail is one of the main domestic investment drivers. Billions of dollars are spent yearly on upgrading China's existing rail network. Tens of billions more are being spent every year creating a new high-speed rail network that traverses the longest distances by rail in the world. It is already a larger network of high-speed rail than even the famed bullet trains of Japan or Europe's multi-country system.

Rail not only includes long-distance high-speed rail, but also urban transportation in the form of light-rail, subway, and even high-speed Maglev trains linking transportation hubs. Knowing that a car for every person—or even just one for every family— would gridlock the cities, China's local governments install subway lines that are among the newest, fastest, cheapest (to ride) and most expensive (to build) in the world.

Building China's new cities sustainably is one of the biggest challenges China faces. As well, its decades of being the world's manufacturer have taken a toll on the environment. That is why the next *sustainability supertrend* is so important to China's future.

## THE SUSTAINABILITY SUPERTREND

China's impact on the environment, at least in terms of manufacturing, had been negligible until the 1950s. China missed the Industrial Revolution due to its isolationist policies, and its manufacturing base in the 20th century suffered continual destruction from the effects of near continuous war or civil war up to 1949. China was an agrarian society with its carbon footprint the result of burning biomass, not fossil fuels, though methane—another greenhouse gas—produced by rice and pig farming was not insignificant.

It was only with the 1949 formation of the People's Republic of China under Mao that industrialization began in earnest, fossil fuels started to be burned, forests were cut down and the water became polluted. However, for all of the central planning under Mao, China's industry never really caught up with the Western nations, and furthermore, life under Communism was economical and frugal. As per Confucian values, Chinese wasted little, so per capita use of energy and output of waste remained far below that of United States, right up to today, in fact.

This all changed after 1978. Deng's reforms would have a more pronounced effect on China's industrial pollution and consumer attitudes. Now China's growth would be based on unfettered capitalism and open markets, *turbocharged* with FDI, resource- and energy-intensive. People were free to buy whatever they wanted (and could afford). This period of practically unchecked economic growth, from 1978 to 2008, ushered in a new age of China development that saw hundreds of millions of people lifted from abject poverty. It also came with significant consequences for the environment—land, air and water.

It might be said that nowhere else in the world was the pillaging of the environment so great as in modern China, where an entire generation saw everything as owned collectively by the people and untouchable before 1978 then, almost overnight, turned into a paradigm of taking what you could get. After 1978, then, natural resources suddenly became anybody's to do with as they wanted yet with no individual responsibility: in effect, everybody's resources, nobody's problems. The increased impact on the domestic environment, in terms of industrial inefficiency, electricity and water waste, pollution of lakes, rivers, land and air, was unprecedented.

It is hard to quantify pollution and environmental damage during the 1980s and 1990s, because few measurements were taken. By many accounts, pollution was terrible. Large cities were powered by inefficient coal-burning plants just outside, or even inside, the city limits. People cooked their food and even heated their homes with charcoal stoves. Chemicals and all manner of wastes were dumped into the rivers and ocean without treatment. The air was black with soot, and the water was gray with sewage and industrial waste.

China's only major environmental initiative of that time might have been to be part of the Kyoto Protocol. While China did ratify the Kyoto Protocol (which it regularly chides the United States—a non-ratified country—about when environmental issues are raised between the governments), since then it has polluted significantly more, even becoming the world's number one carbon emitter. As a developing country, China was not obligated to the same reductions as developed countries. Today China is the home of many of the world's most-polluted cities.

In the last decade, China saw some of its most visible environmental problems get covered in national and international media. Multiple giant algae blooms ruined some of China's most picturesque lakes; weeds blocked important commercial rivers; even the coastal area meant to host the sailing competitions for the 2008 Olympics was beset by foul-smelling algae. Plagues of rats ravaged farms; and a major toxic chemical spill in northern China's Songhua River effectively shut off the water for millions for several months. The shame from so many environmental problems was, perhaps, a turning point.

China responded by enforcing environmental laws more strictly; upgrading the State Environmental Protection Administration to Ministry status, with more powers and a broader mandate; and making environmental improvement one of the parameters used in evaluating government officials.

It was in this context that, in 2005, the Chinese government formed its 11th FYP which, among other initiatives, put the environment and sustainable development at the forefront. China is trying to turn its environmental situation around by becoming one of the leading producers of green tech and enforcing policies that put developed countries environmental policies to shame.

While those steps were good for China, it was increasingly noted that China's industrial activity was also polluting neighboring countries. In fact, there was factory fallout from China in places as far away as Denver. No place on Earth, it seemed, was beyond the reach of China's mounting environmental catastrophe.[8]

Nevertheless, China is not willing to put the environment ahead of its economic development. For example, when it comes to the issue of greenhouse gases and global warming, China refuses to heed calls to reduce its pollution at the same rate as the developed countries. It relies on the argument that Western developed countries are imposing their post-development standards on developing nations by forcing them to, in effect, foot the bill for pollution that Western countries emitted during their own industrialization. China is trying to find a fragile balance between the environment and the economy, but there is a line it will not cross.

China is responding to the environmental crisis by maximizing the speed at which it responds, and it is combining industrial policy with environmental policy so its companies can still win by being green. Finally, the newly affluent people of China are influencing the government to clean up rivers, towns, even entire industries, in order to enjoy a better quality of life. This has quickly become the *new China normal* and it is China's path to sustainable development. It is also, not surprisingly, providing a great deal of business opportunities under the *sustainability supertrend.*

### Jieneng Jianpai: Save Energy, Reduce Waste

There are two main directions that the *sustainability supertrend* is taking, summed up by a Chinese government catchphrase—*jieneng jianpai*—save energy, reduce waste.

As it currently stands, China is one of the least-efficient industrialized nations on the planet. Countries such as Russia are actually worse but, on the other end of the spectrum, countries such as Japan and Germany are much more efficient. Russia, energy-rich in oil and natural gas, can perhaps afford to be inefficient. China, with only coal and some oil (and not enough of it), must become more efficient.

China's 11th Five-Year Plan's initiative with the strongest environmental impact was undoubtedly the pledge to reduce electricity usage per unit of GDP by 20 percent. It nearly achieved that target with a 19 percent reduction in energy intensity, but this was a struggle during the 2006-2007 high growth period. The 12th Five-Year Plan continues China's focus on greater productivity and efficiency with a 16 percent energy savings target.

China's energy policy is also becoming more environmental, promoting the adoption of more clean energy generation, especially hydroelectric, wind, and starting in 2012, a new emphasis on solar energy.

When it comes to reducing waste, pollution is often a symptom of both inefficient production and usage. China faces natural resource shortages of almost every industrial material, and it doesn't even have enough fresh water.

Lack of sufficient water supply is a big problem because generation of electricity takes a lot of fresh water, not just for hydroelectric power but also because China uses coal for the vast majority of its energy generation, and water is needed to be boiled for steam that runs the turbines. As well, there are China's inefficient agricultural practices, which tend to waste a lot of water, and huge number of manufacturers that all may require water for cooling and cleaning. Finally there are the 1.3 billion thirsty people. A persistent drought in Yunnan province affected millions from 2010 to 2012. Compounded by desertification and depletion of the water tables, many parts of the country are already in a permanent state of drought. China's officials estimate that two-thirds of Chinese cities have a water shortage. Considering China is building even more hydroelectric power, reducing the flow on rivers, this problem is expected to get worse as the water tables—which took millennia to fill—are depleted this century. Solutions such as the South-to-North Water Diversion Project, a greater than $40 billion infrastructure project, will only alleviate some of the problem.

China must, therefore, become more efficient, find new ways to save water, use all materials more efficiently, generate cleaner electricity, and reduce pollution—all at the same time. This broad range of challenges and opportunities form the basis for the *sustainability supertrend.*

## THE AFFLUENCE SUPERTREND

While China is far from wealthy on a per capita basis, pockets of wealth and extreme wealth do exist, especially among the entrepreneurial class and within the cities. By global standards, these people are very well off.

Many of China's state-owned companies, often thanks to their monopoly or duopoly business environments inside China, have joined the ranks of the world's top corporations. Most are enormously profitable, are cash rich and can draw upon huge amounts of additional capital through the state-owned banks.

Private enterprises are not doing badly either, though they have been having a rough time in the past few years as China's central government puts more emphasis on picking industry winners and supporting the state firms. But when entrepreneurial companies are successful, they do so in a market that is growing at 9 percent or more a year, where some cities and provinces are the size of some European *countries*, allowing them to grow fast and attain scale in their markets.

Finally, the government of China itself could perhaps be thought of as the best turnaround success story of all time. From one of the poorest countries pre-1978 to one of the richest post-2008, China is making money hand over fist. Tax revenues are growing faster than GDP. Foreign exchange surpluses grew to become the largest in the history of the world—more than $3.2 *trillion*. And China's GDP appears to be on a growth path of at least 7 percent until 2015 by following its national target from the 12th FYP.

In short, some Chinese people, some Chinese companies, and the Chinese government have all become extraordinarily wealthy. The problem of too much money—inflation—is the impetus driving China's search for new outlets for its own wealth. Wealth is the *new China normal,* and the *affluence supertrend* is how China is going to spend it.


FANRONG HUA: PROSPERING

The amount of wealth generated in China during the last 30 years has been staggering. It is also projected to grow further in this decade as China continues its upwards trajectory of 7 percent or greater GDP growth.

Stock markets to land prices, corporate profits to personal incomes, government tax revenues to government investments—all are up. Yet this sudden prosperity is not without its problems as China's new economy has started to develop wealth bubbles in everything from fine wines to garlic to *pu'er* tea that bring rapid inflation, and could bring disastrous and sudden deflation when they burst. Also, China's wealth, unevenly divided, is a source of increasing tension. So, the opportunities within this *supertrend* are great, but so are the risks.

*Tiny Bubbles*

For individuals other than entrepreneurs, the best way to get rich in recent years has been to either buy real estate or invest in the stock market, preferably both, but rarely at the same time since their prices often change counter-cyclically.

Such opportunities did not exist during the early years of reform. Stock markets did not reopen until 1992, and private real estate ownership was first allowed in the mid-1990s. From then, up to the early part of the first decade of this century, China was a story of tiny bubbles and tiny busts. Since 2004, when China's economy kicked into overdrive, tiny bubbles became hot-air balloons, and the risks to China's economy increased dramatically.

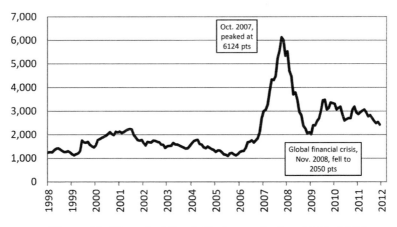

*Figure 12: Shanghai Stock Exchange Index, 1998–2012*

As the economy began to speed ahead, real estate and stock prices followed. By 2007, it was clear China was on a roll. In 2007, when the Shanghai stock market's main index was the best performing major index in the world for the second year running (97 percent growth in 2007, 130 percent growth in 2006), the economy was at the high point of 14.2 percent growth. Like so many bubbles in so many places before it, it seemed like the boom would never end.

The year 2008 was a terrible year for markets around the world, China included. China's property prices were stagnant. Stock markets were down. The benchmark Shanghai Composite Index lost two-thirds of its value at the lowest point of the crisis but, by mid-2009, China's stimulus package started to kick in. Few predicted what would happen next: China's real estate market essentially doubled in value. Whether it was pent-up demand or state-owned enterprises using stimulus money to buy real estate, *happy days were there again.*

From the trough of the downturn in 2008 and early 2009 to the peak at the end of 2011, growing regions in many Chinese cities saw a doubling of property prices. It was not unheard of for individual developments' properties to treble (or, if they were starting from a very low base, to quadruple) in price. By 2010, it became clear that real estate investment was so out of proportion to the rest of the economy that the central government had to move in with a slew of new policies designed to return prices back to Earth. The policies did not result in a significant decrease but, starting in 2012, supply and demand appeared to reach equilibrium: prices finally stabilized in the downtowns of first-tier cities and even began to show signs of a correction in their suburban districts.

China's stock markets, for their part, have returned to the fluctuations of the past. China equities went from being one of the top global performers in 2010 thanks to the massive stimulus package, to one of the worst in 2011 once the money had run out.

## China's Government Gets Richer

It is not just the real estate and stock market speculators of China who are getting rich on the booming economy; the government is still the biggest investor around, thanks to its legacy holdings of state-owned enterprises (SOEs). Though the government privatized or restructured many of the least efficient and unprofitable SOEs in the 1980s and 1990s, it has strategically held on to majority control of more than a hundred of the biggest money-makers—the utilities, oil companies, mining, heavy industries and telecom—as well as tens of thousands of smaller SOEs still on the books. The centrally managed SOEs alone, a small subset of the total SOEs (which includes local and national), brought in profits to the state of 917 billion yuan ($146 billion).

Many of these centrally managed SOE companies are names that Western investors might recognize from blockbuster stock market listings in the past five years: China Mobile and other telecom operators, PetroChina and other energy-related firms, several Chinese airlines, metals producers, and China National Tobacco among many others. The State-owned Assets Supervision and Administration Commission (SASAC), the central government's SEO management organization, stated that, in 2011, the largest 120 centrally managed SOEs generated profits of more the 917 billion *yuan* ($146 billion) on revenues of 20.2 trillion *yuan* ($3.2 trillion).

China uses these SOEs to generate government revenues through dividends. About 10 percent of profits go into the public finances as dividends (though for certain sectors, such as banking, this can be considerably higher, up to 40 percent), and the rest is reinvested. Given their monopoly, duopoly or oligopoly status, many of them are very profitable. These same SOEs, however, are often criticized for being non-transparent, inefficient, and slow. With only a business unit being listed overseas (not the holding company or conglomerate it is in), the true financial performance of many of these SOEs is unknown to all but SASAC.

Another way China's government has become rich is by increasing the amount of taxes it collects. In 2011, it grew its overall tax base by 22.5 percent in a single year, while GDP grew at only 9.2 percent. Who is paying all this extra tax?

Quickly rising wages have contributed to a larger personal income tax base. China harmonized taxes on foreign companies, making more foreign companies pay tax where before they had generous tax holidays. Taxes for many companies—foreign and domestic, especially small and medium enterprises—are now collected electronically, allowing China to prevent tax evasion that had amounted to billions of dollars lost a year. Finally, China has been producing ever-larger quantities of goods, growing the value-added tax base.

To offset traditional government income from land sales, some local governments have started to implement property taxes. All of these things mean that China's central government has a steady income that is not dependent on SOEs alone, as once was the case. Local governments, on the other hand, are still dependent on land sales to generate the majority of their operating income. This has resulted in a number of social problems, including land seizures. But, overall, China's national and local governments are getting richer due to higher taxes and continued development of the real estate sector.

Finally, China's holdings of foreign currency mean that China is now a force in global finance, taking a bigger role in the IMF and calling for changes to the international monetary system while keeping its own currency, the *yuan,* from floating or being traded on international markets.

With the people, companies and the government of China enjoying new prosperity, some of the richest opportunities of the Olympic Decade are to be found within the *affluence supertrend.*

## SUMMARY: AN INTRODUCTION TO THE SUPERTRENDS

This chapter has introduced the *supertrends* and how they are related to the *drivers* and the *turbochargers*. The *supertrends are* the biggest trends that will contain the most valuable opportunities during the Olympic Decade:

The New Manufacturing Supertrend

The Urbanization Supertrend

The Sustainability Supertrend

The Affluence Supertrend

Each of the following chapters focuses on one *supertrend*, explaining which industries, companies, and individuals are best placed to take advantage of the trends.

## Chapter 5

# THE NEW MANUFACTURING SUPERTREND

## 价值化 - 革新化
### *JIAZHI HUA - GEXIN HUA*
### VALUE-ADDING AND INNOVATING

China has been an industrial nation for only the last 60 or so years. Starting under the leadership of Mao Zedong, the country attempted to emulate Soviet-style industrialization while upholding Marxist principles of Communism: the means of production were to be in the hands of the people. During this time, the country went through several aborted attempts at large-scale industrialization, notably the Great Leap Forward (1958–1961), a program aimed at improving agricultural productivity and jump-starting China's production of industrial goods, such as steel.

As described earlier, one policy of the Great Leap Forward had farming communities build small-scale steel mills in the country-side. The furnaces used excessive amounts of coal, wood, and anything else that could be burned, and produced only minor amounts of poor-quality steel. In the process, entire communities may have melted down their only tools as scrap, taking away their means of growing crops and making a living. No exact figures are known, but it is estimated that tens of millions died of starvation.

## THE CHALLENGES OF MANUFACTURING IN CHINA

Manufacturing in China is still growing and, in the short term, will not slow down, as the domestic market grows to balance the export market. High foreign investment and the new sophistication of China's own exporters will propel China's export-driven economy to greater heights. Nevertheless, the world's workshop is facing challenges that affect all companies, both foreign and domestic.

In 2008, during the financial crisis, uncertainty about China prevailed. Then a Booz Allen survey of American manufacturers in China highlighted how perception of the benefits of manufacturing in China—low cost being the most common perception—was changing, and what this meant for the future. Nearly 20 percent of the companies surveyed indicated they would relocate their manufacturing base to other countries, the vast majority stating the main reason for doing so was the disappearing low labor-cost advantage and loss of tax holidays.

By 2012, in a survey from the American Chamber of Commerce in Shanghai, about 90 percent of American companies thought China was losing its low cost advantage, with an increasing amount of low-value manufactured goods being produced outside China or inland. However, the benefits of staying in China's growing market had also become more apparent: for two-thirds of companies surveyed, China operations were growing more quickly than in other regions, and 77 percent of companies would increase their investment in China in 2012.[1]

In fact, costs were up for every business—foreign and domestic—but, for the domestic companies, leaving the country was not an attractive option, if it was even possible. They are stuck in an environment of increasing wages and more regulation. Foreign companies are facing increased taxes as tax holidays expire, and new rules mean foreign expatriate workers are no longer exempt from paying Chinese social welfare deductions. The challenge of increasing costs has forced all China-based manufacturers to rethink their business models.

Compounding the problem, China is also trying to restructure its economy in a number of ways. Most significantly, it is de-emphasizing the export sector in favor of domestic consumption. In terms of employment, the government is deemphasizing manual labor for higher-value added or technical work and pushing the creation of the higher-paying service sector. This is putting manufacturers in a difficult spot. They need to restructure their production to be more suitable for domestic use, while being forced to look outside of urban areas for cheaper labor.

Nevertheless, manufacturing is still China's most important economic activity. Just before the start of the Olympic Decade, in 2007, the industrial output grew by 13.4 percent, while the service sector grew 11.4 percent, meaning that manufacturing and related industries actually became a bigger part of China's overall GDP, continuing a trend since 2005. In 2010, China's GDP by sector was about 47 percent for industry, 43.6 percent for services and just 9.6 percent for agriculture. As urbanization increases and urban jobs become the norm, the service sector's pace of growth will surpass the growth of the manufacturing sector. By the end of the Olympic Decade in 2018, the service sector will have surpassed manufacturing in importance to the Chinese economy.

CHANGING BUSINESS ENVIRONMENT

China-based manufacturers must go from business as usual to proactively or reactively dealing with the changed business environment under *new China normal* scenarios.

*New Emphasis on Value-added*

In the 1980s and 1990s, China had begun to produce many labor intensive hand-made products, which took market share from products previously made elsewhere in Southeast Asia. Such products were only suitable for lower-end segments of the market domestically or elsewhere. After joining the WTO in 2001, China started to replace that low-end production with more capital-intensive manufactured products using equipment and machinery, but still sometimes with a large amount of hand-finishing and assembly. This was done on a sourcing model: foreign companies would come to China to look for the products they needed off-the-shelf, or to be produced by an OEM or perhaps a joint venture. At the start of China's Olympic Decade, these products were becoming more technologically sophisticated and had a growing degree of value added within China. By this time, many foreign manufacturers were starting to set up their own factories rather than relying on a Chinese OEM or joint venture partner. This led to the second characteristic of *new China normal* for manufacturing.

*Higher Labor Costs*

The second effect is increasing labor costs inside China. In answer to the slow markets at home during the global financial crisis, foreign companies were still in 2012 producing more things in China than ever before. All of this increased manufacturing puts pressure on manufacturing wages, especially in coastal areas that have traditionally attracted most foreign investment. While it is true that China still has much excess capacity and surplus labor to utilize before its cost-advantage runs out, this, too, is changing quickly with worker migration patterns.

While the rapid economic growth of China since 1978 is truly remarkable, it has been built on the backs of labor. China has quadrupled its GDP over the past two decades, much faster than other previously high-growth Asian countries such as Japan in the latter half of the 20th century (which took 40 years to quadruple). Going back further, it had taken the United States more than 60 post-war years to quadruple the size of its economy. Back further still, it took more than 100 years for the British Empire in the 19th century.

As China's growth barrels on, wages have been stagnant by comparison. According to government statistics, the *real* wages for general laborers in the Pearl River Delta region, which includes Guangdong province, where many exporting companies and foreign manufacturers have based their operations, have increased less than 10 percent over the same 30-year period.[2]

Further compounding the wage issue is that the coastal region has received far more investment and growth than the inland regions. Consequently, labor rates have gone up much faster in coastal areas before 2011. Recently, wage growth on the coasts has tapered off (having reached a high and livable wage for most workers). Inland wage growth has increased but wages there will take some time to catch up to the wages on the coast. China's internal difference of labor has led the central government to discourage coastal investment in low-tech manual labor and encourage high-tech capital intensive industries instead.

If manufacturers are not happy with the high labor costs, they can move production inland, where wages are lower and tax benefits are newly available. However, many multinationals are instead moving to a so-called "China *plus one*" strategy, where the *plus one* refers to another even lower-cost of labor country, such as Vietnam or Bangladesh, partly as a backup should China production falter or become too expensive.

*Increases in Other Costs*

Other non-production-related expenses are going up as well, such as those due to environmental and worker safety regulations. China's equivalent of the U.S. Environmental Protection Agency is the Ministry of Environmental Protection (which, before 2008, had been called the State Environmental Protection Agency). It has been taking its job more seriously since air quality and other issues became global news during the 2008 Olympics and 2010 World's Expo.

Additionally, commodity prices and raw material costs are increasing globally (partly due to China's own voracious appetites), from basics like iron and copper to oil and plastics. When labor is the biggest factor in production cost, China has an advantage. But, if the products are energy- or material-intensive, China's advantage diminishes significantly. For example, during much of China's rise from 1978 to 2004, oil was priced in the $10–$30 a barrel range. Starting in 2004, coinciding with China's impressive growth expansion, oil rose steadily to a peak of about $145 a barrel in 2008. While that peak price might have been an aberration, 2012 has seen a return to $100 or more per barrel prices, which affects many aspects of China manufacturing.

It is not all bad news for China exporters, however: a glut of shipping containers as a result of decreased global demand has made exporting from China much cheaper.

*New Emphasis on Quality*

Since the start of China's Olympic Decade, there has been a new emphasis on quality and product safety.

While, to some extent every newly industrializing country in Asia has gone through a period where its products are seen as inferior—think Japanese cars in the 1960s and 1970s until Toyota revolutionized the industry with its Total Quality Management, or how "made in South Korea" used to be associated with poor quality electronics until the likes of Samsung and LG became consumer favorites in high-tech gadgets and appliances—Chinese products have retained an air of low quality that they can't seem to shake off.

Chinese products, from a United States consumer's point of view, might often be found in places such as Wal-Mart and dollar shops; they are cheap and you get what you pay for. However, the 2007 cases of poison pet food and lead-tainted toy recalls marked a change in how Western consumers see Chinese goods: no longer just cheap, but now potential health hazards as well.

A reputation for poisoning beloved family pets and endangering the lives of children with toys is serious news to a nation that relies on exports for a large portion of its GDP, so the government is pushing quality more than ever before.

It is ultimately, of course, a consumer-driven need. Western consumers demand quality or stop buying, and there is also significant pressure from the domestic Chinese consumers who are newly flush with disposable income. They are faced with a multitude of domestic and foreign brands vying for attention, and are able to do Internet research online and buy gray market or authorized reseller versions of almost anything on China's leading eCommerce companies Alibaba (for B2B commerce, along with Taobao for C2C and its B2C site, Taobao Mall) and 360Buy. Savvy retail shoppers are even using their smartphones at the point of sale to check product popularity rankings, quality and price. Thus Chinese consumers, too, are becoming more discerning, and now have the purchasing power to influence companies to improve their quality.

*From "Made in China" to "Made for China"*

Products are increasingly created by China-based manufacturers for China's domestic market. In the recent past, Chinese and foreign manufacturers might have made their products *in* China, but those products were not really *for* China, they were for export markets. This situation is changing quickly. The previously mentioned American Chamber of Commerce survey for 2010–2011 indicated 71 percent of companies have or would produce products uniquely for China—made *in* China *for* China.

Today, the *new China normal* is creating products not only *in* China but *for* China as well. This means *Sinification*, adapting Western products to Chinese tastes, as well as original Chinese innovation of new ideas. China does not want to get ahead of itself, but it hopes those same products will eventually be for *the world* as well, using the *reverse globalization turbocharger* to retain its position as an export powerhouse while still having one of the most desirable consumer markets.

In order for China to become an innovator, much work needs to be done. One barrier to innovation in China is that the education system, based on rote learning, does not encourage creative thinking. As a Chinese saying goes, the nail that sticks up gets hammered down. It is more important to be part of the status quo than it is to think differently. As mentioned in Chapter 3—*China's Roadmap*, China is using its national plans to focus more on research and development as one of the country's core competencies.

This is not an entirely new trend. China has, for two decades, been trying to develop its own technology to varying degrees of success. It has yet to achieve a breakthrough that is recognized around the world as a true and useful Chinese invention or innovation, but some examples illustrate how well it is progressing.

*Case Study: The China Video Disc*

When China first introduced a player for Video Compact Discs (VCDs) in the early 1990s, the Western world barely blinked. VCD was an almost unknown and unused standard developed by Philips and Sony to put video on regular compact discs. Western markets were going to make the leap from VHS to DVD directly—skipping over the intermediate (and inferior) VCD format—but China found that the players and the media could offer many advantages over either the VHS or DVD platforms, and it quickly became the global leader in a market few outside Asia even knew about.

The VCD media was cheaper and more durable than VHS tapes, especially in high-humidity regions. Furthermore, the VCD hardware licensing cost would be much cheaper than for DVD players, free in fact, possibly because the holders of the IPR—Japanese companies—thought the market for VCDs inconsequential or because it was not worth badgering China over when they had so many other opportunities to pursue.

Whatever the case, Chinese producers and Chinese consumers made the platform a hit, selling up to 22 million players a year in China alone, and in 2005 it was estimated as many as 200 million Chinese households owned a VCD player.[3] It is impossible to know how many VCD movies were sold because the vast majority of them were pirated (VCDs had no copy protection scheme) from VHS tape or filmed in the theaters. DVD players and official DVD movies would be too expensive for Chinese consumers for many years to come, giving VCD a strong market share in China.

Wanting to move up the value chain, China's government began working on its own technology standards for video and a host of other consumer products. The Chinese video disc standard was eventually called a Super VCD (SVCD) and the video players were not only sold inside China but also exported throughout Southeast Asia. Some of the success of the VCD/SVCD formats was owed to its application in the karaoke industry, allowing the replacement of the expensive and bulky LaserDisc (LD) format. Adoption of VCDs elsewhere and in other applications was negligible.

At the peak of the VCD/SVCD product adoption cycle (1998–2001), the DVD format began encroaching into both consumer and producer channels. DVD players were coming down in price to the levels Chinese consumers could afford, and pirated DVD movie copies became widely available after the DVD encryption system was cracked. On the producer side, DVD players were increasingly made in China under OEM agreements (or produced by Chinese manufacturers without paying royalties to the patent holders). The growing DVD market looked attractive enough for China to again try to create its own national standard, the Advanced High Density Disc System (AVD), which was later combined with a Taiwanese standard, the Enhanced Versatile Disc (EVD), but this project failed to gain traction before the price of DVD players and licensing came down to levels that made AVD/EVD uncompetitive.[4]

Unable to get around the DVD standard, China's latest foray was into the realm of High-Definition DVD. The battle between Sony's Blu-ray standard and Toshiba's HD-DVD may be over (Blu-ray won and has since become the global standard for high-definition DVD), but China had one more card left to play: the CH-DVD.

Short for China High-Definition Video Disc, this format is based on the HD-DVD standard supported by Toshiba. Development of the CH-DVD has had many twists and turns, and started at least as early as 2005. Toshiba was said to have courted Chinese manufacturers to pick its DVD standard over Blu-ray, but this did not satisfy the most important criterion for China's electronics industry: avoiding paying large license fees to a foreign consortium, as they were supposed to be doing for DVD players and other electronics.[5] As a result, China worked with a Toshiba researcher to develop the Chinese standard, which would have additional Chinese intellectual property and use different encoding and copy protection formats to make it a Chinese-controlled architecture.

Today the CH-DVD has been rebranded as China Blue High-Definition (CBHD) and the players are sold mostly in China. There they outsell the more expensive foreign-brand Blu-ray players by a three-to-one margin.[6]

Unlike VCD, officially released titles are being produced for the format by the likes of Warner Brothers at prices that Chinese consumers should find affordable, about 50–150 *yuan* ($8–$24) for titles such as the Harry Potter series.

If, like they did with the VCD players, Southeast Asian and other markets can also accept the CBHD standard, the final chapter for Blu-ray may yet turn out differently.[7]

～

From the development of the Chinese video disc industry, several common themes become apparent, and will become more frequently seen in the next decade of China's growth. These themes include development of China's own intellectual property to avoid paying foreign license fees (and to eventually be able to *receive* license income, it is hoped); cooperative research between various Chinese government institutions, universities and companies to develop standards (sometimes with foreign companies desiring an entry into China's huge market); and using its massive domestic market to achieve economies of scale that enable its manufacturers to sell cheaply in the domestic market before expanding to other regions.

## Other Technology Innovation

While it remains to be seen whether this model can work in other industries, China is still going to try to develop its own standards in any technology it can. Some reasons China is pursuing a policy of developing its own technology might include instilling a sense of national pride, establishing non-tariff barriers to keep foreign competitors at bay in the domestic market while China exerts pressure to ensure its own standard becomes dominant, and creating a type of subsidy from the government to producers (who would not have to develop their own technology or deal with licensing issues) and consumers (who could buy lower-cost China-made products).

Another example of this policy and approach might be the case of magnetic levitation ("Maglev") train technology, which originally came to China just a decade ago through a foreign consortium of manufacturers who were willing to grant China favorable terms to use their solution, thinking it would lead to much more business down the line, so to speak.

At the time of the project's launch, commercially operating Maglev trains were unproven and the Chinese were the first who were willing to build and operate a line. The attractiveness of this opportunity encouraged the main partners, German companies Siemens and ThyssenKrupp, to invest much time and resources. The German government even kicked in a loan for about 15 percent of the $1.33 billion cost for the 30.5-kilometer (19-mile) line that would run at 430 kilometers per hour (267 mph) and be the fastest operating train on Earth. That was in 2001; the line went into operation in 2004 and has been running smoothly, if under capacity, ever since. It did not work out so well for the consortium members; they were unable to sell any other systems, in China or even in Germany, and in May 2008 the partners announced the dissolution of the venture. Some speculated the technology would be sold to China, but the announcement was careful to specify that the core technology would remain with Siemens and ThyssenKrupp.

However, based on all of the technology transfer and practical implementation experience that took place in the construction of the Shanghai Maglev line, it took Chinese companies less than a decade to start using the technology themselves.

In January 2012, a Chinese company announced its own variation on Maglev train technology, a light-rail edition that would be running at maximum operating speeds of 100 kilometers per hour (62 mph); be targeted at urban light-rail markets because of its low cost; and be environmentally friendly with low noise and zero emissions.[8]

Finally, demonstrating this trend is going to continue, for any number of the reasons mentioned above, China has also developed its own standards for other technologies including mobile telecommunications.

For example, in 2009, China launched its own 3G mobile phone transmission technology, known as TD-SCDMA. Following China's pattern of obtaining the initial technology standards from elsewhere, TD-SCDMA was also based on technology that has been developed by other countries and companies. It was also directly supported in its development by Siemens, so it is not an entirely Chinese invention. However, it has enough Chinese technology and development in it to allow Chinese companies to adopt it without paying foreign licensing fees. The only problem was that nobody wanted it, neither the consumers nor even the network operators.

Lacking even domestic demand, China once again used its coordinated industrial policy to ensure that the biggest of its mobile operators (and the biggest in the world), China Mobile, adopted the technology and rolled it out nationwide. At the same time, it gave 3G licenses to two other companies that used international standards such as WCDMA and CDMA-2000. The experiment let the market decide. By 2012, the market had spoken. As was apparent during the testing phase, consumers didn't like the TD-SCDMA system. It was slow, dropped calls and did not have the latest phone models (especially the iPhone). Customers left China Mobile in droves to sign up for 3G plans on China Unicom, China's number two mobile operator, which offered the 3G iPhone. China Mobile was not happy about the situation, of course, but it had no choice. At this time, it is essentially waiting for 4G licenses to be approved and has already invested a huge sum in developing a Chinese standard for 4G called TD-LTE. It seems clear that China's TD-SCDMA experiment is going to fail, much as China's DVD standard, the CVD/EVD. But, like the CBHD high-definition DVD format, which *has* become successful in China, TD-LTE could do the same.

Whether China can compete with foreign standards and ultimately win in the international marketplace is quite uncertain. China has the advantage of a huge domestic market to test and grow new technologies, and its market is attractive enough to bring global technology companies willing to offer their best ideas for a piece of the action. China's policy of innovation and support of domestic industry is one of the most important of the *new manufacturing supertrend.*

### Fashion Made Fashionable by China

Clothing made in China usually has an image of being low-cost and mass-produced, but this sector is also moving up the value-added chain, as well as growing overall. The narrative of China moving out of low-value-added goods, such as textiles and apparel, because labor costs are becoming too high to remain competitive is misunderstood. In fact, China is not losing its position as the top manufacturer of textiles and apparel to other countries, it is simply restructuring internally by automating or by sending those factories inland.

China's exports overall, with the exception of 2009, have been steadily growing for decades, frequently at annual rates above 20 percent. When it comes to textiles and apparel, in 2011 China's total exports were nearly $250 billion, growing more than 20 percent from 2010 (when they were at a still astounding $200 billion). This makes China the world's largest exporter of textiles and apparel, with about 30 percent of the global trade.

Clearly this is one of China's most important export industries, but China is not assured of its continued dominance in the next decade as new "Asian Tigers" such as Vietnam, Cambodia, not to mention South Asian countries such as India, Pakistan and Bangladesh will increasingly compete for low-value-added products by encroaching on China's low-cost labor advantage.

Raw materials costs are going up too. Cotton hit a record price in 2011, and China's demand for cotton increased by 86 percent in 2010.[9] Other factors affect the price of cotton, including planted acreage and crop yields on the supply side and demand from other countries. But any changes in price affect China proportionately.

Finally, increasing labor costs, along with health, safety, and welfare expenses are making Chinese products less competitive.

In response, some Chinese factories are adapting in a number of ways, such as by automating the production process, adding more design services, producing more expensive up-market goods or changing from using OEM mass-production under their clients' brands to launching their own brands domestically and, increasingly, internationally.

Chinese factories can now offer the best of both worlds: low-cost handwork, combined with the latest high-technology manufacturing practices connected into Internet-enabled supply chains, to produce ever-smaller runs at efficient cost. In order to become the workshop to the world, China not only needed large quantities of labor, it also needed the most modern equipment to automate processes, produce quickly, and change frequently to meet the requirements of the many different brands and companies a single factory might supply for. This path of industrial development has been honed through years of working with companies such as Hong Kong's Li & Fung, which in turn supplies the clothes to companies such as Wal-Mart and global clothing companies. This has made the Chinese factories' capabilities formidable.

So, after years of producing other companies' designs to exacting standards, on-time and at ever-thinner margins, many Chinese factories themselves are now ready to leave the nest. With the addition of some designers—often Chinese who were trained in fashion centers such as France or Italy—to their payrolls, the Chinese apparel manufacturers can offer a surprisingly good combination of original design at competitive prices.

Many of these designers are now able to launch their own self-brand labels, riding on global interest in Chinese art and fashion. While Hong Kong and Taiwanese designers, such as Jason Wu (a favorite of First Lady Michelle Obama) and Shiatzy Chen, have already made this leap into international fashion, the next wave of Chinese designers will come from the mainland in a *reverse glolabization* manner. This means that—as with China's modern artists—China's fashion designers will initially be more famous abroad than at home, embraced by the Western consumers, especially if the designers show a penchant for Chinese iconoclastic styles. Perhaps the Zhongshan suit (known as the Mao suit in the West) will emerge as a dinner jacket, or *qipao* (cheongsam) dresses might become the next must-have item in a wardrobe of a Western fashionista. Mainland Chinese consumers, for the most part, will still be most interested in famous international brands, but as with the current mainland Chinese infatuation with domestically produced modern art, Chinese fashion designers will eventually be embraced at home, once their designs are expensive enough.

For former Chinese OEM subcontractors suffering from ever-lower prices and ever-higher commodity and production costs, moving upmarket—either as a higher quality OEM or by producing their own brands—is the approach Chinese apparel manufacturers of all kinds are now attempting.

It is a well-guarded secret in the luxury goods business that an increasing number of luxury products—in whole or in part—are already made in China: guarded because it does not suit the image of a luxury brand to be associated with mass production, low-cost labor and sweatshops. The top brands avoid this fate by producing only parts of the whole products in China, assembling elsewhere with a certain percentage of value to qualify for the treasured "Made in a Country-Other-Than-China" label.

Mid-tier luxury brands are not so shy, especially when it comes to bags and accessories, which China excels in. Coach, maker of handbags and apparel, has retained the status of a luxury brand in China even as many of its products are produced in the country, rather than imported. Coach and other luxury brands may not necessarily come to China just for the price difference (which is negligible in high-quality fashion where materials and brand are the largest components of value) but for reasons of manufacturing flexibility and the ability to meet deadlines. Chinese OEM manufacturers are learning to supply to these companies' even higher standards.

This is not exactly a Faustian bargain for luxury brands: they are gaining other benefits from producing in China. Unlike the luxury workshops of Europe, Chinese factories may take fewer vacations, and operate during Western holidays as well. Increasingly, international luxury brands are also manufacturing in China because it allows them to significantly shorten the supply chain and speed delivery to retail shops—China is the source of much of the raw materials used in apparel and accessories, and is already the world's first- or second-largest retail market for many luxury products (depending on which industry association's definition is used).[10]

The final way in which China's textile and apparel manufacturers are adapting and competing is by launching their own brands.

Sporting goods and apparel company *Li Ning* is just one example, now beginning to compete with rivals Nike and Adidas. Other shoe manufacturers in China, formerly famous for running sweatshops that served Nike and other global brands, are now competitive on their own. They are subject to trade restrictions in the EU because their products are such good quality and so inexpensive that they are putting what is left of the European Union shoe industry out of business.

In fact, Chinese-made running shoes have been dominating the Western countries' shoe markets for two decades, either under the names of famous brands or under their own, lesser-known brands. Just ask Sara Bongiorni, author of *A Year Without Made in China,* how easy it is to find running shoes not made in China: she tried in vain to find a reasonable alternative to a $10 pair of Chinese-made children's sneakers, going from store to store in her Louisiana town, before she finally ended up paying $68 by mail for a pair of Italian running shoes with ugly Velcro straps.

Dongguan, a light-goods manufacturing city in Guangdong province, has factory after factory of Chinese shoe manufacturers, making millions of running shoes each year for shipment over-seas at rock-bottom prices, such as those ending up as $10–$20 pairs of shoes at Wal-Mart.

As in a *kung fu* movie, the Chinese OEM students have be-come the masters. More Chinese OEMs in more sectors will be moving up the value chain in a similar way. First they will become original design manufacturers—ODMs—sub-contractors that design and build according to another compa-ny's specifications, for products sold under the client's brand. Finally Chinese companies will develop their own brands and stop offering OEM and ODM services, cutting out the non-Chinese brands altogether.

Apparel and luxury products are just two areas where Chinese manufacturers are moving up-market, as OEMs for more sophis-ticated brands, by becoming an ODM or by launching their own brands. Another sector is personal electronics, such as computers or mobile phones. Before China gets to the point of being able to consistently design its own products and develop its own brands in *any* sector, however, many of its manufacturers have to overcome a very big hurdle—that of intellectual property.

KNOCKOFFS, CLONES AND COPIES, OH MY!

The line between a knockoff, a clone and a copy is thin indeed, especially when you are talking about consumer devices like the Apple iPhone. The words themselves are not precise.

In design (fashion or industrial), a *knockoff* is generally some product intentionally or unintentionally made to look similar to another product. For example, a fashion designer's Milan runway show might "inspire" the design themes of a lower-end off-the-rack line of clothing. This is somewhat of an accepted practice in fashion, with mainstream brands taking their cues from luxury designers for what will become the next season's hot look.

In technology, a *clone* PC used to be something that was made to mimic the IBM-designed PC's proprietary built-in software called the BIOS. In order to avoid claims of being a copy, the process started from the ground up by re-engineering the BIOS in an isolated lab thereby giving the clone PC identical functionality without violating IBM's intellectual property rights.[11]

A *copy* is what many things manufactured in China often are: an exact duplicate of something without regard to intellectual property rights. For example, pirated computer software minus the copy protection, sold from a cart on the street; a copied DVD movie (complete with DVD extras and new Chinese sub-titles, often amusingly mistranslated); or the opening credits of *Late Night with Conan O'Brien,* blatantly ripped off by a Chinese talk show.

It is not just creative works; endless numbers of manufactured products are copied by China's factories. Copies could be made of anything from high-tech electronic device to a pair of Levi's jeans or Nike shoes. The copies appear almost exact in their reproduction down to the labels and packaging (possibly because they were made at the same factory in a phantom shift—an additional shift of workers producing the same products with the same machines in an authorized OEM factory producing an unauthorized run).

Sometimes the copies are superficially the same but are completely different under their covers. A phone once sold in China through online auctions and other gray-market channels was the HiPhone, a detailed copy of the iPhone from Apple, right down to the box and an ersatz Apple logo (with the bite out of the wrong side). Externally, it looked like an iPhone. Internally, the operating system and software was written to cleverly mimic the look and feel of Apple's iPhone user experience, but was written with completely different unlicensed code. It was an Apple product in appearance only; it did not connect to iTunes.

This is the negative side of China's counterfeit goods industry: legions of fake products, everything from fake watches to fake Chateau Lafite Rothschild wines. A set of fake Ping golf clubs can damage both the original brand and likely the golfer's game.

However, a newer kind of product is increasingly being seen in China, with better quality than the original—at a lower cost, and only just pushing the boundary between knockoff and copy without breaking it.

When a Chinese company launched a line of MP3 players that looked a lot like the iPod designs, down to the popular white casing, many wondered what exactly they were—very good knockoffs, or just copies.

*Case Study: Meizu MP3 Players and Phones*

Meizu, a Chinese company, came to the attention of American consumers when some of its products were featured on gadget blogs such as *Engadget* and *Gizmodo* around 2007. Some of Meizu's products looked suspiciously familiar.

When it was first released, the Meizu M3 Music Card MP3 player may indeed have confused some consumers. It looked a lot like the first-generation iPod nano—elongated, with a small video screen at the top—but it had no ability to sync with iTunes. Its technology and software were, in fact, those of a generic MP3 player, of which China makes hundreds of millions a year both for domestic and overseas consumption, including for Apple itself through the OEM Foxconn.

A short time later, in 2007, the Meizu M6 miniPlayer was released. It looked something like the third-generation iPod nano—a cross between the classic hard-drive-based iPod and a second generation iPod nano, squat and with a bigger screen. The M6 had no hard drive, so it wasn't like the classic iPod, and it had a bigger screen than the new third-generation iPod nano, so it wasn't really that either. It was, if anything, the best of both.

While the M3 and M6 were definitely knockoffs in respect to design aesthetic, did they violate any of Apple's patents? Apple has never sued over those devices, but that is far from the end of the story.

Meizu's next generation of products—the M8, M9, and MX— were all smartphones that looked and acted too much like Apple's iPhones for Apple's comfort: it sued Meizu in China over the M8. The dispute is not clear-cut, in that Chinese manufacturers contend that Apple's Chinese patents are too broad and describe a relatively generic device. The suit may yet be thrown out, giving Chinese manufacturers, at least in China, the go-ahead to compete directly with Apple.

Meizu is clearly not giving up, and is getting ready for the market showdown. Its latest product, the MX (an Android-based smartphone), was released in China just a few weeks before the iPhone 4S in January 2012. It has almost identical specifications, from screen and camera resolution to size and weight.

Once a low-end manufacturer of cheap electronics, Meizu has quickly achieved a manufacturing capability comparable to one of the world's most successful high-tech giants. How much of that achievement is from standing on the shoulders of the giant and how much is stealing the giant's ideas and intellectual property, as Steve Jobs wrote about Meizu, is likely to become a defining issue for Meizu and for the tens of thousands of Chinese manufacturers that have been serving Western multinationals for a generation. [12]

*A Shanzhai By Any Other Name*

Meizu's products are emblematic of a trend in China. While Western business models often utilize extensive branding to add perceived value in the minds of consumers, many of China's products compete on a functional or price basis alone. The extreme example of this is a product that essentially copies everything, up to and including the design and packaging, but sells at a much cheaper price. Western people might call them fakes, counterfeits or copies. In China, they are often called *shanzhai.*

The word *shanzhai* (or sometimes *shanzai*) originally referred to a mountain village with a reputation for harboring thieves or bandits. In its modern colloquial Chinese usage the word refers to a class of brands or products that could include knockoffs or look-alikes, fakes or copies. Examples are everywhere in China, anything from bizarre Potemkin Villages of false-branded storefronts with logos that look like famous brands, to people resembling famous celebrities, such as the *shanzhai* President Obama (a look-alike actor) selling *real* KFC in Hong Kong or the "real" President Obama (a pasted-in photo) endorsing a *shanzhai* "Blockberry" smartphone. Some *shanzhai* products are legitimately competitive, in the way that Coca-Cola led to Pepsi-Cola, China's Wahaha created its own "Future Cola" (though the latter's can once looked somewhat suspiciously like Coke's red can with the white swooshes). Other *shanzhai* are complete rip-offs of the original. For example, Starbucks logos and shop designs have been copied numerous times and, in 2011, an entire *shanzhai* Apple Store was found operating in the western Chinese city of Kunming, complete with employees who apparently thought they were working for Apple.

While such examples seem humorous, crudely designed, or even offensive to Western brand marketers and consumers, *shanzhai* do not always have a stigma attached when seen from Chinese eyes. China—with a historical tradition of students duplicating the works of masters to develop skill—is possibly more culturally tolerant of something that appears to be copied without attribution. Chinese consumers may not even be familiar with the original Western brand that is being *shanzhai'd*, so the fault is not theirs in overlooking a *shanzhai*, but more with market regulators for failing to enforce trademarks adequately or the original brand owners themselves, who do not adequately pursue the violations.

An important implication of the *shanzhai* phenomenon is that, while the products may begin as pure copies or poorly functioning knockoffs, more and more often the companies that produce them are maturing and improving, to the point where one day they may introduce actual competitive offerings.

This process may be considered a type of disruptive innovation, a term coined by Harvard professor Clayton Christensen, whereby new entrants produce something for the low end of the market, too cheap or under-functional for the original incumbent producer to care about, but then begin to gradually climb the quality and capability ladders and eventually challenge the incumbents. Christensen used the example of how cheap microcomputers from Apple grew to eventually disrupt the market for expensive minicomputers from Digital Equipment Corporation.

With much basic technology becoming commoditized and mired in overlapping patents, Chinese *shanzhai* products may be disrupting on the basis of brand and design, taking on just enough of the look-and-feel of a successful brand or product, but selling it much cheaper because they produce entirely in China in the most efficient way possible and, of course, pay no R&D or licensing fees. This somewhat follows in the tradition of Japanese companies such as Sony and Matsushita (better known as Panasonic in the West) that made "cheaper, smaller and better" into a manufacturing credo that allowed them to become the foundations for the Japanese electronics industry that would eventually overtake the incumbent American and European leaders.

Copying the brand or the design may seem too blatant, but unless Western manufacturers are more aggressive and persistent about protecting their intellectual property *inside* China, the *shanzhai* firms will continue to develop their know-how within China's huge market by selling to China's unaware, apathetic, or price-conscious consumers. The worry that Western companies should have is not about the short-term loss-of-sales effect from *shanzhai,* but rather from the long-term disruptive effect the *shanzhai* makers are going to have on their industries as they gradually improve products through research and development.

MOVING R&D TO CHINA

In research and development (R&D), which spans almost every industry, foreign companies are also giving Chinese manufacturers a helping hand by willingly setting up research and development facilities inside China, sometimes as independent wholly owned enterprises, sometimes in joint ventures with Chinese partners. Other R&D models include contracting with local Chinese technical research institutes or universities to work on assigned projects, or establishing technology centers in China to work on the projects directly.

Foreign companies are creating new R&D operations in China at a surprising rate. There are four main reasons for this growing trend: lower salaries for Chinese researchers, localization of international products for China, tax breaks being offered to foreign companies by the Chinese government, and cost and time savings offered by an R&D center being close to a manufacturing center.

First, there is a cost savings for researcher salaries. A typical Ph.D. researcher in many Western employment markets may receive $150,000 annual salary, bonus and benefits (which can amount to greater than 50 percent of the salary). In China, the average *total* employee cost for an equivalent Ph.D.-level researcher (a local hire rather than a returnee Chinese or foreign expat) is merely $50,000 per year—meaning in China three or four researchers can be hired for the price of one Western researcher. It is no wonder so many MNCs are setting up R&D centers in China—China's cheap labor extends to Ph.Ds.

Second, by locating an R&D operation inside China, and by having it primarily staffed by local Chinese employees, a foreign company will be more likely to quickly localize a Western product for the Chinese consumers' needs or even develop new products that satisfy their needs better. This need not be limited to fast-moving consumer goods, such as food and personal care products. Increasingly, big-ticket items, such as mobile phones, computers and cars, are being modified or created just for China. The R&D centers where these products are designed will become a source of intellectual property arising from the localization or development processes. As mentioned in Chapter 4— *Introduction to the Supertrends*, China as a country is no patent slouch: it is currently creating new patents at a furious rate and a decreasing percentage of those are foreign-company-registered patents. China's local companies, in other words, are out-patenting their foreign-owned peers inside China.

Third, the tax breaks for R&D centers in China rival or exceed those of Western countries, and they give a significant advantage against both domestic Chinese and foreign companies in China. The basic corporate tax of 25 percent can be reduced to 15 percent for operations classified as high-tech enterprises and, if they locate themselves in preferred industrial parks or geographic locations (e.g., inland), they can take advantage of two years of operating tax free, followed by three years at 50 percent of the prevailing corporate tax rate. For R&D centers in particular, there are additional tax credits—from 50 percent up to 150 percent for the formation of intangible assets—on R&D expenses. R&D centers can also avoid paying import and VAT on R&D equip-ment.[13]

Finally, for foreign companies, especially those with existing manufacturing operations in China, setting up a nearby R&D center provides other advantages since local governments are eager to attract such enterprises and can offer a variety of local incentives in addition to the national tax benefits above. Having an R&D center and a manufacturing facility in the same country can even save executives' travel time.

China's own manufacturers are not sitting idle while foreign R&D centers gain many of these benefits. They are receiving their own kind of assistance from the central and local governments.

China's government has pledged to increase spending on homegrown R&D activities from about 0.6 percent of GDP in 1995 and 1.5 percent in 2005, to 2.5 percent of GDP by 2020. By that time, two years after the end of the Olympic Decade, China's GDP will have surpassed that of the U.S. and it will be the world's biggest spender on research. As indicated by China's 12th Five-Year Plan, research investment should be spread across key strategic emerging industries in areas such as biotechnology, environmental services, space exploration, communications and information technology.

Chinese companies may benefit directly from government policies and subsidized research (e.g., the TD-SCDMA, TD-LTE, and CBHD technology standards discussed in the previous section), and at the same time may also be receiving technology transfers and outsourcing deals from foreign companies. Finally, Chinese companies themselves are waking up to the idea that innovation can bring new growth, so they are investing significant amounts of money in their own research. A case in point, China's NYSE-listed WuXi PharmaTech is less than 12 years old, but already employs 2,500 researchers and scientists.

Chinese corporate R&D is still a relatively new trend, but it is being encouraged by the central government. Throughout the 30 years following the start of Deng Xiaoping's reforms, much technology was transferred from abroad by foreign companies. Since the opening of China's markets following the nation's entry into the World Trade Organization in 2001, many foreign companies see China as a more attractive place to do R&D since they can now avoid working with a Chinese joint venture partner in more industries.

*Meet the New Neighbors: Foreign R&D Centers*

The number of research centers in China established wholly or partly by multinational companies (MNCs) in China has increased significantly since the start of China's Olympic Decade in 2008. Then, China's Ministry of Commerce noted there were about 1,100 R&D centers operated by MNC. Today there are more than 1,300 (one MNC may open one or more centers). The investments have been getting much bigger as well, from millions or tens of millions of dollars in the early 2000s to hundreds of millions, even billions of dollars being invested by some of the biggest firms today. Traditionally, the R&D centers were located in the first-tier cities close to the MNC's China headquarters, but this is starting to change.

With labor and facilities costs rising in first-tier cities, such as Shanghai and Beijing, a new pattern emerging is for MNCs to keep their headquarters in one of those prestigious locations and have R&D or other operations in nearby second-tier cities that are gaining in prominence and talent but lower in cost. For example, a Beijing headquarters might locate its R&D facility in Tianjin or Dalian. A Shanghai headquarters has many choices, including Suzhou, Wuxi, Nanjing, Ningbo and Hangzhou. Many of these cities are now connected by high-speed rail that takes less than an hour to commute to.

Here are just some of the R&D investments of the hundreds that have been set up in China since the start of the Olympic Decade:

> *General Motors:* In 2007, GM announced an investment of $250 million in GM Park in Shanghai, an R&D facility that would include alternative fuel vehicles as one of its prime research objectives. GM intended to be a leader in hybrid car technology in China. One financial crisis, bankruptcy, and a $20 billion IPO later, GM was doing consistently well in China. Its success selling its enormously popular cars in China was one of the only bright spots for GM globally during its tough years of restruc-

turing. In 2011, it announced the first phase of the research center was open, a 65,000-square-meter facility for more than 300 employees. Interestingly, GM also announced new research projects in electric cars, which tie into *China's Roadmap,* the 12th FYP's call for battery and other electric car components.

*Pfizer, Lilly and Merck:* In the pharmaceutical sector from 2009 to 2011, Pfizer, Lilly and Merck all announced big changes to their China R&D strategies. Pfizer would take both the *Sinification* and the *Going West* approach simultaneously by establishing a new R&D facility in central China's Wuhan together with its Chinese partner. It would do this while maintaining its commitment to its Shanghai R&D operations, which already employ more than 340 people. Lilly announced in October 2010 that it was closing down its large Singapore-based R&D facility. A short time later, Lilly announced a big expansion in China R&D instead. The company cited lower researcher wages as well as the need to develop a bigger footprint for growth in China. Merck is possibly making the biggest commitment to China, announcing in late 2011 a $1.5 billion five-year investment plan. The plan's main focus is establishing Merck's Asia R&D Center in Beijing by 2014, with plans to employ around 600 people, up from 260 in 2011. Interestingly, both Lilly and Merck announced that a focus would be diabetes research, a disease that is increasingly afflicting Chinese, which ties into the *consumption growth engine* and some of *China's demographic supertrends:* as China gets richer, its consumers live longer and get fatter, increasing the risk for diabetes and other diseases.

*Genzyme:* In biotech, in 2010, industry leader Genzyme started construction of an R&D center in Beijing meant to eventually host about 350 researchers, only its second lab outside of the United States. Investment in the venture was listed at about $100 million.

*Microsoft:* In 2010, Microsoft opened a 7,000-person capacity research and technology facility in Shanghai. The employees are working in a state-of-the-art LEED-certified complex, which cost more than 700 million *yuan* ($111 million). It already has more than 1,500 researchers and technologists working there and will expand rapidly in the coming years, as it is Microsoft's biggest R&D center outside the United States and meant to lead non-U.S. innovation for Microsoft. At the same time, Microsoft is not just limiting itself to one R&D center in a country as large as China. In November 2011, it announced a major new center to be established in Beijing, focusing on its Bing search engine, advertising and mobile Internet, among other services.

*Symantec:* The company best known for its anti-virus software announced in 2008 it was also *Going West* to Chengdu in Sichuan province to set up a $50 million R&D center, which will eventually have a staff of 1,000. By this move, Symantec is possibly acknowledging the growing number of computer viruses and computer security threats originating in China and wants to be close to the action, and at the same time acknowledging that China's coastal wages for software professionals are significantly higher than in the inland regions. Symantec was an early leader in taking incentives to establish operations in such an inland region. One possible reason is that programmers and other technologists in first-tier cities now have salaries that rival Western countries' levels, while Sichuan, with lower salaries, has millions of potential employees.

*Caterpillar:* In 2012, heavy equipment manufacturer Caterpillar announced, similar to Microsoft, that it was expanding its R&D operations in China, making China the company's second-largest research investment globally. Based in Wuxi, a fast-growing second-tier city near Shanghai, the center already has 500 staff members and plans to add several hundred engineers, with a target of innovating advanced heavy equipment for China's expansion, part of the *urbanization supertrend*, which it can then leverage across the Asia Pacific region.

With so many foreign companies investing billions of dollars in research and development in China, what are the Chinese companies themselves doing? As mentioned earlier, China is not sitting idle, but it is important to remember that much of China's R&D is being nationally directed through the Five-Year Plans and preferred industry lists, as well as other state regulatory controls. Much R&D is publicly funded, directly by the government or indirectly through large state-owned enterprises and banks. Under this model, the central government provides vision and financing, and the local government executes the vision by rallying the public and private stakeholders, such as academic institutions, state-owned enterprises and private industry.

An example is the December 2011 announcement that China would—according to the guidelines set out in the 12th Five-Year Plan—establish a cloud computing research and production facility. The facility will be based in a Beijing technology park and will combine an R&D center, related technology manufacturers, server farms and operations centers in a sprawling three-square-kilometer (1.2-square-mile) area meant to eventually host a staff of 50,000. A pipe dream perhaps, but the plan is clear at least.

*To Localize or Not to Localize R&D*

An important strategic question for foreign manufacturers operating in China is whether to do original R&D in China, as the companies in the previous section are; do none at all, perhaps because a company has a commodity product or service; or take a middle path that is often referred to as localization. Localization in the manufacturing sense usually means taking an existing product, process or service and modifying it for the needs of the local market, rather than building something new.

As mentioned in Chapter 1—*China's Growth Engines*, the *new China normal* marketing strategy is *Sinification* (i.e., localizing products and services to specifically better satisfy *Chinese* consumers' tastes and needs). The context there was in terms of attracting consumers (by using localized advertising, for example).

Here, in the *new manufacturing supertrend,* there are three *Sinification* issues foreign companies selling in China need to be concerned with.

The first issue is whether the product, process or service actually needs to be produced in China at all in order for it to be sold there. Some manufacturers will find local production in China an asset for logistical, regulatory, or operational reasons; other manufacturers may not. For example, a software development company could hire programmers in any country (but the company's website or downloads could be blocked by the Great Firewall—the colloquial name for China's Internet censorship infrastructure).

The second issue is how much *Sinification* is needed. The range could go from *none at all* to *extensive* (but not to the point of creating a new product—that would be *invention*, not *Sinification*). This decision may include, but is not limited to, the brand and external appearances; it could mean fundamental changes to a product, process or service at the design or manufacturing level.

The third issue is, if *Sinification* is necessary, who does the *Sinification,* who makes key decisions about *how* to change a product, process, or service? Under *new China normal,* these decisions are increasingly made in China by Chinese managers. Up until 2008, this was not often the case. Before China's rise in prominence following the global financial crisis, decisions were often made at the global headquarters level. This frustrated many China-based employees and it was simply an extension on the

"West to East" product and technology flow. The head office told the China subsidiary what it should be doing, how, when and by whom (and the subsidiary knew not to ask *why*). Under *new China normal*, a Chinese subsidiary is often the tail wagging the dog. It might tell the head office what should be done, and ask for approval. And very independent subsidiaries are now given free rein for fast market response.

The positions on these three issues determine a company's affinity for and success using *Sinification.*

*Sinification* can actually be thought of as a derivative of an Asia-wide trend. Before mainland China was the market of choice, Japan was an attractive market due to its affluent consumers. The question of product localization was of great importance. Certain failures of Western multinational companies in Japan may, in fact, have started the change of the once-prevalent attitude that Western products and services could be sold as-is for Eastern markets. For example, how GM and Ford at one time tried to sell large American-made gas-guzzling cars with steering wheels on the left to Japanese drivers, who preferred smaller, fuel-efficient cars with steering wheels on the right. While some models may have sold as-is in limited numbers because of a cachet of Western style or imported appeal, real successes (if they could be called such) only occurred after the cars were localized to Japanese needs.

Today in China, *Sinification* has been adopted by a number of successful foreign companies such as Yum! Brands, the owner of KFC, Pizza Hut and other restaurants. Yum! uses *Sinification* by changing flavors, sizes and other elements of its core products to make them more appealing to Chinese consumers. It also devises new products for China at its Shanghai R&D center. For example, China KFC outlets serve congee and egg tarts. Dunkin' Donuts has a pork-flavored donut for the Chinese consumer's savory tastes.

Not localizing products at all is a viable strategy for those wishing to keep their foreign image value, which is sometimes quite significant. So far, this approach has been adopted by a number of luxury brands, especially ones made outside of China in places such as Italy or France. The adage *if it ain't broke, don't fix it* would seem to apply. However, the Year of the Dragon, which started on January 23, 2012, was a paradigm shift: suddenly every luxury company seemed to be introducing a localized model for Chinese buyers. Nokia's luxury brand Vertu introduced a hand-engraved dragon on a specially designed mobile phone; watchmaker Piaget launched two dozen dragon-themed watches in China, ranging from $25,000 up to $1.7 million for diamond-encrusted twisting dragon watch; even that quintessential luxury car, the Rolls-Royce, created a special-edition "Dragon" Phantom model in 2011, which quickly sold out.

This is the first time in China's modern history that Western luxury brands have attempted this degree of association with a Chinese theme, in this case the lunar calendar. It is possible that previous years' animals were not considered "marketable" from a Western perspective. For example, in China, pigs are thought to be very lucky and the richest of the animals—yet most Western luxury brands would balk at putting an image of a pig onto their luxury bags and watches. From the Western perspective, certain animals that might seem appropriate, such as a tiger (whose lunar calendar year last occurred in 2010), are actually negative images to some Chinese people. For example, a tiger might be considered a beautiful animal by Western standards, but a Chinese woman would never want to be identified as a tiger—a *mulaohu* (母老虎)—which has a fierce connotation.

Nevertheless, the Dragon Year seems to have brought with it a new willingness on the part of these luxury brands to use *Sinification*. Where are they doing the manufacturing? Most presumably are still manufacturing abroad in their existing workshops. Chinese consumers will buy them as imports—luxury tax and higher prices connote greater value and give *face* to the buyer—so there is no need to manufacture in China yet. How much *Sinification* are they using? It would seem they are not making fundamental changes to their products, simply changing superficial elements of design. Who is making the decisions about how much *Sinification* is needed, who will do it, and so on? That is unknown for the most part, but one would hope they at least did some market research and created the products with care, lest they be accused of pandering or, worse, trying to cash in on the Year of the Dragon.

Chinese buyers are very sensitive about how their national symbols—especially the dragon—are used by foreign companies. Advertising agency Leo Burnett once learned this to its detriment by creating an advertising concept that portrayed a Chinese dragon slipping down a pillar that had been painted with the product of its client, Nippon Paint. So great was the backlash that a Leo Burnett spokesperson apologized to *the Chinese people,* all 1.3 billion of them.

## OUTSOURCING EVERYTHING ELSE

Moving up the value-added ladder means that China is not just a place to outsource basic manufacturing needs; it is increasingly handling more advanced products and services and even R&D. What is left? China's outsourcing capability is even going virtual.

### VIRTUAL SWEATSHOPS

Perhaps it is not surprising that, with just about every physical product that can be outsourced already being manufactured in China, it was only a matter of time before China would start manufacturing virtual products as well. Ironically, many of China's "real" farmers have become "virtual" farmers.

In China, Massively Multi-player Online Role Playing Games (MMORPGs), large-scale online gaming worlds of adventure and fantasy where users can meet and cooperate in a virtual environment, are very popular, played by tens of millions of Chinese. MMORPGs include both global games with localized Chinese versions, and games developed just for China's domestic market. Due to the popularity of MMORPGs and the sheer number of players in China, the country is one of the top markets for games such as Blizzard Entertainment's *World of Warcraft* (WoW) series. While players in many developed countries play the game for fun, and find the usage fees a reasonable value, some players in China play for profit. One might even say they are working *inside* WoW's virtual world.

Most MMORPGs have an in-game process and rules that, in effect, mean players have to put in effort in order to progress to higher levels and more challenging adventures. One can gain experience and treasure by actively playing the game by going on quests, and can also gain passive "income" by having their avatars make clothing, grow food or dig for gold—which can then be sold or traded for things such as magic potions or weapons. It is this latter activity that has created a virtual economy that connects to the real world through offline transactions.

In order to serve players who would rather pay than put in the sometimes arduous task of building an avatar's experience-level, some users will sell their weapons and magic objects—in some games even their entire avatar with all its accumulated experience and possessions—on eBay or other auction sites. This is enabled by the selling of passwords for real dollars or arranging an in-game exchange and a real world money transfer via a medium such as PayPal. In China, the in-game economy has created an entirely new type of job: gold farmer.

In gold farming, as it is practiced in China and emerging markets elsewhere, Chinese individual players and companies employing vast numbers of "slave players" essentially labor for days online to gain the gold, experience-points or items that may them be sold at a premium offline to players who want a shortcut. It is a play on the classic international difference of labor. Buyers, who are often from developed countries, and whose time is more valuable, buy from sellers, often Chinese players in inland provinces, who are much more numerous and have low labor costs. What started as a friendly transaction between players has become a business.

Entrepreneurs in China realized there are arbitrage profits to be made simply by hiring some unemployed workers in the lower-tiered Chinese cities to sit in an Internet cafe all day doing the equivalent of online digging for gold. In extreme cases, it is alleged that some Chinese prisons run in-prison gold farming operations where prisoners are literally forced to play or face harsh punishment: it is slave labor in a virtual world.

Aside from the moral issue, this manufacturing of virtual property has a real-world economic effect. With so many Chinese players involved in virtual labor rather than the actual playing of the game for fun, the value of the virtual currency and other items inside the game begins to weaken because of too much supply. Virtual labor in a virtual world has created virtual inflation. Like central banks, the game developers need to enact a form of monetary policy to restrict the virtual money supply, or try to ban the activity. But such moves have not been successful or popular. Many players like being able to pay to progress more quickly and gold farmers have adapted to new regulations (such as a ban on selling items or characters, or making gold harder to find) by shifting their efforts to other games or just by working harder, longer and faster. Gold farming and other types of virtual production will continue in China and are, in fact, a growing new—if virtual—industry.

*The World's First Virtual Property Crash?*

The once-popular and predominantly U.S. online game *Second Life* saw another type of virtual economy develop thanks to China: virtual real estate development. *Second Life,* unlike the MMORPGs, which are based on game play and adventure, is about ideas of community-building and social exchanges, all in an online world. The users of *Second Life* have the ability to augment their avatars with clothes and accoutrements, build virtual houses to live in, and operate stores and small businesses. Virtual objects can be bought and sold, services performed, and online assets—such as virtual real estate in prime areas of user interaction—have become increasingly valuable. Through the gaming interface, new objects could be created. In its heyday, from about 2005 to 2008, companies such as IBM had meetings in-game; American Apparel and Dell opened stores and showrooms; fashion shows were held; news bureaus were opened; offices and homes were built. People could even work in-game and get paid in virtual currency.

The currency of Second Life is called Linden Dollars, after the name of the company—Linden Lab—that created the game. Through a mechanism akin to a central bank, Linden Dollars are managed by the company through exchange rates and can be bought in and exchanged out of the game for real currency. All in all, the virtual economy seemed to be flourishing. The challenge, and opportunity, with all the virtual economies design and development is that the creation of the *virtual* objects still takes *real* time and effort. That was where China came in.

The international difference in labor works just as well online as it does offline. So, when one online entrepreneur—Anshe Chung, a pseudonym for the real-life Ailin Graef—announced she was the first real-world millionaire as a result of activities based in a virtual world, people took notice. It turns out there was an interesting connection to China in the story as well.

Anshe Chung Studios has set up a real production office in Wuhan, in central China.[14] By hiring low-cost labor in China to design and build virtual property that would be rented or sold in an online game popular in the United States, Anshe Chung Studios was taking advantage of the same cost differential that many MNCs seek when they come to do business in China. That it was achieved in one of the most cutting-edge industries in the world—virtual real estate development—says something about the outcomes possible under China's innovation drive. In this case, it was the real-to-virtual-to-real currency conversion that turned this business model into a real, rather than virtual, success. By 2012, however, the Second Life economy had changed significantly, and there were signs it was not as profitable as before.

Independent "analysts" noted a "crash" in the "property" market—dedicated users could identify a significant number of virtual homes unoccupied, offices empty, and shops closed—with entire communities even left abandoned: virtual ghost towns. As a private company, much of Linden Lab's operations, information and decisions affecting the game are obfuscated or confidential. It is thought by bloggers that, lacking a critical mass of new users and the real world economic crisis, there was little incentive for many to go on with their "second lives." The evidence was visible in-game as early as 2008. In fact, American Apparel chained its door, a bank suffered a run and collapsed, the popular activity of gambling was banned and other indications of a decrease in real world investment into the virtual game were apparent. Even so, Second Life continues, as does Anshe Chung Studios.

With gold farming and Second Life design services, China has proven that there is a business model in online virtual manufacturing. Furthermore, it has a consistent labor advantage that is likely to remain for some time (the large number of Western technology companies investing in low-cost inland Chinese cities attests to this). While such *virtual* economies may collapse overnight on the whims of a private company (or a computer virus), fortunately for China there are many other industries where it has a *real* economy advantage.

## THE FASTEST GROWING INDUSTRIES IN CHINA

Based on the innovation and value-adding themes of the *new manufacturing supertrend,* the following sections profile some Chinese manufacturing industries that are set for the greatest growth for the remainder of the Olympic Decade. These are the industries that are rapidly upgrading their production through technology and innovation, and casting off the low-quality mass-produced or labor-intensive practices of the past in favor of world-class high-tech value-added practices. Among these industries are those favored by the Chinese government as pillar industries, such as the automotive industry, strategic emerging industries under the 12th FYP, or sectors that will grow as a result of one or more of the *supertrends*. The *urbanization supertrend*, for example, requires transportation infrastructure—along with more trains, planes, and automobiles to use it. *China's Political Supertrends* (the third volume of the *China Supertrends* series) will come back to examine the geopolitical implications of China developing its own aerospace industry but, from the perspective of the *new manufacturing supertrend*, aviation is also an important industry for its ability to push China's national strategy of having a more innovative and value-added manufacturing base.

CHINA GETS READY FOR TAKE-OFF

While China has been developing aircraft since the early 1950s, the story of how China developed its own large passenger jets in a matter of years instead of decades is a tale of two cities, Shanghai and Tianjin.

During Mao's long march to industrialization of China post-1949, airplanes were one of the strategic pillar industries targeted to bring China into the class of industrial heavyweights.

Initially relying on the USSR for much of its technology, China borrowed, bought or received working aircraft from the Soviets and had little need for its own aircraft. When that relationship began to sour, China saw its lack of aircraft production capability as a military weakness and began to develop its own capability to manufacture aircraft. Military aircraft are something that China had success with over the decades. But in the long history of false starts for China's own large passenger aircraft, the homegrown planes never really did get off the ground, literally.

In the 1970s Shanghai was an early base for production of a failed passenger aircraft, the Shanghai Y-10, and has remained a key location to produce aircraft ever since. Before China would be ready to produce its own passenger jets, it had to learn something about passenger jet manufacturing and testing, and that is the story of Tianjin's role in the development of China's aviation industry.

For years China had been campaigning to have Boeing and Airbus set up factories for producing aircraft in China, but little progress had been made. There was some understandable concern that, as a strategic industry for both the EU and the United States, it was too valuable to let another country muscle in. This was not the same as producing clothing or injection-molded kitchen goods: producing any part of a major passenger jet, much less the entire aircraft, in China would mean billions of dollars of investment, and important high-tech jobs and technology would all be taken away from Boeing's or Airbus' home markets. It was a difficult business *and* political decision.

In what may be termed a factory-for-jets kind of quid-pro-quo, in 2007 it was announced that a joint venture between Airbus and a consortium of Chinese aerospace companies would establish an A320 assembly line near Tianjin.[15] At the time, China's large and expanding airlines had more than 370 Airbus A320s on order, likely creating some incentive for Airbus to agree to the request to set up a Final Assembly Line (FAL) outside of Europe for the first time. The business case was simple: China's already-ordered jets could literally be rolled off the assembly line, tested and delivered in China. Of course, the ultimate benefit for China would be the technology and knowledge transfer.

The FAL in China would be responsible for putting together all the major components of A320 series aircraft (which would be shipped in pieces to the facility). The FAL would build up the fuselage, attaching wings, pylons and installing the interior cabin. Then the engines and other major components would be added, and the entire aircraft would be extensively tested. Finally, it would be painted and delivered to the customer—ready to fly.

The FAL in China produced its first Airbus A320 in 2009, and by 2012 it was proficient enough to deliver three complete jets each month. Initial deliveries are going to Chinese airlines, but this could change as the venture grows. Airbus's Chinese partner in the FAL—the Aviation Industry Corporation of China

(AVIC)—must be thrilled: while the FAL showed that jets could successfully be produced in China, one of its subsidiaries, COMAC—the Commercial Aircraft Corporation of China, was just getting ready to launch not one but two large passenger jets, designed and engineered to go into operation during the Olympic Decade.

## Flying Phoenix, Hidden Dragon

When Airbus was to shutter and sell a number of European factories in a company restructuring in 2007, many European politicians feared that a Chinese company would buy them, strip them, and ship everything to China to help China's own industry develop even further than Airbus had already allowed with the Tianjin FAL. They need not have worried. In December 2007, the first "Flying Phoenix" 90-seat regional jet rolled off its Shanghai assembly line, ready for testing. It seemed the Chinese didn't need the European factories or technology after all.

The ARJ21, nick-named "Flying Phoenix," has a range of 3,700 kilometers (2,360 miles) and is comparable in specifications to other regional jets from Canada's Bombardier and Brazil's Embraer S.A. It is based on a McDonnell Douglas MD-90 design, and many of the major components come from international aviation companies. It is expected to fly short-haul regional flights when it goes into operation. It flew for the first time in 2008, and, if it passes certification by Chinese and American regulators, it might go into service by 2013. It has already received more than 240 advance orders and purchase options, almost all of them from Chinese airlines, but General Electric's aircraft leasing company gave the ARJ21 great face by being one of the first overseas pre-orders (General Electric, perhaps not coincidentally, also provides the ARJ21's twin jet engines).

Despite being a mostly foreign-technology aircraft, much of the ARJ21's design and engineering, and certainly the assembly and testing, is done in Shanghai. Also impressive is that the ARJ21 project was conceived in 2002, part of the 10th Five-Year

Plan: just 10 years—and about $900 million in investment—later, "Flying Phoenixes" are indeed flying. The ARJ21 is expected to be a strong contender in China's domestic market—where state-owned airlines dominate—and which is estimated to need an additional 800–1,000 regional jets by 2020.

In the symbolism of Chinese marriage, the phoenix is always paired with the dragon, symbolizing the bride and groom. Since the 1970s development of the Shanghai Y-10—which never went into commercial operation—China had longed for a dragon: a large aircraft that could fly long haul flights and compete with the Boeing–Airbus duopoly. However, the "Flying Phoenix's" groom-to-be dragon was late to the wedding.

*China's Hidden Dragon*

The Chinese aviation industry is a complex web of state-owned research institutes, manufacturers, and airlines that are geographically dispersed and further mired by connections to the secretive Chinese military. The industry and its largest players retain much of their Communist-era bureaucracy and duplication.

That's why, in May 2008, China directed its two largest state-controlled aircraft developers, called AVIC I and AVIC II, to form a consortium, to be called the Commercial Aircraft Corporation of China, the aforementioned COMAC. COMAC would become the father of the bride *and* the groom, overseeing both the ARJ21 and the new narrow-body 150-seat jet, to be called the C-919.

To get the phoenix and the dragon off to a good start, COMAC was capitalized with more than $8 billion by government entities, such as the massive State-owned Assets Supervision and Administration Commission (which oversees most of China's major state-owned enterprises) and the government of Shanghai, which would host the headquarters and factories.

A much more complex aircraft, the C-919 would use more Chinese components but still have significant amounts of foreign technology, including the engines and avionics. Interestingly, it appears designed, in part, to compete with the Airbus A320 series now made in Tianjin, with similar specifications including a maximum range of 5,555 kilometers (3,452 miles) in a long-range version and 4,075 kilometers (2,532 miles) in the standard configuration).

At the 2010 Zhuhai Airshow in China, COMAC announced it had received a total of 100 pre-orders and options for the plane, and by 2012 this increased to 215 orders or options. Most of those, again, come from Chinese airlines and a lone foreign order from General Electric (which again, provides the engines, this time through a joint venture with a French company). The lack of foreign orders is not a big concern to COMAC, which estimates China's own market needs an additional 2,800 large jets by 2027.

While both the ARJ21 and C-919 represent great leaps for China's aviation industry, neither have gone into commercial operation and both have faced numerous delays, not to mention critical components such as engines all being foreign imports.

Seeking to move itself up the technological ladder and improve its international aviation competitiveness, AVIC has been trying to build its own aircraft engines since 2009. In 2012, it announced an 8 billion *yuan* ($1.3 billion) engine assembly and testing center in Shanghai. Analysts believe China is a long way off from developing its own engines, much less fully Made-in-China airplanes. Nevertheless, the distance COMAC has come in the 10 years since China's 2002 national pledge to develop a domestic aircraft manufacturing capability shows how much priority China places on the industry. Given that the biggest incumbents—Boeing, Airbus, Bombardier and Embraer—have been producing passenger jets for decades, the ARJ21 and C-919 will likely face new competing models even before they ever carry passengers. However, China's large domestic demand for passenger aircraft and a strong willingness—if not imperative—by state-owned airlines to "buy local," all but guarantee a strong market for the "Flying Phoenix" and *hidden dragon*.

## BABY, YOU CAN DRIVE MY CAR

There seems to be no stopping China's new-found love of cars. The once-vaunted *Kingdom of Bicycles* has become the *Capital of Cars*.

Regarded as another pillar industry by the Chinese government, and widely desired by the urbanizing and higher-income population segments, cars are big business in China. China became the world's biggest market for cars in 2009—Americans weren't buying cars at the height of the financial crisis—continuing a growth trend since 2005, when Chinese consumers started to buy cars in earnest.

China, like all global auto markets, suffered a poor last half of 2008 as the financial crisis began. But, looking at the years before and after, the difference is still huge. In 2007, Sino–foreign joint venture and domestic automakers in China sold approximately 6.3 million passenger cars (or about 8.8 million vehicles total if trucks and light commercial vehicles are included) with a year-on-year growth of more than 20 percent from 2006. In 2009, China sold 13.5 million vehicles, according to the China Association of Automobile Manufacturers. Of those, about 10.3 million were passenger cars, up 4 million units from the 2007 figure.

China is simply crazy for cars. With just over 100 private motor vehicles per 1,000 people (versus 750 cars per 1,000 in the United States and 120 per 1,000 globally) China's personal car ownership market is expected to grow quickly in the coming years. Some point out, however, that the world would not be easily able to handle the commodity demand or pollution if Chinese were to own as many vehicles per capita as Americans. China's streets would not be able to handle that either, so the government is taking steps, such as heavily investing in high-speed rail to connect cities, and subways within the metro areas to avoid a grid-locked, smog-filled fate.

While not wanting to choke the domestic market, China needs to encourage its domestic manufacturers to grow and begin exporting overseas so that the industry will be more robust. To do this, it has relied on a series of state-owned enterprise ties with foreign manufacturers to build cars together. At the same time, domestic Chinese companies have been developing the capability to create their own vehicles, continuing the innovation and value-added themes of the *new manufacturing supertrend.*

CHINA'S AUTO MANUFACTURERS

Similar to China's aerospace industry, the automotive industry is characterized by state-control of agencies and entities, some of which have been in existence almost since the establishment of the People's Republic of China in 1949. Initially using technology and know-how from the Soviets, these large industrial giants served for decades as *iron rice bowls*—stable lifetime employers for millions of workers. As a result, the industry was slow to change and innovate, creating few products that consumers in a free market would actually purchase. In the 1980s and 1990s under Deng Xiaoping's reforms, many faced restructuring and massive layoffs with the ending of lifetime employment. These dark years also saw the rise of a new hope: foreign joint ventures brought new investment and technology. The ambition today is to cast off this last dependency to create a national automotive champion that could compete with General Motors or Toyota.

The most symbolic of China's automotive rise, fall, and then rise again in China's Olympic Decade is, perhaps, the *Hongqi*—Red Flag—brand of China's First Automobile Works (FAW). Red Flag sedans were the luxury models that carried top foreign and domestic political leaders throughout much of the People's Republic of China's early decades. After Deng's reforms, the Red Flag brand languished as a taxi and cut-rate businessperson's car in the face of competition from foreign luxury models in the 1990s and the early 21st century. On October 1, 2009 the Red Flag limousine made a triumphant return, seen on hundreds of millions of Chinese television screens as it carried President Hu Jintao on his military inspection tour at the 60th anniversary celebration marking the founding of the People's Republic of China.

Other than FAW, China's three other large automotive companies are the Shanghai Automotive Industry Corporation (SAIC)—the biggest of the four—producing about 3.6 million units in 2011; Chang'An Automotive, producing more than 2.7 million units; and Dongfeng Motor Corporation, with about 2.4 million units. Each has ties with several large foreign manufacturers, sometimes more than one with the same company. For example, SAIC has two major joint ventures with General Motors. At the same time, it also has a major joint venture with Volkswagen, plus a number of smaller ventures with other foreign companies.

### China's Car Industry Going the Wrong Way?

The goal of China's auto manufacturers is to eventually be able to build their own cars with their own technology, similar to many other pillar and strategic industries already discussed. China is doing this by limiting foreign participation to joint ventures and technology transfers; promoting domestic research and development of purely Chinese models, as is the current practice under the 12th Five-Year Plan's electric car initiatives; and the purchasing or licensing of foreign car designs. Each of these strategies appears to be working in its own way, with numerous successful joint ventures, successful domestic models, and at least two successful purchases of foreign auto companies by Chinese manufacturers.

After buying technology and designs from Britain's MG Rover prior to its collapse in 2005, SAIC made news in 2007 when it launched the Roewe, its first self-owned model based on the Rover 75 technology it had purchased. The Roewe, incidentally, is based on the name Rover (which was not purchased) and is known in China by its Mandarin name, *rongwei*, pronounced "Wrong Way," which would be an amusing coincidence if it weren't for the fact the Roewe is actually selling very well in

China as a Chinese luxury model built with foreign technology. That is not the end of the story, however.

At the time of launch, Roewe sedans were to compete with Nanjing Automobile Group's MG-branded sedans, also based on the same Rover designs from MG Rover Corp, which Nanjing ended up purchasing outright in 2005 when it went bankrupt. The market confusion that arose from the use of the same design by two different companies under different names—the Roewe and the MG—was solved when the two companies again made news at the end of 2007 by announcing they would merge. SAIC would absorb the smaller Nanjing Auto when it combined with Nanjing Auto's parent, the Yuejin Motor Group. The Chinese automotive industry is complicated indeed.

The merger of SAIC with Yuejin Motor Group would mean the merged entity would have joint ventures with GM, Volkswagen and Fiat; majority shareholdings in South Korea's number-four automaker; and a number of domestically developed brands. It is perhaps odd to consider the degree to which these joint venture cars and domestic-branded cars are all competing with each other under one corporate umbrella.

The pace of joint venture formations, consolidations, and restructurings continued throughout the past decade, with all of China's "Big Four" participating. SAIC's main partners are GM and Volkswagen. Dongfeng has Kia, Nissan, Honda and Peugeot-Citroen. FAW's main partners are Volkswagen (again) and Toyota. Chang'an works with Ford, Suzuki and Peugeot-Citroen (again). This is just China's "Big Four" state-owned auto groups; a number of smaller state-owned companies also have joint ventures. The privately owned automobile manufacturers may not be able to use joint ventures for competitive reasons, though they are being active in acquisitions and sourcing from foreign companies. For example, Geely purchased Volvo in 2010 (the second major foreign acquisition for a Chinese automaker after MG Rover), BYD uses engines from Mitsubishi in many of its cars, and Chery—maker of China's most popular mini car— purchases from and has joint ventures with many auto components manufacturers. All three companies compete against the "Big Four" and can be said to be significant players in China's domestic markets.

In the flurry of merger and joint venture activity, some foreign manufacturers realized they and the Chinese were essentially *sharing the same bed with different dreams,* as the Chinese expression goes. In the case of SAIC, it was essentially competing with itself via joint ventures, and any number of its models overlapped in the market. Aside from the possible conflicts of interest, SAIC's foreign partners might have worried that intellectual property and strategy secrets could be leaked to other manufacturers by a partner who was in bed with everyone.

Some foreign manufactures noted a lack of motivation on the part of their Chinese partners or redundancy with other joint ventures they themselves pursued for greater market access to China. Around the time of the merger of SAIC and Yuejin, for example, Fiat and Nanjing Auto announced a breakup of one of their joint ventures, while Fiat would keep its other two joint ventures (for the Iveco truck line), one with Nanjing Auto and the other with SAIC, intact.

Before the Olympic Decade is out, more of these joint ventures will likely have outlived their usefulness (to one or both partners). While some separations will be amicable—to preserve other business opportunities for the foreign partner—others may end acrimoniously—Wahaha–Danone-style—with contrived reasons used to warrant a breakup of the joint ventures that no longer serve China's interests.

## Built for China, Sold Abroad

China only exported less than half a million vehicles in 2007 before the start of the Olympic decade, and progress is still slow. By 2011, exports were only up to 850,000 units. China's auto industry is overwhelmingly built on domestic sales unlike, for example, Japan's, which produces cars for export far in excess of domestic market consumption. China is slowly increasing its exports but, for the moment, domestic sales are the greatest focus. There are some early signs, however, that China's market is influencing international trends.

General Motors is a case in point. It has consistently invested in its joint venture partnership with SAIC, including significant investments in R&D. For the first time, in 2011 GM's China sales (about 2.4 million units) were greater than its sales in the United States (about 2.2 million units). This trend is likely to continue, meaning that GM will do more development of new models in China and some of that will transfer back to the United States and other foreign markets.

Chinese-preferred features, such as a longer wheelbase and roomier back seats, have already made their way into models that are being sold outside of China. It will not be long before more Chinese design considerations influence production decisions. Whether these features will be accepted by non-Chinese buyers remains to be seen, but with China as the number one market and likely to continue being so, *what's good for China is good for GM*.

As with the aviation industry, China will also seek to build more of the components, especially engines, using Chinese-developed technology. To that end, China's automotive manufacturers also pursue joint ventures with companies such as Cummins to produce engines in China.

Finally, China's domestic auto companies, state-owned and privately owned, are now large enough to begin acquiring foreign companies or to establish factories abroad, as a way of alleviating trade imbalances and avoiding tariffs, much the same way as Japan's auto manufacturers did in the 1980s to relieve trade pressure with the United States.

## IS THIS THE END OF CHEAP CHINA?

With China's *new manufacturing supertrend's* components being value-adding and more innovation in strategic and pillar industries, a lot of businesspeople have been asking if "cheap China" is coming to an end. It is not.

"Cheap China" and the "China price" are one and the same, both referring to the idea that China's costs were cheap. In many industries and sectors, this was assuredly true for many years, and it still is. China's Olympic Decade may see the end of "cheapest" in some sectors but "cheap" is still to be found in many manufactured products for many years.

The challenges highlighted at the beginning of this chapter—increasing wages, increasing costs for raw materials—attest to the fact that China manufacturing is facing a challenge.

For manufacturers looking for cheap, or even the absolute cheapest price, there are still options that do not involve packing up and leaving China. Below are six strategies and points of caution that manufacturers are using to avoid losing cost competitiveness in their China operations:

> *Going West:* As Symantec, Pfizer, and dozens of large MNCs and scores of smaller companies are showing, locating factories in China's central and western provinces is a viable strategy that will lower costs. Migrant workers, who formerly worked on the coast, have returned inland and seek jobs there. *Going West* policies that started under the 11th FYP are expanded under the 12th FYP. For example, the government supports companies going west with tax breaks, and has removed incentives in traditional MNC locales of the Yangtze River Delta (Shanghai, Zhejiang and Jiangsu) and the Pearl River Delta (Guangzhou). The local governments in western provinces provide additional subsidies, cheap land and other benefits. Wages there are lower than the first-tier cities (although wage *growth* is higher, they are starting from a smaller base). It is also important to find good logistics; many of these regions are still developing.

> *Labor intensive:* Paired with *Going West,* labor intensive industries are still an option in China and it is not too

late to consider switching to a more labor-intensive strategy—hand-made custom goods, for example. There are still several hundred million workers being paid wages of less than $400 a month. Products that are labor-intensive will still be relatively cheaper to produce in China than in Western markets. On the other hand, the labor supply in any given region is subject to change due to *the urbanization supertrend,* and so-called "mass incidents"—worker demonstrations or riots—are on the rise.

*Increase productivity:* The converse of labor intensiveness is increasing productivity through automation and technology. In the past it was easy for MNCs to "set it and forget it" by outsourcing to Chinese OEMs. The *new China normal* means establishing quality *improvement*— not just quality control—programs; and buying new equipment, even installing robots, as Foxconn, the world's largest OEM electronics manufacturer, is planning to do. Workers may need more training to make effective use of the equipment.

*Research and innovation:* Investing in China and doing more research will qualify many organizations for a special tax reduction or subsidy that will lower costs. However, balancing this is the need to protect intellectual property.

*More value added in China:* If the amount of work done in China for a given supply chain can be increased, *total* cost can often be reduced. For example, R&D in China lowers design cost, sourcing and production in China lowers logistics and manufacturing costs, selling inside China (i.e., made *for* China, not just made *in* China) lowers delivery costs, and so on. Total cost, not just individual product cost, should be the new focus. If there is a risk to this strategy, it is the investment risk, since it is an expensive option.

*Industry development zones:* In the past, MNCs would locate in an economic zone, such as the coastal cities of
Shenzhen, Zhuhai or Xiamen. Then, export processing
areas such as Shanghai's Waigaoqiao Free Trade Zone became common in almost every coastal city. Today it is the
industrial development zone, such as the cloud computing center being set up near Beijing. These zones are setting up on the outskirts of first-tier cities—and inside tier-two and lower-tier cities—and will combine like-
minded university and research institutes, suppliers, talent and infrastructure to allow *network effects* (lower costs
due to being part of the zone). The worry here is that
some zones are pipe dreams in the minds of the local
mayors, who may be competing with other cities to attract investment. Whether a given zone can attain critical
mass is often a question mark.

So, during China's Olympic Decade, the China price and
"cheap China" will still be reliable, but there will be areas of
China's economy that need to restructure. Within the context of
that restructuring—whether it is due to wage increases, materials,
logistics or government policy—there will be manufacturing
winners and manufacturing losers. China will create a new
position for itself as the cheap place to do innovative and value-
added manufacturing (especially on the eastern coast), and move
the cheapest place to do low-value-added or labor-intensive work
further inland. Throughout China's Olympic Decade, there will
always be a "cheap China" somewhere.

## SUMMARY: THE NEW MANUFACTURING SUPERTREND

The *new manufacturing supertrend's* themes are *value-adding* and *innovating*. Sourcing or manufacturing in China is no longer just about the low-cost, mass-production paradigm: the next phase of opportunities in manufacturing must follow the themes by either moving away from low-tech, low value-added, mass-produced products, or by moving that kind of manufacturing inland. *New China normal* for manufacturing during the Olympic Decade will bring other changes as well:

> *Sinification:* If a new product cannot be made for China, localization—changing characteristics such as color, size or functions—is the next best option to attract buyers. Products that are "Made *for* China" will be more successful.

> *Chinese product standards:* From TD-SCDMA and TD-LTE phones and switching systems to Chinese high-definition media players, China's government is setting standards to reduce patent licensing costs. If adopted outside China, this will be another case of *reverse globalization*—China's products and ideas going outward instead of the world's coming in.

> *Pillar and strategic industries:* China is using all manner of strategies to grow its pillar industries—aerospace and automotive. It has also introduced strategic emerging industries—clean technology, biotech, and others. Growth is high, so is risk.

Much of China's *new manufacturing supertrend* will depend upon how well China's new cities attract investment and infrastructure; whether labor moves into the cities from the farms; and if enterprises can provide enough jobs. Those are the keys to the *urbanization supertrend.*

## Chapter 6

# THE URBANIZATION SUPERTREND

## 新城市 - 基础发展
### *XIN CHENGSHI - JICHU FAZHAN*
### NEW CITIES AND INFRASTRUCTURE DEVELOPMENT

U rbanization is a global trend and has been an ongoing process in China for several decades. But, since the start of the Olympic Decade, it has become in China a political and social imperative unlike in any other country, except perhaps India. China's population is so large, its economy so unbalanced between urban and rural, and its wealth divide so dramatic that China must expend extraordinary resources to urbanize quickly and efficiently. With hundreds of millions of people needing to be moved into cities, existing cities need to be expanded and new cities need to be created. That is the first theme of this chapter: *new cities*. The second theme, *infrastructure development,* describes how to get people into the cities, how to improve commerce between cities and how to create a platform that will allow China's economy to successfully develop as a consumer-oriented society rather than the current, export-oriented, one.

There is an oft-noted progression that—as labor costs rise, consumption grows and the newly affluent express a desire for better living standards—developed countries lose certain lower-value and polluting industries and the service industry rises to take their places for job creation. This is one part of how the unique relationship between the United States and China has developed. It is also happening within China itself.

Considering that many Chinese provinces and megacities have economies as large as smaller European countries, moving work from one place to another can be equivalent to a Western economy offshoring its work to emerging economies. China's major coastal cities—Shanghai, Tianjin, Guangzhou to name a few—are the "developed countries" within China. Anhui and Sichuan provinces are like the "emerging economies."

The pattern is to first move factories outside the city, then to neighboring smaller cities and development zones, and finally to other provinces and regions. Shanghai first created the Pudong New Area in the 1980s. Later development zones were created within and on the outskirts of Pudong itself. As Pudong became too expensive, companies moved to Shanghai's surrounding cities such as Suzhou. Finally, many of these businesses (domestic and foreign) started *Going West* to the central and western provinces of China, such as Anhui and Sichuan.

There, companies find a number of *new cities,* even giant metropolises such as Chongqing. Formerly known in the West as Chunking, Chongqing has taken on new importance in China's Olympic Decade as it consolidates nearby towns to become China's largest metropolitan government, a city-state that has more than 30 million people.

In order to attract foreign and domestic companies to these less-developed regions, new *infrastructure development* is needed. This infrastructure includes energy and transportation, as well as the offices, factories and residences millions of urbanizing workers require. That is why *infrastructure development* is the second theme of the *urbanization supertrend.*

China is using billions of dollars to construct extensive infrastructure and fast transportation systems. From the Three Gorges Dam for energy, to thousands of miles of high-speed rail for transportation, China is investing in the infrastructure it needs to support its urbanization drive. As a result, it is leading the world in the use of raw materials (such as iron and cement) and developing new technologies as discussed in Chapter 4—*China's Roadmap*. But, in a country of 1.3 billion people, there is one kind of infrastructure that will help China to urbanize more quickly, and that is the transportation infrastructure.

The process of developing *new cities* and *infrastructure* will clearly take some time on a countrywide basis, but China has already made good progress. The growth opportunity is that, as of 2012, urbanization is only half done. The *urbanization supertrend* will bring tens of millions more into cities in the Olympic Decade.

## CHALLENGES OF URBANIZATION

Urbanization in China is both difficult and at times controversial. The scale is heretofore unknown: due to the incomplete process of urbanization, mass migrations of hundreds of millions of people occur each year as migrants go to and from their hometowns. Cities of 10 million people can grow in a decade or two. Some of the most common problems frequently receive the majority of coverage on China in foreign media, sometimes with good reason, as they are serious social problems that threaten China's continued smooth growth.

China, in terms of its labor allocation, has been an agrarian economy more than an industrialized economy right up to the present day: there are so many hundreds of millions of people still classified as working in agriculture that China can reasonably say it is still a developing country—an emerging economy—despite all the skyscrapers and the world's fastest trains. It is these people who must undergo a radical change in lifestyle if China is to meet its urbanization goals.

In trying to relocate so many hundreds of millions of people into cities, the methods employed are often more expedient than considerate: the window-dressing of compensation and the promise of better lives in the city mask a number of social problems that China must deal with if it is to successfully urbanize its vast rural population. To each problem, however, China is endeavoring to find a solution.

## FORCED RELOCATION AND LAND-GRABS

While urbanization has a number of positive aspects for society, such as efficient city-based distribution of goods and services, the way many rural residents are forced or coerced into the system has been criticized inside and outside China.

Sometimes land is undeveloped, unproductive (China has some of the lowest agricultural productivity in the world), or even unused—making a case for reclaiming the land "for the public good." Sometimes it is justified for officials to monetize the property held by farmers into new developments—residential, industrial or commercial. At other times, land in productive use supporting residential communities is unfairly taken.

Land grabs by the government are increasingly common in China as the country seeks to meet its urbanization targets, as well as generate sufficient revenue for local governments to operate. This is more than just rezoning. The existing residents are often urged, persuaded, pressured or forced to move off the land, with or without fair compensation.

In the good cases, a large payment (equal to many multiples of agricultural yields) is offered, sometimes together with a new residence in a multistory apartment block on or near the land being reclaimed, *if* the farmers willingly agree to vacate their land. In the medium cases, a payment at less generous rates is offered and relocation might be to a new location far away. In the worst cases, residents are barely compensated and are forcibly evicted if they refuse.

Many times, the process is rife with corruption, as governments try to get farmers to accept the lowest possible compensation and have developers pay the highest possible amount, pocketing the difference for the city (or themselves), getting kickbacks from developers, and using enforcement—including hired thugs—to kick people out of homes, in which they may have lived for decades, that are then literally bulldozed in front of the former residents' eyes.

Proponents of urbanization and relocation policies state that the new residences provided by the government, though sometimes in new towns and cities a far distance from their traditional community, provide a higher quality of living. From the perspective of the relocated, however, it is not only a different place, it is a different *way* of living—from farm to apartment block and city jobs—that many older rural workers may not be able to adapt to. Sometimes it is not rural people that are being relocated but urban residents, when their properties within the city need to be rezoned and replaced by office buildings, infrastructure, parks or more high-rise apartment blocks. At times these urban residents are hardly better off than their rural cousins and may be asked, persuaded or forced to move. Some are fighting back.

*Case Study: House on a Stick*

With all rural and urban private property having been abolished by the Communist government policies after 1949, residents were assigned a place to live through their communes in rural areas and usually through their work groups (known as a *danwei*) in the cities. When China's private property rights began to return in the 1990s, existing residents in urban dwellings were often given squatter's rights to continue living where they had been assigned. Some single-family dwellings passed smoothly into private ownership and secondary property markets while other, larger multi-family dwellings are still today often mired in competing claims and have never been resold.

Those dwellings are sometimes in the form of traditional Chinese architecture, such as low-rise *hutongs* (lane dwellings) or *shikumen* (four-sided courtyard dwellings), and can comprise more than 50 percent of the housing stock of a city. While China preserves some of these dwellings for heritage or aesthetics, there is no great desire to preserve them all, inasmuch as they are often inefficient low-density buildings in central locations, putting city planners into a quandary: demolish them or preserve them.

A standard redevelopment process in China's cities, especially for areas covered with too many of these less-than-efficient living structures, is for the government to designate areas that require expansion for the *common good*. In other countries this may be referred to as eminent domain, and is seldom invoked except for cases such as when a highway is to be built through a rural property. Property to be claimed in such a manner would undergo a lengthy and transparent legal process, usually resulting in the landowner being compensated and the government building its highway.

In China the process is somewhat different. For those buildings not lucky enough to be labeled as historic sites, their fate is almost certain in China's modern cities. First, a new area is designated (often outside of the city center) for the residents to move into, then a high-density apartment building built, and residents of the to-be-demolished district are concurrently asked to choose a new apartment, take cash compensation, or sometimes both. Most people accept an offer, and some even enjoy their new, modern accommodations—even if they are less conveniently located. Other residents are choosing a new option: neither.

Common reasons given for rejecting the offer include insufficient compensation, or simply not wanting to move. Courts, as an administrative unit of the government rather than an independent judiciary, may be of little help to the landowner. These residents refuse to vacate even on an eviction notice and demolition order, holding out in their dwellings as their neighborhood is knocked down around them. Their homes are known as *nail houses*, because they refuse to be hammered down.

The civil court may be one thing; the court of public opinion is another, increasingly important, forum to air grievances. In 2007, a now-iconic image of China's urbanization dilemma swept across the Internet in China and even internationally. The image could best be described as showing something akin to a house on a stick: a house precariously perched on a 30-meter pillar of earth, around which the surrounding land had been excavated, resulting in a vast pit, perhaps to accommodate foundations of a skyscraper or underground parking garage. The house looked as if it would topple into the abyss at the first big wind but, if one looked closely, you could see a banner that had been hung by its current occupants, stating "No violation of legitimate private property!"

Since the concept of private property is still relatively new in modern China, residents of older parts of China's cities frequently do not have any rights to their properties beyond a type of squatter's rights that establish residency but do not include a 70-year land lease or title, as with other private property in China. Disputes among family members living at the same location are frequent, and it is not easy to sell a property with conflicting claims. So, when the government says to move, it allocates compensation based on the number of actual claimants. For this reason, some couples will divorce and cohabitate, hoping to get compensated twice. The residents usually accept the compensation offered and move into much more modern, newly built low-cost housing on the outskirts of the city.

Mrs. Wu and her husband Mr. Yang were not such people.[1] Taking their squatter's rights seriously, they occupied their dwelling and refused to accept the compensation offered by the developer which, in Wu's estimation was insufficient compared to the true property value when neighboring properties or the post-development value were considered.

This case was seen as a test of a number of legal issues in China, including the level of government collaboration and interference in private real estate transactions, whether squatter's rights could be enforced, the progress of market reforms in the property sector and how much the people deserved to be compensated versus the interests of the public and private businesses.

After the "nail house" protest had gone on many weeks, Wu and Yang accepted compensation and dropped their court case, but the government, by allowing the excavation of surrounding properties to take place before all claims had been settled, was found to have been unfairly pressuring and endangering the life of Yang (who had climbed the pillar of earth, hung the banner and occupied the home in spite of the surrounding excavation work). The local government also made the situation worse from a publicity standpoint, in warning the people that such acts of private rebelliousness would not be tolerated. The national government reacted harshly against the local government's position and swiftly acted to strengthen property rights with the promulgation of the new Property Law on October 1, 2007.[2]

## Disneyland Millionaires

In the rural areas, as opposed to the cities, it is not always the case that redevelopment means an unfair deal for the residents. In fact, around the major cities owner-farmers are not always farming. Some rural residents who were lucky to have been near a developed first-, second- or even third-tier city have already left their land, became part of the nearby urban economy and, as landlords, rented out their property to migrant peasants who come from poorer parts of China. Besides collecting rent, farming landlords may enjoy a number of other lucrative opportunities. The outskirts of some major cities have become extremely valuable as the city spreads outward. If the land is to be reclaimed, the owners (not the renters) will still receive a one-time payment and possibly one or more new apartments for a family that wasn't even living on the land. Other so-called urban farmers may turn to organic production to supply the city's white-collar health-conscious elites; eco-tourism and "pick-your-own" fruits and vegetables businesses; farmers' restaurants; or may just leave the land fallow, waiting to sell to the inevitable developers that come calling as the city's sprawl reaches ever outward.

Such was the case with the rumored mainland China Disneyland, an on-again-off-again project since 2005, after the first China Disneyland was opened in Hong Kong. During a long process of negotiation with the Chinese government, national and local, each time the project appeared to be on, property prices in the area would shoot up and farmers would rush to establish residences on undeveloped land (an occupied parcel of land would be more valuable in terms of compensation). These residences were, more often than not, illegally constructed shacks, but the true residents were richly compensated when Disneyland finally decided to set up its second China Disneyland in Shanghai's Pudong New Area district.

FORGOTTEN SENIORS, KIDS AND SPOUSES

The movement of labor away from farming was not necessarily all government-led initiative. In fact, migration had already been voluntarily occurring ever since the reform and opening up policies began in 1978, as young workers willingly sought better lives and higher-paying jobs in the cities. This vast migration of labor—known as the floating population and numbering in the hundreds of millions—acted to hollow-out traditional farming communities of their most productive young workers. Though these teens and young adults often returned for harvests or, if there were no harvests, for the traditional Chinese New Year and other holidays, the old, the infirm and the children unable to otherwise work increasingly became the left-behind.

It is estimated that nearly 60 million children are left behind in rural hometowns while one or both parents work in manufacturing or city jobs. These children may be left with older relatives—themselves either too old or lacking skills to work factory or service jobs—and have poor access to education, health and welfare due to the lack of development of those sectors in rural areas.

The migrating parents are often not considered permanent residents of their working location. Left-behind children often cannot join their parents in the cities because of the need for a *hukou* residential permit. The *hukou* is a legacy of the more rigid Communist period. It was used to control migration and ensure that China's agriculture producers would remain tied to their land (in a people's commune) and the urban workers tied to their factory (in a *danwei*). At one time, working in a city would have been impossible without a residency permit, but today migrants are given temporary licenses to work in the cities. Recently, progressive cities, such as Shanghai and Beijing, have moved to liberalize the system, with Beijing announcing a new type of residence permit for migrant workers in 2012, which would likely give additional rights beyond the temporary permit but not full *hukou* permit rights.[3] This is significant for China's major cities, which have several million migrant workers each: without a full residence permit in the city they work in, parents may bring children but often cannot enroll them in local schools or attain other social benefits.

Under these circumstances, many parents opt to leave their children behind. This is one of the reasons for the massive migration that occurs every Chinese New Year: the best that parents can do to maintain a presence in their children's lives is travel home once or twice a year during that time or on the National Day holiday.

The children, elderly parents, other relatives and even left-behind spouses are increasingly living in poverty as the country modernizes around them. Some children and elderly end up as beggars on the streets, forced to supplement their meager pensions or transfers from relatives working in the cities, whose paychecks are increasingly squeezed by inflation.

China needs to solve both the urban and rural challenges if it hopes to have a satisfied populace. It is employing a number of strategies to do this, including building *new cities* closer to rural areas and building *new transportation infrastructure* to connect the eastern developed areas with the western areas.

## CHINA'S NEW CITIES

China is building new cities across the country, especially in the western areas that have lagged behind the coastal eastern side. This will reduce the need for migration.

The western city of Chongqing is one example. Currently it is, by official population, China's largest city, and one of only four that are granted a special city-state status to self-govern as a municipality—the others are Shanghai, Tianjin, and Beijing—with the same rights as a province. Chongqing, formerly known as Chunking, was the temporary capital of Chiang Kai-shek's provisional government during World War II. It has grown from a mere 400,000 people to the point where its population is listed as nearly 32 million people.

This would actually make Chongqing the biggest city in the world, a fact which Chongqing's promotional materials never fail to mention, but its population is not directly comparable with the official populations of other world cities since its status as a city-state has allowed it to consolidate a large number of nearby towns and villages as well as the rural areas in between. With the population of the municipality being only about 45 percent urbanized, more conservative estimates of the population in Chongqing city proper range from 8 to 12 million, which is smaller than Shanghai or Beijing. So Chongqing has its own process of urbanization to undergo, whereby 4 million additional residents will be brought into the city itself within 10 years and the surrounding rural populations will be consolidated in the surrounding satellite towns.

Nevertheless, Chongqing is still a massive undertaking and part of a civil planning experiment by the National Development and Reform Commission to test a balanced urban and rural development model. In fact, this is not the first time China has built a made-to-order megacity: the prototypical example is mainland China's answer to Hong Kong, the former fishing village of Shenzhen.

The fourth largest city by GDP size, with an official population of about 8 million and millions more in floating residents, Shenzhen is within a short commute of Hong Kong. Pre-1980, Hong Kong was a major hub for many manufacturing industries. Manufacturing was 25 percent of Hong Kong's GDP in the early 1980s. It was well-known for producing export products of textiles, toys, watches and electronics. Today, manufacturing represents less than 4 percent of the Hong Kong's GDP, with much of the manufacturing industry long ago moving to nearby mainland Chinese cities including Shenzhen. Designated as the first Special Economic Zone (SEZ) in Deng Xiaoping's post-1978 reforms, Shenzhen transformed from a fishing village with only 70,000 people in early 1980s, to a modern city today. Shenzhen's rise is the pioneering example of success in China's process of urbanization, a city where everyone is from somewhere else.

Shenzhen and Chongqing are just two of the dozens of large cities that are already well on the path to development as international-class cities, but there are literally dozens more being planned and built to accommodate the 300 million new residents from the countryside who will urbanize in the next 20 years. Those cities are going to need a lot of *infrastructure development*—which is the second theme of the *urbanization supertrend.*

### SUPERLATIVES, CHINESE STYLE

While biggest, tallest, or fastest does not always mean best, some of China's megaprojects and feats of business-daring make for interesting concepts or experiences as part of the process of urbanization:

> *Fastest passenger train in operation:* The Shanghai Maglev train connecting the Pudong International Airport to the middle of... Pudong! Though many would wish it could connect all the way into Shanghai downtown proper, the line is short so the Maglev runs at a top speed of 432 kilometers per hour (268 miles per hour) for only about 30 seconds before having to start slowing down.

> *World's biggest exhibition site:* Currently, Hanover Germany's Hanover Fairgrounds—at just under 500,000 square meters (5.4 million square feet)—is the world's largest exhibition area, but Shanghai will build one just a bit larger, near its Hongqiao International Airport, to

take the number-one spot in 2014, tripling the size of China's current largest exhibition center (also in Shanghai, in the Pudong New Area).

*Highest cellular tower:* The importance of communication infrastructure cannot be understated, so China has one of the most advanced and far-reaching cellular networks in the world. Nary a village or rural district is without coverage and even Mount Everest, 6,500 meters (21,324 feet) above sea level, has a mobile phone transmission tower to provide service to the handful of mountain climbers and Sherpas at the stations to the summit.

*Biggest Shopping Mall in the World:* In a sign of possible over-building and irrational exuberance, the South China Mall in Dongguan, Guangdong, at 660,000 square meters (7.1 million square feet) of leasable retail area, was built to be the world's biggest—but has ended up being one of the emptiest, as it was practically a ghost town as recently as October 2011, when a journalist went to visit. Fortunately, China also has the second biggest mall in the world, in Beijing, the Golden Resources Mall, at 557,000 square meters (6 million square feet) of leasable area.

*World's tallest hotel:* Depending on when you set the bar, prior to the 2008 Olympics, the world's tallest hotel was the Grand Hyatt Shanghai on the 88th floor of the Jin Mao Tower, but it was surpassed by the 93rd floor Park Hyatt in Shanghai's bottle-opener-shaped World Financial Center in July 2008, and then by the Hong Kong Ritz-Carlton Hotel in 2009. Sometime around 2014, China will again top its own record by placing a hotel in the Shanghai Tower which, at 632 meters (2,073 feet) high, should become the world's second tallest building after the Burj Khalifa. Significantly, Shanghai Tower's largest tenant will be the Chinese-owned J Hotel, part of the Jin Jiang International Hotels Group.

*Longest ocean-crossing bridge:* The Hangzhou Bay Bridge, joining Shanghai and Ningbo, 36 kilometers (22.4 miles) long at a cost of $1.7 billion, was opened in 2008. Perhaps in a case of bridge envy, northern province Shandong opened the eight-lane 41.48 kilometer (25.8 mile) Jiaozhou Bay Bridge in July 2011 at a cost of $2.3 billion, cutting off 20 minutes from a previous route.

*Busiest Airport in the World:* Comprised of three terminals, Beijing Capital International Airport includes Terminal 3 which, at 2.95 kilometers (1.83 miles) long and 1.3 million square meters (14 million square feet) of floor space, is in a neck-and-neck race with Dubai International Airport's Terminal 3 for the title of world's largest terminal. In terms of passenger volumes, it is expected that the Beijing Capital Airport's 850 million annual seat volume will overtake Atlanta's Hartsfield-Jackson International Airport's 870 million seats to become the world's busiest airport in 2012.

While China's seemingly endless drive to build bigger, taller, faster and larger shows no sign of abating, some megaprojects seem to be in excess, such as the above-mentioned Dongguan South China Mall; Inner Mongolia's ghost town in Ordos City; and government buildings of small towns or provinces all over China that are built so grandiose as to be nick-named "White Houses" after the one in Washington. Many questions remain as to how well they will be utilized and whether or not they will ever make a return on investment that would justify their original costs. Until that day of reckoning, the world should actually thank China for continuing to build; its real estate construction boom has helped drive China's economy forward and, for that reason, may be considered one of the world's most important drivers as well.

## TRANSPORTATION INFRASTRUCTURE

China's other major tactic to connect the migrant workers, bring more companies west, and spur economic development is to build transportation infrastructure. The theory is that the cities can create economies of scale, while hundreds of millions of peasants spread sparsely throughout the country's massive area cannot. So it is of paramount importance to create ways to get to the cities from the countryside, get around in the cities and connect the cities to one another. Making these solutions as sustainable as possible is another consideration, which reduces the desirability of certain transportation options, such as the automobile.

Certainly, giving people roads and highways, and letting them buy cars is a possibility, and it worked wonders for the development of the U.S. economy after World War II, with the Interstate Highway project. But, as previously mentioned, China and the world lack the resources to give every person in China their own automobile, electric or otherwise. Some of China's biggest cities are already suffering from too much traffic: two of China's largest cities, Shanghai and Beijing, are using different methods to try to control the number of new cars going on the roads.

### THE WORLD'S MOST PROFITABLE DMV

Since 1994, in a bid to keep Shanghai's high-spending consumers from flooding the roads with cars, Shanghai has had a cap on the number of new license plates. At present, it releases about 5,000–10,000 new plates per month, which it sells at a monthly auction.

In many years, the amounts raised from this activity are significant, as much as half a billion dollars or more for the city to use on subsidizing public transport. More importantly, the system acts as a disincentive on the purchase of new cars, reducing road congestion and pollution. It is not without controversy, being opposed by car buyers, while most transit users support it.

The controversy mostly arises from a lack of transparency as to how the funds are being used.

In 2007, the once-a-month license plate auctions generated about $500 million in annual revenue, while the 2010 auctions raised a total of $659 million for the city, probably making it the most financially lucrative Department of Motor Vehicles in the world. Most of this money was used to improve local public transportation facilities and subsidize public transportation costs. The amount left over each year is published, but detailed spending figures are not yet available.

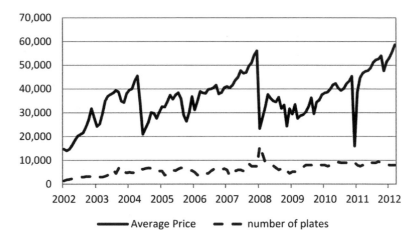

*Figure 13: Shanghai's car plate auction results, 2002–2012*

With the car craze unabated, monthly auctions during the last two years saw high demand and high prices for plates. In fact, the price of a plate can be as much as eight to 16 months' salary for a typical office worker, yet consumers seem willing and able to continue to pay the high tax. Sixes and eights are important in Chinese numerology, so plates with auspicious numbers such as 888 are even more expensive and can go for astronomical amounts.

Prices rose to a record average price of 58,625 *yuan* ($9,305) per plate in March 2012. This price level can actually eclipse the price of an economy car, such a Chinese-made Chery QQ, which goes for about 51,000 *yuan* ($8,095). With the plate nearly doubling the cost of a small car, many people try to register their cars in nearby provinces where the plate costs are lower. But, in recent years, this circumventing of the rules has become more complex and expensive. In fact, the high plate prices in Shanghai could actually be having a negative impact on the environment: many consumers use the high plate price as a justification to get a more expensive car, which will likely have a higher displacement engine and emissions, increasing China's carbon footprint and local pollution. It is a good example of the sometimes unintended consequences of an economic policy. On the one hand, fewer cars are on the road. On the other hand, the cars that are on the road are bigger and less fuel-efficient.

Nevertheless, using this plate system, Shanghai has been able to limit itself to 80,000 to 110,000 new cars on the road each year, and make a lot of money in the process. That one of China's largest cities is able to do this is probably a good thing, considering the Chinese nationwide are purchasing more than 10 million vehicles a year now, and China is the world's largest market for automobiles. In 2012, Shanghai had about 1.3 million public vehicles and 1.2 million private cars on its roads. Without the controls on new plates for cars purchased by Shanghai's 22 million residents, Shanghai would likely find itself overwhelmed with cars, much the same way Beijing already is.

THE WORLD'S WORST DMV

Beijing, once a city of bicycles in a country of bicycles, has now become a car city. In 2010, it issued 750,000 plates, about eight times the typical yearly quota in Shanghai.

Unable to cope with the smog and the constant traffic jams plaguing Beijing in the run-up to the 2008 Beijing Olympics, the local government finally begun to rethink its policy of allowing an essentially unlimited number of new cars on the road each year. At first it introduced various traffic management plans to keep some cars off the road each day. For example, if your car had a license plate ending in 4 or 9, it would not be allowed on the roads on Tuesdays. Or cars with out-of-town plates were prevented from entering the city ring roads during daily rush hours.[4]

When that was not enough, Beijing decided to tackle the problem by controlling the number of new cars being put on the road each year through a quota system similar to Shanghai's. It had people up in arms, however, over how the plates would be distributed, essentially at no charge and by lottery. With prospects of plate arbitrage dancing in their heads, nearly 400,000 people applied for a monthly lottery in which only 17,600 plates were being granted, a one in 23 chance. Most of those people did not even want cars, but entered on behalf of family members to increase the chances of winning.

Aside from the fact that people who don't need cars are entering the lottery, some agencies have apparently found loopholes in the system. The scams can become quite complex. For example, one method involves the "winner" of a plate in the lottery being sued by the person who actually wants the plate (and is willing to pay an under-the-table fee to the agent and the lottery winner). In the court case, defendant loses but cannot pay compensation; the aggrieved party (i.e., the buyer) agrees to take compensation in the form of the plate instead. The money for the under-the-table payment could be as much 100,000 *yuan*—double Shanghai's average plate costs of more than 50,000 *yuan*—or as little as half that figure. But, either way, it transfers what could be revenue to the city into the hands of consumers and companies, and therefore may not discourage new car buyers as much as Shanghai's plate auction does. Other somewhat shady methods of bypassing the system involve buying the rights to use another person's plate by indemnifying them against claims via a personal contract, which must be extra-legal if not illegal. It will be interesting to see how such cases are treated in the court once the inevitable disputes arise.

It is not clear why Beijing decided to adopt a system that was different from the one that was already being successfully used in Shanghai. In addition to missing an opportunity to generate income for the city, Beijing's system is also struggling to be as fair and transparent as Shanghai's.

NEW AUTOMOBILE BUSINESS MODELS

Some other positive effects of the plate quota systems include the development of the car rental market. In Shanghai, for example, 1.7 million people own cars but there are more than 4 million people with licenses. Avis and other car rental companies are already in the market.

On the green front, car-pooling should be a no brainer. But liability fears are on drivers' minds, and black taxi services— charging people for a ride—are illegal and strictly punished. In China carpooling is usually not free. Only one person may have a car, so it is assumed by the police that anybody transporting people is probably receiving some kind of compensation, for gas or otherwise. So car-pooling hasn't really taken off with consumers. Several sting operations have infuriated drivers: undercover police posing as stranded commuters or even injured parties lure cars to stop, then arrest the would-be Good Samaritans for offering them a ride. Again, here it is assumed that people would not be altruistic and anybody stopping to pick somebody up must be doing it for a fee. Drivers caught by this type of sting have protested—to no avail—that they were just trying to help and were completely baffled that the police thought they were trying to run a black taxi service. To be fair to the traffic police, the problem of black taxis is endemic in Shanghai and other cities. Merely standing on the sidewalk outside a station will attract touts running illegal car pool services. It is not uncommon to be propositioned in IKEA by illegal drivers, hoping to carry you (and your furniture) home for a tidy fee that bypasses the taxi waiting lines.

Community car sharing services—where a fleet of cars is shared by members in a club, similar to U.S.-based Zipcar—may have high growth potential once the parking spaces can be found. With both real estate and cars being highly prized in most large cities, parking spots are a rarity in many downtown areas.

One bright spot was a 2011 announcement by the Ministry of Science and Technology, together with the National Development and Reform Commission, that "new energy" cars would be exempt from some plate restrictions in Shanghai, Beijing and 23 other large cities. Many of these will be Chinese-made electric cars, such as those made by BYD (which Warren Buffet has invested in).

With the gridlock that has developed in many large cities, the pollution, the lack of parking spaces and the expense of cars and plates relative to per capita income, China is looking at other transportation options for the nation's masses. It will still build more roads and highways to create a more efficient transportation infrastructure, which is especially necessary to improve the economic connections between inland cities and the ports, but China has recognized the limitations of allowing cars to take the place of mass transportation. Instead it is encouraging more use of rail transportation—high-speed between the cities and light-rail and subways inside the cities. China will also build airports to satisfy the need for speed within China's large geographic land mass as well as internationally, to promote more trade and travel with the global community. In all, China is using its national policy tools to establish a transportation infrastructure that is second to none.

## MOVING PEOPLE AROUND THE COUNTRY

Transportation infrastructure is one of China's future competitive advantages due to the fact that much of it is relatively new, built since 1978. Prior to 1978, China's ports, highways, airports and other infrastructure were all far behind the West's. Its rail network was comprehensive but it was built using Communist-era technology and systems, some of which are still in use today.

The *new China normal* is to update transportation infrastructure no matter the cost. The financial viability of a transportation asset itself is not usually a pressing concern to local and national leaders, who see GDP growth as a key metric of success, and who put more emphasis on the *public good* argument to justify even small increases in efficiency. Before it was stopped, Shanghai nearly built a Maglev train line to the neighboring city of Hangzhou at a cost of tens of billions of dollars, even though a high-speed rail line (using traditional railway technology) had just been built the same year.

With a desire to reach national targets, state-owned banks are directed to lend money at low and uncompetitive interest rates to support new airports, rail, bridges, highways and public buildings—whether they will make money or not. Sometimes projects are built at the direction of government officials as a sort of *Field of Dreams* economic stimulus for regional growth: build it and they will come. Keynesian economic policies for state development are quite at home in modern China.

*Fast Pace of Infrastructure Development*

In addition to the state-controlled banks making funding easier, China's government authority also allows it to overrule local concerns, including those of the residents. A controversial policy of relocations has dogged many of China's largest infrastructure projects, while China has been able to build faster than almost any nation on Earth.

*Case Study: Comparison of Chinese, Japanese and Indian Infrastructure Development*

When it comes to large infrastructure projects, few are as big as hydroelectric power. China has built giant canal systems that will bring water from south to north, and is damming its rivers faster than any nation. Looked at one way, this prevents flooding and generates clean electric power. Looked at another way, large dams are costly and flood vast areas of formerly inhabited land, forcing the relocation of millions of people. Despite the size and complications of some projects, China has had some success with hydroelectric engineering, compared with India, another large populace country with a focus on hydropower.

India's Narmada River Dam hydroelectric projects (the largest being the Sardar Sarovar Dam at 163 meters (535 feet) in height) involve a potential total resettlement of 1.5 million people and have been off and on again since 1979. In India, political wrangling, citizen lawsuits, corruption and other controversies have all played a part in delaying the projects.

Roughly comparable to the Narmada's Sardar Sarovar Dam is China's Three Gorges Dam, the world's largest hydroelectric project at 185 meters (607 feet), involving the relocation of about 1.3 million people. The Three Gorges was approved in 1992, began construction in 1993, and was completed almost two years early in 2007, at least 15 years (and counting) faster than the Sardar Sarovar, which has not yet been completed.[5]

When it comes to transportation infrastructure, China is also building its ports, rail, and airports at a pace other countries can only dream of.

In a famous case of citizen opposition to new airport infrastructure, in Japan's Narita Airport area, a group of farmers and residents held up construction of a second runway for more than 30 years. By comparison, when Shanghai decided to build Shanghai Pudong International Airport in the 1990s, it was started in 1997 and completed by 1999 (and with some irony for the Narita Airport expansion, funded largely by a development grant from Japan). A second runway was built by 2005, a new terminal and third runway opened in 2008, and a third terminal and two more runways are to be completed by 2015 so the airport can meet its target of 80 million passengers per year and 6 million tons of cargo.

At Beijing's Capital International Airport, Terminal 3 was completed in just four years by 50,000 laborers working 24 hours a day. It opened in February 2008, in plenty of time for the Olympics, without any of the glitches that London's Heathrow International Airport's new Terminal 5 suffered when it started operation in March 2008 after nearly 19 years of discussion, planning, design and building. In terms of actual construction time, Beijing's terminal took two years less and cost half as much as Terminal 5, and is bigger than all five of Heathrow's terminals put together. The concrete had barely had time to set when discussion began in Beijing on a plan to build a fourth runway or start construction of a second international airport for the city, possibly both.

⁓

When it comes to transportation infrastructure for what the government calls China's masses, airports are not the best option: the tickets are simply too expensive for many. What is more important, China has something of a rail culture, a history of using trains, that give trains sentimental as well as practical value: there are no other practical means to travel long distances besides rail. Cars or buses would take too long and be too expensive on the still-developing and highly-tolled highway systems. That is why China is still, and may always, be a nation that runs on rails.

## CHINA'S RAIL AMBITION

Rail is a popular means of travel in China and the network carries a total of about 2 billion passengers a year. This compares to about 210 million passengers using air travel inside China, showing that rail is truly the people's choice. During the 40-day-

Chinese New Year travel season, more than 3 billion trips take place by road, rail, air and boat. Of those, road travel by car, bus, even overloaded scooters accounts for about 90 percent of the trips. The rail network, however, is the only affordable alternative for long-distance travel for tens of millions of migrant workers. A single day may see as many as 6 million people using intercity trains, while 230 million passengers total travel by rail through the entire holiday season. Trips by boat along China's Yangtze, Yello and other rivers account for about 44 million trips, and 35 million trips are undertaken by air. This yearly travel rush is called *chunyun,* which in English could be translated as the New Year rush. [6]

In addition to rail being a domestic priority for general transportation, China also sees rail as one of the key drivers of urbanization. By establishing new railways and stations linking cities, those cities can become economic centers and drive development. By doing so, they also take away from development in rural areas and may exacerbate the wealth gap. But, on balance, China believes that by encouraging urbanization and concentration in cities that are connected by rail, social welfare and commerce will increase. China is therefore committed to the use of rail to speed development and urbanization. It already has the longest high-speed rail system in the world in terms of length of track and, increasingly, the most high-tech as well in terms of top speeds (China's trains are the fastest in operation, faster than Japan's bullet trains), amenities (some carriages have been criticized for being too luxurious) and engineering (through inhospitable environments, high altitudes and long distances).

China hopes its rail industry will be a pillar for the economy, eventually developing one or more national champions similar to Bombardier or Siemens. With a large rail network sale planned to nearby Malaysia, and even an agreement to produce trains for the U.S. network under contract by General Electric, things were looking up for China's rail ambitions until late July 2011, when China suffered a major rail accident.

The accident occurred in the suburbs of China's manufacturing hub of Wenzhou in Zhejiang province, not far from Shanghai, when a train rear-ended a stopped train on the same line. In the aftermath, confusion reigned as the government, apparently worried about a loss of face, tried to get the line operating again as quickly as possible—even as people were still being pulled from the wreckage. The haste with which the government tried to dismantle the wreckage upset many, and was widely criticized, especially after a rescuer who seemed to disregard an official's orders to stop searching went in again nearly 21 hours after the crash and came out with a toddler still alive. In the accident, 40 people were killed, including the toddler's parents, and nearly 200 injured.

Far from finished developing its rail network or being deterred by the accident, in many ways China is just getting started. Under the 12th Five-Year Plan, China will double its spending on rail to 2.8 trillion *yuan* ($438 billion) from 2011 to 2015. If all goes according to plan, from 2010 to 2020, the total network will have increased from 91,000 kilometers (56,500 miles) to 120,000 kilometers (74,600 miles), a 30 percent increase.

Where will the greatest growth be? From 1978 onward the fastest intercity trains ran 50–160 kilometers per hour (31–99 miles per hour), and it was only in the late 1990s and early 2000s that some of China's trains hit 200 kilometers per hour (124 miles per hour). *New China normal* is all about the need for speed.

## MAGLEV TRAINS

Maglevs are the ultra-high-speed trains that literally float on the tracks, balanced on a rail of electro-magnets. Their name is derived from the method of magnetic levitation they employ. This technology is also being developed in Japan and the United States, but Germany helped China build the world's first Maglev train in commercial operation, from Shanghai's Pudong International Airport partway to the city, a short eight-minute journey. The Shanghai Maglev track, with a length of about 30 kilometers

(18.6 miles), cost $1.2 billion total or about $40 million per kilometer ($64.5 million per mile). Although it will probably never return its investment in ticket sales, the public relations value has been enormous, and many visitors to Shanghai get a thrill traveling at 432 kilometers per hour (268 miles per hour) at ground level.

Japan also plans to build a maglev train to replace parts of the aging *Shinkansen* (Bullet Train) fleet, with a single line from Tokyo through central Japan. It will take until 2025 to construct, and cost nearly $45 billion to build the 290-kilometer (180-mile) track, about $150 million per kilometer ($250 million per mile). This is possibly an indication of Japan's more stringent regulatory requirements, but the difference seems large enough that China's cost advantage seems to apply this kind of advanced technology, not just labor-intensive industries, as many believe.

Projects such as the Shanghai Maglev only tell part of the story of China's use of rail transportation. One must also consider China's adoption of municipal subway and light-rail lines, high-speed *Shinkansen*-style long-distance rail links, and advanced engineering to fully understand the magnitude of China's use of rail infrastructure and the belief that rail will lead China's economy forward. It is, in many ways, on a par with the importance of the U.S.'s development of the Interstate Highway System after World War II, except that China is developing one of those as well, at the same time.

SUBWAY AND LIGHT RAIL

China's use of subway and light rail has accelerated, with eight cities in mainland China currently using them and an additional eight scheduled to start using them in the next decade. In 2006, there were only 10 lines in use in the entire country, while there were already 37 lines in use in 2011. There are so many projects in progress throughout China that, according to planning documents, there will be as many as 86 lines in China by 2015. It is fair to say that Shanghai jumped on the subway far sooner and more enthusiastically than other Chinese cities.

Shanghai has expanded its system from three lines in 2004 to five lines in 2006, eight lines at the start of 2008, and 11 lines and 400 kilometers (249 miles) by the 2010 start of the World Expo hosted in the city. By 2020 it will have 18 lines, according to the transit plan. It took New York and London a century to reach the 400-kilometer (249-mile) mark, while Shanghai did it in only 20 years. From 2007 to 2008 alone, the total line distance increased from 145 to 234 kilometers (90 to 135 miles) and the daily passenger flow increased from 2.3 million to 3 million. Few subway networks in the world will boast as many lines, stations, or passengers as the future 2020 Shanghai network, but there is one: Beijing, which is working hard to solve the problem of an ever-expanding city overwhelmed by cars.

Beijing now has six ring roads circling the city, and traffic congestion on the roads is a daily problem, so it is hoped the subway can alleviate the vehicle gridlock. Beijing set its standard subway fare to anywhere on the network to 2 *yuan*, about 25 cents, as a way to further encourage use of the subway rather than cars.

Subway transportation is still a new choice to many Chinese people, who may be used to buses, cars or bicycles. Subway networks are great for increasing livability (and property values) of places nearby the stations, but may have fewer stops than buses—and fares can be more expensive. Consequently, many lines in other Chinese cities have trouble attracting the volumes of riders needed to reach the planned capacity. In China, many companies provide free buses for their workers, and stores, such as France's Carrefour, may have a fleet of buses that ply the roads looking for shoppers.

For other cities, it is affordability of the network itself that is becoming a barrier to success. Underground subway trains (rather than above-ground light rail or trams) seem to be preferred by city planners. With a cost of about 500 million *yuan* ($75 million) per kilometer (800 million *yuan* or $121 million per mile), in cities where the per capita income is low, the financial viability of a subway is sometimes put aside for the desire to have a modern state-of-the-art system: keeping up with Shanghai and Beijing, so to speak. Of course, local government borrowing from state-owned banks and issuing of bonds are both frequent solutions to funding shortfalls but that does not change the fact that many of these systems probably shouldn't be built when there are cheaper alternatives available.

HIGH-SPEED RAIL

Japan and Europe have historically led the world in high-speed rail links, but to paraphrase Elton John, *that train don't stop there anymore*. China has made high-speed rail a priority and, despite the major crash in 2011, is on the way to achieving the target of having the most expansive, modern network in the world by 2020. In 2011, China had actually planned to invest upward of 745.5 billion *yuan* ($118 billion), even after investing more than 700 billion *yuan* ($111 billion) in 2010. The crash and subsequent investigation (which unveiled a corruption scandal) acted to scale back investment, to about 470 billion *yuan* ($74.6 billion) for 2011. Even with a reduced projected budget of 400 billion *yuan* ($63.5 billion) in 2012, an additional 6,366 kilometers (3,956 miles) of lines will go into operation, according to the new Railway Minister Sheng Guangzu. This is the equivalent of building more than half of the entire European high-speed network in a single year.

While Japan and Europe have had high-speed rail for decades, it was just since the middle of the last decade that China embarked on its plan for modern high-speed rail. Before this time, the effort was focused on improving the speed of existing lines by, for example, switching from diesel to electric, to get China's first 200-kilometer-per-hour (124-mile-per-hour) trains into operation. Through a series of "Speed Up" campaigns since the 1990s, coordinated with the Five-Year Plans, China has been steadily advancing its adoption of high-speed rail at ever-higher speeds.

The first milestone was reached in 2010, when China had installed more than 8,300 kilometers (5,157 miles) of track to make China's the longest high-speed rail network in the world. At average speeds of 250 kilometers per hour (155 miles per hour) and the fastest lines running at 350 kilometers per hour (217 miles per hour), it is also one of the fastest.

One of the lines, in particular, is a model of China's ambitiousness. Put into service in 2011, the 21-station 1,318-kilometer (819-mile) line between Beijing and Shanghai is the longest continuous high-speed rail line in the world and cost 221 billion *yuan* ($33.4 billion) to build. It was built in just 38 months and even opened one year ahead of schedule in order to be ready for the 90th anniversary of the Chinese Communist Party. With a top operational speed of 380 kilometers per hour (236 miles per hour) and a typical operating speed of 350 kilometers per hour (217 miles per hour), that is about 30 kilometers per hour (18.6 miles per hour) faster than the operational speeds of Japan's fastest bullet trains or France's TGV trains, making it the world's fastest long-distance high-speed train. It cut the travel time from Beijing to Shanghai from about 11 hours to just over five, comparable to the time needed for a flight—if the airport waiting time is included. Airfares between Shanghai and Beijing even started to come down as a result of the new competition, so successful was the line.

The investment was financed by the Railway Ministry, local governments where the line passes through, and several Chinese investment funds, including more than $3 billion to compensate residents needing to be relocated along the route.

China has announced plans, by 2020, to have more than 15,000 kilometers (9,321 miles) of high-speed track among its total 120,000 kilometers (74,565 miles) of rail nationwide.

RAIL TRAVEL AT THE TOP OF THE WORLD

Long-distance rail meets advanced engineering in China's new Beijing-Tibet railway, known as the Beijing-Lhasa Express, which opened on July 1, 2006. The 4,000-kilometer (2,485-mile) line is a three-day journey, reaching the world's highest elevations by rail, as it crosses the permafrost on the roof of the world to reach Lhasa, the Tibetan capital. The train had to be specially designed to accommodate the changes in altitude, both for the passengers and the engines. Additional oxygen is supplied inside the cars using airplane-style oxygen tubes that dangle from the ceiling to keep passengers comfortable as they adjust to the altitude changes. At the highest altitudes on the final day of the trip to Tibet, custom-designed General Electric locomotive engines are added to the train to pull it up the final leg, the only engines in the world capable of doing so.

The ticket prices are comparatively high but still a bargain considering the distance, with a range of seating and berths relatively comfortable and appointed with small luxuries such as flatscreen TVs. But the scenery is so spectacular during the day that the TVs are typically only used at night. More recently, China built another rail project in China's western region between Chongqing and Wuhan with engineering that must be considered world class.

Neither snow nor ice nor mountains nor gorges nor even cost nor return on investment shall stop a train line from being built in China, it seems, with the completion of this new line in 2011 that would cut travel distance between western Chongqing and the up-and-coming central city of Wuhan from 22 hours to just five hours. It required 159 tunnels and 253 bridges and was completed by 50,000 workers. The cost per length of track was double that of the technically challenging and remote Qinghai-Tibet Railway, at 60 million *yuan* ($9.5 million) per kilometer (97 million *yuan* or $15.4 million per mile).

Cost is no object to China's rail ambitions, and perhaps shouldn't be in a nation that sees billions of riders each year. Whether it is the pace of change or the rate of travel on the rails, is there anything that can slow down China's seemingly endless need for speed?

CHINA'S GREAT RAIL LEAP FORWARD?

The July 2011 crash, mentioned earlier, was one of China's most serious rail accidents ever, and only the second high-speed rail accident to occur anywhere. This caused serious introspection in China on the social and financial costs of China's high-speed rail plans. On a more general level, people questioned China's too-rapid pace of development.

The investigation concluded that the accident was caused by design flaws at the system level that resulted in a confluence of human errors, including errors in emergency response, though neither of the drivers themselves nor the train's technology were blamed.

Following the accident, the Ministry of Railways' seemingly unending desire for higher speeds and more comprehensive networks was called into question by the public and even the media, which ignored gag orders. Repercussions were still being felt in 2012 as the central government examined construction standards and stopped work on lines that seemed financially questionable.

Soon after the accident, for example, several ongoing construction projects were delayed from several months to a year, including a major 840-kilometer (522-mile) section in the north-south route between Guangzhou in the south and Beijing in the north. A larger and longer-term investment, the 300 billion *yuan* ($47 billion) 2,066-kilometer (1,284-mile) line between the southwestern Yunnan's provincial capital of Kunming and Shanghai, was abruptly stopped with no indication of what effect this would have on the planned March 2015 opening.

While public transportation inconvenience is one outcome, the bigger worry in the short-term is that millions of workers will be unemployed while these lines are under review. An official from the China Railway Tunnel Group pegged the number of layoffs at 3 million, and said he feared that the work stoppage and halt in wages could lead to social unrest.[7]

Financially, things appeared to go from bad to worse as the ministry was hitting borrowing limits with the state-owned banks in 2011. It was rumored that the Ministry of Railways needed a bridge loan of more than 800 billion *yuan* ($126 billion) in November 2011 to refinance debt and supply new working capital. The ministry has issued more than 2 trillion *yuan* of debt ($312 billion) thus far, about 5 percent of China's annual GDP, and up two and a half times the 868 billion *yuan* ($138 billion) in 2008. Its debt and financial performance are backed by the central government directly as a state-owned enterprise, and indirectly through the state-owned banks, fueling fears of a non-performing financial money pit.

An analysis by the Shanghai Daily showed that, if run at 80 percent capacity, the Beijing-Shanghai line alone would suffer an operating loss of 7.5 billion *yuan* ($1.2 billion) a year. High energy costs were the single biggest expense, but debt repayment amounted to nearly 5.5 billion *yuan* ($873 million) a year, showing debt's choking effect on the potential rail returns.

Other controversies plagued the Shanghai–Beijing line's initial year, including the opulence of luxury reclining seats in the VIP section (which were later scrapped) and several high-profile cases of trains malfunctioning and stalling on the tracks for several hours, delaying the entire system.

Finally, corruption scandals have been uncovered up to the highest levels of the ministry. In February 2011, its former head, the Minister of Railways himself, Liu Zhijun, was arrested and accused of embezzlement of more than 800 million *yuan* ($127 million), receiving bribes and keeping up to 10 mistresses.

In 2011, after the Wenzhou accident, it seemed as if China's government and its people were finally considering the tradeoff between progress and safety, if not the question of financial performance. Some consumers, citing fears of accidents, stopped riding the high-speed lines. Airlines increased their fares, welcoming the returning passengers. Editorials in China and abroad questioned China's Great Rail Leap Forward as an unsafe, unnecessary and unsound investment.

However, it was not long before China was once again on track to higher speeds. The latest high-speed train was unveiled in December 2011. Designed to resemble an ancient Chinese sword, the train has more than double the power of the world's fastest train (the CRH380s operating on the Shanghai-Beijing line) and would theoretically top speeds over 500 kilometers per hour (311 miles per hour) in commercial operations, according to its maker, CSR Corp, China's largest train maker. It seems there is only one place in the world where swords are faster than bullets.

ROADS AND HIGHWAYS

China's road system is probably less developed and less utilized than those of major industrialized countries, but China has made progress there, too, and now has the second largest expressway network in the world at 53,000 kilometers (33,000 miles) with an estimated cost of $122 billion, a program it started just three decades ago. However, its highway network is 3.4 million kilometers (2.1 million miles), with approximately half of that at a very low level of quality and in need of upgrade, according to a Chinese government official. The same official also highlighted the need to add another 1 million kilometers (620,000 miles) of road by 2020.

If China's roads are to be used for logistics, they need to be improved, which is one reason China continues to make the investments. Another reason to be investing significantly in highways is development of the western regions of China, linking them through commerce to bring prosperity to China's poorest areas and, not coincidentally, reinforcing national unity in China's far-flung and predominantly ethnic regions, such as Xinjiang and Tibet.

The rush to build new expressways, highways, roads and bridges often means corners are cut, as with the Xinsan motorway in Yunnan, opened in July 2011—like the Beijing—Shanghai high-speed railway—in time for the 90th anniversary of the Chinese Communist Party on July 1, 2011. Perhaps it was too soon, as part of the road collapsed in a rainstorm, killing two, resulting in the closure of the road just a few days after it opened, causing it to be dubbed by Chinese netizens as the shortest-lived motorway in history.[8]

~

China's *urbanization supertrend* is primarily concerned with the creation of *new cities* to host the tens of millions more people that will be urbanized within the remainder of the Olympic Decade. The process of urbanization, however, is slow. The United Nations estimates that, by 2050, China will only be about 75 percent urbanized. China, undoubtedly, would like to have that happen faster. To that end, it is investing incredible amounts of money on infrastructure—including airports, roads, and rail—in order to get people to the cities, transport them within the cities and improve China's capability to grow as a domestic-consumption-led economy.

Doing all of this sustainably, in the sense of having enough energy, water, food and other resources, as well as preventing pollution and environmental degradation, is China's next challenge, and the main topic of China's *sustainability supertrend.*

## SUMMARY: THE URBANIZATION SUPERTREND

The themes of the urbanization supertrend are new cities and infrastructure development:

*New cities:* China is building dozens of new cities to be home to more than a million people each, and expanding many older cities, such as Chongqing and Shenzhen, so that they can become megacities with tens of millions of residents.

*Relocation:* As part of the urbanization process, rural residents are sometimes relocated into cities, and urban residents are sometimes relocated from the middle of the cities to the outskirts of the cities. This process is sometimes fair, sometimes not.

*New buildings:* To support its urbanization drive, China is creating many large-scale buildings—including skyscrapers, giant shopping malls and airports—often the world's largest.

*Transportation infrastructure:* China is building new infrastructure to transport people to and from the cities. The preferred type of infrastructure is rail, including subways, high-speed and even maglev technology.

The *urbanization supertrend* will potentially last until 2050, so it is the longest of the *supertrends,* going beyond the Olympic Decade.

**Chapter 7**

# THE SUSTAINABILITY SUPERTREND

## 节能减排
### *JIENENG JIANPAI*
### SAVING ENERGY AND REDUCING WASTE

Before China's recent decades of post-reform modernization, the nation's impact on the environment was limited by the incomplete modernization occurring during the Mao years in addition to the burning of biomass, methane emissions from animal farming and rice paddies, and some use of coal and fossil fuel for heating. That is not to say China's impact on the environment was small—its large population ensured a major impact on resources—but its *per capita* use of energy and output of waste had been low. Further back, China largely skipped over the Industrial Revolution of the 1800s, due to the isolationist policies of the Qing Dynasty. Other than pockets of factory production located in colonial-era Hong Kong and mainland treaty ports such as Shanghai, China avoided developing a large fossil fuel carbon footprint. This was true, at least, until the 1912 revolution that overthrew China's last dynasty.

Thereafter, industrialization occurred under the reformist policies of Chiang Kai-shek's Nationalist Party, the Japanese occupiers pre-World War II, and finally Mao Zedong following the formation of the People's Republic in 1949. China's consistent and large-scale industrialization under Mao caused China's environmental footprint to grow, yet it has not—to this day—reached the level of energy usage or pollution per capita that Western countries have today. But its pollution output is increasingly steadily, along with its pace of industrialization and urbanization.

China and other developing countries make a case that they are due their hard-earned success, and their growth should not be shackled. On the other hand, allowing growth to proceed unabated could create something of a conundrum. For example, China is the world's largest market for cars, yet if China had the same number of cars per person as the United States does, China's cities would be gridlocked. By the same token, in absolute terms, China is already the world's largest emitter of carbon dioxide—the most common greenhouse gas—but if it reached the same per person emissions of the United States, its current carbon footprint would more than *quadruple*, possibly causing a devastating increase in the rate of global warming.

The environment-development trade-off is especially acute during China's Olympic Decade. The nation needs massive amounts of electricity to fuel its factories and new cities, yet its own energy resources are limited. It has huge reserves of coal and, consequently, legions of coal-powered generators, which supply more than 70 percent of China's electricity needs (versus about 50 percent in the United States).

Unfortunately for China's air quality and global warming, the pollution from this form of energy is arguably the worst, combining carcinogens released in the atmosphere (many generators are said to turn off scrubbers when regulators are not looking, to increase profits) with massive amounts of carbon dioxide, which contribute to global climate change. China also uses oil and natural gas for a large part of its remaining needs, with hydroelectric power a very distant third.[1]

One of China's challenges today, which it shares with the United States, is an inability to provide enough of its own energy to be self-sufficient. Even coal, for which China has abundant reserves, is partly imported from Australia. Since 2011, China is the world's largest importer, producer and consumer of coal, simultaneously. In fact, importing from overseas is actually cheaper than shipping it by truck and train from north and northeastern China—where the coal is found—to where it is needed—the southeast and eastern coastal regions. This also says something about the imperative for upgrading China's road and rail transportation infrastructure, mentioned in the *urbanization supertrend*. The quality of China's coal is not ideal. Furthermore the efficiency of coal extraction—often coming from illegal mines that see frequent cave-ins—is low. Finally, China's aging thermal generators and the inefficiency of the long-distance power transmission grid means that China's coal-powered infrastructure is insufficient for China's future growth. China makes up for the difference by importing higher quality coal from Australia.

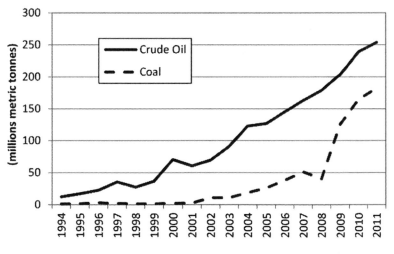

*Figure 14: China's oil and coal imports, 1994–2011*

A second energy shortage China shares with the United States is of oil. China is a net importer of oil, and is growing its demand faster than any other major economy. This was not always the case. Until the early 1990s, China was a net *exporter* of oil and, in fact, had used oil exports in the post-1978 reforms to generate essential foreign currency. China was in this position thanks to the discovery in 1959 of a major oilfield, named *Daqing*. Its name, which means Great Celebration, stands for the joy it gave the nation to finally be able to power forward its development without relying on the Soviet Union for oil. The joy did not last for long. By 1993 China had started to import oil to cover the increasing demand. Today China is actually the world's fourth largest oil producer, but that covers less than 50 percent of China's total demand. The rest it imports, and more every year. In 2010, China's oil imports covered about 56 percent of its requirement, up from 51 at the start of the Olympic Decade in 2008.

One bright spot for China's energy resources is the relatively new type of natural gas extraction known as horizontal drilling. So-called shale gas is found in abundance in certain geologic formations and early—though unproven—surveys seem to indicate China has vast amounts of the gas trapped in rock. Projections indicate China's estimated recoverable gas reserves—25 trillion cubic meters—could be double those of the United States' estimated 13.8 trillion cubic meters of recoverable reserves. This would be more than enough to make China self-sufficient in natural gas and, if it wanted to, offset a large amount of coal-based energy generation. In fact, China's natural abundance of shale gas could be even larger, since the vast areas of Tibet and Qinghai were not included in the survey.

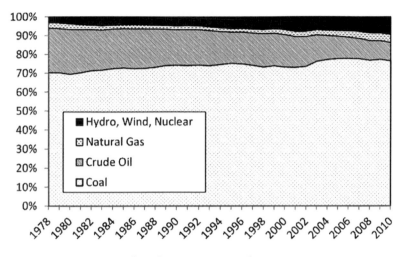

*Figure 15: China's energy usage by type, 1978–2010*

When it comes to energy, China would like nothing more than to increase its reserves of any type of natural resource other than coal. With onshore resources landlocked and far from the coast, the search for offshore oil and natural gas drives many of China's geopolitical activities in the South and East China seas. There, islands and territorial waters are in dispute with the Philippines, Vietnam, South Korea and Japan. The South China Sea—including Taiwan and the narrow Taiwan Strait—is especially crucial to securing sea routes for Middle Eastern and African oil and Australian minerals, a topic to be further examined in *China's Political Supertrends*. Of course, with the exception of Taiwan, it is not so much the islands themselves as the extension of sea borders and the possibility of striking new oil and gas fields under the ocean floor that draws the nations' attention. As long as those areas are in dispute, no large-scale extraction will be possible.

What about hydroelectric or nuclear power? These two comprise most of the balance of China's electricity needs after coal. China is home to two of the world's longest rivers, the Yellow and Yangtze, and has built dozens of large hydroelectric dams, most notably, the world's largest, the Three Gorges Dam project that has so far resulted in the relocation of more than a million people and may eventually force 6 million in total to urbanize because of unplanned effects from erosion around the edges of the reservoir. China is *damming* its rivers in increasing numbers, thereby possibly *damning* them to problems such as silting, flow reduction and loss of natural flora and fauna—including China's fabled *Baiji*, the freshwater white dolphin.[2] But it needs the power for newly developing areas, such as Sichuan's Chengdu and the massive city-state of Chongqing. Therefore China is, in effect, *dammed* if it does, and *damned* if it doesn't. Nuclear power is a viable, less-polluting alternative for China. But, with so much coal available, China is unlikely to make large investments in nuclear power generation in the short term.[3]

As a result of China's poor quality and quantity of many natural resources, China's energy policy must pay special attention to securing overseas coal, oil and natural gas. Lacking viable alternatives to finding new reserves within its own borders (natural gas fracking shows some promise but remains largely unexplored in 2012), China is now encouraging the use of clean energy, such as solar and wind. Unfortunately, despite the fact that China will become the largest producer and user in the world of both solar and wind energy within the Olympic Decade, neither type can be installed fast enough to keep up with China's energy growth. Like GDP, China's energy needs grow 5–10 percent a year or more. To make up for the shortfall, China is building more coal and nuclear generation capacity. In order to mitigate those huge investment costs, China is going the only other route it has left: saving energy and reducing waste. This policy is part of China's Five-Year Plan, and is known by the catchphrase *jieneng* (save energy) *jianpai* (reduce waste), which are also the two themes of the *sustainability supertrend.*

## CHALLENGES OF SUSTAINABILITY

More than any other country today, China faces environmental and sustainability challenges in almost every conceivable way, including air pollution harming people's health and creating acid rain; land contamination, over-farming and desertification; and water pollution in the rivers, lakes and seas.

### FENG SHUI: WIND AND WATER

The ancient art of geomancy, better known inside and outside of China as *feng shui,* is making a comeback in mainland China. Once banned and persecuted as one of the "four olds" under Mao, *feng shui* survived in Hong Kong, Taiwan, and overseas Chinese populations. In today's modern China, it is beginning to thrive, with the newly affluent Chinese homeowners buying properties and laying out rooms that suit their personal readings. Businesspeople and restaurants put water elements—usually a tank of fish—in their lobbies, to absorb *qi*—the Chinese concept of an ethereal energy that permeates the natural world, part of *feng shui,* *qigong* meditation and *tai chi* exercise—as it flows in through the door. In 2012, the so-called Dragon Fish—the Arowana—was the most prized: a single grown specimen with the desirable golden or red glows fetched thousands of dollars. It is unlikely that anyone would be willing to part with one in a Dragon Year, which the Arowana is symbolic of: selling one's own Dragon Fish in the Year of the Dragon could bring ill fortune.

*Feng shui* literally means wind and water, two of the elements of geomancy. In the context of the *sustainability supertrend,* they highlight China's two most pressing challenges: air and water pollution.

### Air Pollution

China, known for poor air quality, is home to 14 of the world's 20 most-polluted cities, according to the World Bank in

2007. A lot of people who move to China for work end up leaving, sometimes with pollution being the main reason for their departure, especially if their children suffer from a sudden onset of asthma. Some residents in Beijing were understandably skeptical that the city could be awarded the Olympics, based on its poor environmental record.

When it was campaigning for its original Olympics bid back in the 1990s, the city appeared so clean when the Olympic Committee was visiting that people joked that residents and companies must have shut down all the coal burners. In fact, they had: whenever there is a major event held in China—such as when it hosted the APEC meeting in 2001, the Olympics in 2008 and the Shanghai World Expo in 2010—temporary traffic and manufacturing controls are implemented to cut down pollution.

The air pollution problem in the 1980s and earlier was often due to small coal-powered burners, which residents used to cook their food and used for heating in colder northern cities such as Beijing. Today, the pollution is more likely due to the number of vehicles on the road and factories causing smog. Beijing was especially bad so, in order to reduce pollution to levels sufficient to host the Olympics, huge sums of money were thrown at the problem.

Between 1998 and 2002, the Beijing government spent about $6 billion to clean the air and reduce sulfur emissions by controlling auto registrations, improving the coal burners and relocating factories. In 2002, as a result of these changes, the particle mass decreased to about 167 mg / cubic meter, only about 1.7 times that of the comparatively pollution-conscious Japan. After Beijing was awarded the Olympics in 2001, it redoubled efforts, spending $19 billion to clean up pollution before the 2008 Games

For 2008, the Beijing city government had set two especially strict targets for the year to ensure a clean Olympics. First, in terms of reducing carbon dioxide that is produced through energy generation, the energy consumption per unit of GDP would need to fall by 5 percent, which was 1 percentage point higher than the national target of 4 percent a year set under the

11th Five-Year Plan.[4] Second, in a measure that would indicate the combined effects of traffic smog and factory pollutants, Beijing mandated there should be an increase in "blue sky days"—days where the air quality is fairly good—to a target of 256 days, 10 days more than in the previous year, 2007.[5]

In order to ensure the city would meet those two targets (as well as to reduce traffic congestion during the Olympics), the city government initiated the plan to only allow cars with odd- or even-numbered license plates on the road on alternating days.[6] Some affluent residents simply bought a second car so they would have one even-numbered plate and one odd-numbered.

This policy was later modified to become Beijing's permanent traffic control policy, though no longer as strict—20 percent of cars are now to be kept off the roads each weekday, depending on the last digit of the license plate number. It was reported in Chinese media that affluent Beijing residents bought up to five cars and five plates with different numbers to make sure they could whenever they wanted. This loophole was more-or-less closed with the institution of the license plate lottery in 2011, which made it difficult to get multiple plates.

Nationwide, China's total pollution is harder to pin down. Even its global pollution ranking was difficult to ascertain because of lack of good data. A number of estimates, including a 2008 ranking from the Netherlands Environmental Assessment Agency, and rankings from the U.S. Department of Energy's Energy Information Administration, the U.N., energy company BP and a growing number of bodies all rank China as the world's largest carbon dioxide emitter. China's own official statistics still rank it as the second largest producer of carbon dioxide in the world, after the United States, producing about 13 percent versus the U.S.'s 23 percent of the world total. But there is no question that China's pollution *growth* is the fastest in the world. Each year, the equivalent of a medium-sized U.S. state's total power generation comes online in China—usually from coal-powered generators.

The 12th Five-Year Plan from 2011 onward will be even stricter in terms of controlling air pollution. China is using measures that are common around the world as a way to benchmark its current situation and progress.

A common way to measure air pollution is to examine how much particulate matter (PM) is in an air sample. Typical particulate matter, such as dust and sea salt, are found everywhere. Human-made particulates may come from engine exhaust (especially from diesel engines), factories and burning of waste. The PM scale is used to refer to size of particulates. Larger particles are generally less dangerous, since they can be filtered out from the human respiratory system by the mucous membranes and cilia, while smaller particles (PM10) may penetrate into the lungs, and the smallest particles (PM 2.5 or less) can enter the blood and harm the body's other organs.

In 2011 and 2012, China measured and reported PM10 levels. However, also during this time, the PM2.5 standard for pollution became more common after the Chinese public began to notice how China was still using the PM10 standard while other countries used PM2.5.

The shift to greater public awareness of PM2.5 was partly brought about by the United States Embassy in Beijing reporting its independently monitored pollution statistics, which at times contradicted the official Chinese meteorological agency figures. The postings to the embassy's air quality Twitter feed once jokingly rated the air as "crazy bad" because it was off-the-scale. This comment did not help the Chinese public's perception of its own government's standards, nor did it help diplomatic relations between China and the United States.

Not to mention that merely looking out the window and seeing haze and smog which, on some days, blanketed the city like fog, was enough to tell most people that the air quality in Beijing was much worse than was commonly acknowledged. Fog, in fact, was a euphemism and was intentionally used by the local meteorological agency until public outcries forced an end to the misnaming.

*Water Pollution*

The quality of China's drinking water is poor in many regions for two reasons. First, pollution is a persistent problem in virtually every lake and river because of uncontrolled dumping of factory effluent. Second, even water that has ostensibly gone through treatment and purification may still not match the quality of developed countries' drinking water because of China's obsolete treatment equipment and old pipes.

If it is not pollution, then the problem in many parts of the country is hard water—deposits of calcium and minerals—on pots after just a few uses. The strong smell of chlorine from old purification systems forces many residents to choose bottled water.

*Lake Pollution*

Lake Tai (*Taihu* in Mandarin) was formerly one of China's most picturesque bodies of water, being written about in centuries-old poetry and still a popular tourist destination, until 2007 when Blue-Green Algae blooms made the lake unnavigable, undrinkable, and unappealing as a travel destination, much less a subject of poetry.

The blame was placed on a combination of warm weather and too many nutrients in the water, but the root cause was lack of control over the factories that dumped effluents into nearby areas. These seeped into the water tables or even directly into the lake itself. The disaster required millions of dollars to clean. Afterward, questions were finally being asked: how did this amount of pollution get into the water? Why were there no controls?

Examples of outright dumping of toxic chemicals and the prosecution for such are rare in China; most cases of extreme pollution are labeled as accidents. This includes the Songhua River benzene spill in northern China in 2005, and the more recent 2012 spill of toxic cadmium in the Longjiang River, which affected the water supply for more than a million people in southern China. It is still quite common to have factory water (used in cleaning, cooling, or other industrial uses) simply dumped untreated.

Avoiding treatment costs and lack of government enforcement of regulations are the primary reasons significant amounts of water pollution occur throughout China today. With manufacturing and other industrial competition in China being intense due to endemic over-capacity, any cost reduction counts. Often a company that evolved under state ownership lacks government oversight since it is, in effect, an arm of the government and therefore beyond reproach. Entrepreneurs who grew up during the 1970s or early 1980s may simply see pollution control as a hassle cutting into their profit margins. The attitude in China among older generations that grew up in a shortage economy—that you take what you can while you can and do what you can get away with—still prevails in less developed areas of China.

From the government's perspective, officials were rewarded for development, not clean environment. In 2007, when *environmental* GDP growth became one of their key performance indicators, this started to change. Before then, even polluting industries were welcomed. In retrospect, the areas that accepted such factories for the sake of investment are now paying a very high price. Many foreign factories sought to escape financial legislation and costs in their home markets by moving to China in the 1980s and 1990s. In effect, they were exporting their pollution to China, an issue that China regularly points out, such as during climate negotiations in Copenhagen in 2009 and Durban in 2011.

China actually has very strict regulations and laws on the books, but the problem is enforcement. The sheer number of factories and the vastness of China make it doubly hard to catch violators. The former State Environmental Protection Administration (SEPA) was able to catch significant numbers of polluters but, as a federal agency, had little power to enforce directives at the provincial and local levels. The fines that it could impose were often so small that it was cheaper for factories to pay the fines and keep on polluting rather than clean up their acts.

The situation changed in 2007, when both the national government and SEPA acted in conjunction with the major banks to create a polluting-firm blacklist. Firms on the list were not supposed to receive additional financing and had their applications for public listings suspended.[7] SEPA was later turned into the Ministry of Environmental Protection and granted stronger powers. There was also increased cooperation between state and local government to shutter polluting factories in Heilongjiang and Shanxi provinces and Inner Mongolia. In one city, Wuxi, suffering from the effects of the Lake Tai algae bloom, this resulted in 1,340 factories being closed immediately or in the short-term.[8]

*Case Study: Suzhou Creek Cleanup*

Suzhou Creek, meandering for a little more than 53 kilometers (33 miles) through north-central Shanghai, has a total length of about 125 kilometers (78 miles). It is a tributary of the Huang-pu River, eventually feeding into the Yangtze River, China's longest. From the 1920s onward, Suzhou Creek was one of the most polluted rivers in China for four reasons. First, because of uncontrolled dumping of industrial waste during Shanghai's development as a business and industrial city; second, untreated domestic sewage; third, effluents from shipping; and, finally, poor flow, which allowed silting and pollutants to build up. By the 1990s, the smell (horrid, by all accounts) and color (black) was too much for residents to bear. It was a blight on the city's image as well. So, starting in 1998, a program was implemented to clean it up.

Up to 2009, more than $1.4 billion was spent. The cleanup combined building of new water treatment facilities for waste; redevelopment of roads and buildings along the river's edge; and, in the last phase, dredging of up to three meters (9.8 feet) of sludge from the bottom for much of its length to allow the reintroduction of fish. In 2012, some of the hottest property in Shanghai was along this creek, including converted-warehouse offices and artistic spaces, residential units with river views and scenic walkways. That such a project can be undertaken success-fully in a decade at a fairly enormous cost is another sign of China's close coordination between government agencies, business and the public.

## Water Shortages

China, despite its large geographic size (it is the third largest county after Russia and Canada, but is larger than Canada in terms of usable land area) has a shortage of water in absolute terms, and an even greater relative shortage of water once its population is factored in. More than 400 cities in China have a more-or-less constant water shortage, and two-thirds of China's cities lack sufficient water to support growth, according to the Chinese government. This means, for example, that over 300 million rural residents lack access to safe drinking water.

Although China has about 21 percent of the world's popula-tion, it has only 9 percent of the world's arable land and 6 percent of the fresh water supply. In volumetric terms, the water supply in China is approximately 2.8 trillion cubic meters, or about 2,300 cubic meters (81,200 cubic feet) per person (81,200 cubic feet), which is about 28 percent of the world per capita average.[9]

What's more, the water is unevenly distributed, with the southern parts of China receiving a disproportionate amount while in the north per capita availability is only 500 cubic meters (17,700 cubic feet) per person, just 5 percent of the global average. The north is much larger geographically, but it is an arid climate that receives much less rainfall. Some bridges, such as the famed Marco Polo Bridge over the Yongding River, are no longer strictly necessary as the water flow is minimal, if not completely absent, all year round.[10]

The Yellow River, northern China's main source of fresh wa-ter, is China's second longest river, but its average flow rate per year is only 58 billion cubic meters—one-sixth that of the longest and more central Yangtze River and only 2 percent of the total river flow in China. Its namesake comes from the fact that it picks up the largest amount of sediment in the world, 35 kg per cubic meter (2.2 pounds per cubic foot), from the Yellow Earth Plateau. It is a river that is historically noted for flooding and is known as the country's Mother River but also as China's Sorrow. Aside from the fact that high sedimentation makes it much harder to utilize the water for drinking or factory production, the sediment continually settles and raises the riverbed. In some places the river is higher than the surrounding cities, and is supported by dikes and levees, which in the past have flooded more than 1,500 times and, the opposite problem, stopped flowing altogether at least 20 times between 1972 and 2012.[11] With such an imbalance between north and south, China is trying desperately to reduce the north-south water differential though hydro-engineering.

China's dire water situation is the reason water projects are among some of China's largest public infrastructure investments. An ambitious south to north water redirection plan will redirect more than 44 billion cubic meters (1.5 trillion cubic feet) of water per year from south to north by 2050, using a system of pipes and aqueducts, at a cost of more than $62 billion. This is just one of China's major water investments that will occur throughout the final years of the Olympic Decade and then beyond. In 2012, China pledged to invest 4 trillion *yuan* ($636 billion) in water-related projects before 2020. This underlines both the enormous challenge China faces and the huge opportunity for foreign companies such as GE Water, Veolia and smaller water companies providing everything from consulting to filters and water treatment to desalination.

### Desertification

While China's increase in desertification is hard to quantify due to a lack of reliable data, the first official government estimate in 2005 pegged China's desert area at about 1.6 million square kilometers (about 610,000 square miles), roughly the size of Alaska or five times as big as Italy. With the water shortage being dire in that area, droughts are common and topsoil simply blows away. Particulate matter travels thousands of kilometers, and nearby cities including Beijing have sandstorms several times a year that coat everything outdoors in a thick layer of dust. Eyeglasses or goggles are needed to keep out the grit.

China's main defense against desertification is a kind of man-made *Green Wall of China*. These reforestation efforts along the northern parts of China attempt to stop the southward desertification trend. As the Great Wall of China is one of the greatest engineering achievements in the world, the *Green Wall* will likely become one of the greatest ecological projects, if successful.

NOT-IN-MY-BACKYARD POLLUTION

The year 2011 was significant for environmental and health consciousness in China because it saw one of the first social-media-enabled and successful NIMBY protests against pollution.

Previously, NIMBY protests had rarely been reported in state-media and were successful only in cases such as high-tension, ultra-high voltage electric towers that had not yet been constructed or were easy to remove. A single prior NIMBY pollution case in 2007, against a chemical factory in Xiamen, was successful in having the factory relocated. With few precedents, and a general policy of not reporting environmental protests or public protests in general, it was unlikely that a resident-driven movement against a major chemical factory could be reported on, much less succeed. So it must have surprised more than just the residents of Dalian when their protest against a newly built chemical factory worth more than $1.5 billion appeared to be successful.

Dalian, a northern city on China's east coast, and the closest port to mainland Japan, is home to many manufacturers and trading companies. In 2011, a large chemical factory owned by Fujia Chemical along the coast near Dalian came under increased scrutiny after Japan's Fukushima nuclear facility was overwhelmed by the earthquake and *tsunami*. A non-critical dike breach during a large tropical storm in August 2011 made people nearby uneasy enough to begin worrying whether the plant's carcinogenic paraxylene could spill, endangering their health. Facing large-scale protests of tens of thousands of people armed with their mobile phones and blogs, the government eventually agreed to support a relocation of the plant. The protest was covered in China's mainstream media, helped by the social media platforms. It was a rare victory, though residents noticed the plant still operating at the end of 2011. The government responded that relocating such a large operation could not be done in the short-term, but the plant would be moved. For the moment, the expectation of the residents is still for the plant to be relocated in 2012; otherwise it is likely protests will begin anew.

A similar incident occurred in December 2011 in Haimen, Guangdong province, a southern coastal town near the village of Wukan. The residents of Haimen might have been inspired to protest by the success of Dalian's action, or they might have noted that Wukan Village became a media sensation, initially with Western media then eventually Chinese media as well, after enraged Wukan citizens temporarily kicked out their local government and police force over land disputes and the imprisonment of village representatives. Perhaps due to Haimen's proximity to Wukan, the story in Haimen was also picked up by Hong Kong journalists and international media, but the result was somewhat different for the protesters.

The citizens of Haimen were engaged in a NIMBY protest against an expansion of an unpopular coal-fired power plant. Previously, the plant had been known to be polluting, and was blamed by citizens for myriad health problems. Unlike in the case of Dalian, the government in Haimen took a harder line, using tear gas and other action against protesters. While the protests never reached the point of Wukan's outright rebellion, Haimen's protesters and the media attention did finally result in a temporary suspension of the project.

These would be exceptionally successful NIMBY protests by most Chinese standards, since tens of thousands of so-called mass incidents occur each year, and only a handful are known or reported on outside of the affected areas, much less can be said to be successful at achieving their objectives. This is changing as *weibo,* China's most popular Twitter clone, and other social media channels become more popular as forums for airing concerns.

~

China's air and water problems seem daunting, and China's *sustainability supertrend* is threatened by the overreliance on fossil fuels, especially coal, appearing to spell a future with even more pollution. However, China's environmental crises also hold its environmental opportunities, starting with the new cities that are being built from the ground up with sustainability in mind, and finishing with ways to save energy and reduce waste in existing cities.

## CHINA'S SUSTAINABILITY OPPORTUNITIES

China's sustainability opportunities are so large and important that they have become possibly the defining theme of the 12th Five-Year Plan. China's government recognizes both the social need for sustainable development as well as the business opportunity to develop one or more strategic emerging industries with China at the forefront. China is, perhaps unfairly, subsidizing a number of such industries. It promotes technology transfer and foreign investment in key areas, while protecting its domestic energy markets from competition. Like it does with so many other sectors, China is using its large domestic market to develop homegrown national champions. Within the period of the Olympic Decade, China will become a world leader in solar and wind power and electric vehicles, motivated by China's need to solve its energy problems and reduce pollution. These are just a few of the stories of China's *sustainability supertrend,* starting with where it overlaps the *urbanization supertrend.*

Eco-Cities

China is embarking on an ambitious program of green urban development, basically because it must. With hundreds of millions to be moved into cities during the remaining process of urbanization, building sustainable communities is the only way to avoid exacerbating China's already significant problems, such as water shortages and fossil fuel dependence. A second reason it is going green is because it can. Much of China is still underdeveloped, so when the government starts a new city, expands an existing city or decides to completely redevelop an area, there are few private interests strong enough to resist the Five-Year Plan's imperative of going to a sustainable model. Finally, eco-cities may be a platform from which China develops competitive clean technology industries, such as the production of efficient building materials, electric vehicles and solar water heaters. China is using its *roadmap* to guide the development of these and other industries.

In late 2007, the State Council, China's cabinet, designated six experimental zones for pilot projects on energy savings, environmental technology and sustainable social development. These zones included Shanghai's Pudong New District and Changsha, capital of Hunan province.

China is also launching international collaborations. Singapore and China are cooperating to create the Sino-Singapore Tianjin Eco-city. Other countries, such as the United Kingdom (which invested almost $100 million of public funds from the British Environmental Transformation Fund) are buying into China's vision and hope to go along for the ecological ride.

In Shanghai, a local government redevelopment initiative will create a 6-square-kilometer (2.3-square-mile) central business district in the city's Putuo Area that will use green urban planning and ecological construction.

Dongtan is perhaps one of the most ambitious environmental projects. Established on Chongming Island in the Yangtze River Delta near Shanghai in 2005, Dongtan Eco-City was to be a model to test sustainable development, custom-built from the ground up for half a million people. By 2020 Dongtan is to be about a third as large as Manhattan and be home to 500,000 people. The initial development is being coordinated by international engineering firm Arup, and the first phase was to be ready by the 2010 World Expo held in Shanghai.

Among its many laudable green credentials, there were to be no gas-powered vehicles, only electric- or hydrogen-powered ones, and the city would attempt to be a zero waste city by practicing full ecological stewardship of products made and sold there.

In reality, Dongtan may be just another pipedream. In 2012, most construction remained halted since the time of the global financial crisis. It remains a relatively pristine ecological zone, and the plan may yet be revived. More than anything, the apparent failure of the Dongtan Eco-City speaks to the difficulty of establishing such a city anywhere, much less in the most polluting country on Earth.

Dongtan Eco-City was originally part of the overall development of Chongming Island, which sits in the mouth of the Yangtze River. For the purposes of development and urbanization, the island was planned to be connected to the mainland's Pudong New Area of Shanghai by bridge and tunnel. That part of the island's development, at least, has gone ahead and was opened in 2009. A second bridge, connecting the opposite side of the island to the far bank of the Yangtze was opened at the end of 2011, making it possible to traverse the entire Yangtze River at its estuary.

In addition to the bridge and tunnel complex already constructed, a subway line will also connect it with Shanghai and the booming Jiangsu province to the north. At first glance, this appears to be taking the future site of China's hallmark eco-city—not to mention an environmental wetland for birds—and then ramming a bridge, tunnel and highway over, under and through it. Such construction does not make much environmental sense, but from a regional development point of view it is important to ensure the eco-city develops into the integrated and sustainable economy it is meant to be. It could not do that without links to the mainland.

It could be said that this kind of development will be just a blip in negating the massive environmental footprint that China's other new cities are creating, but the fact that it is being attempted will give China a distinct advantage and moral high-ground on the world stage when it comes to reducing pollution.

While China's early experiments at creating sustainable cities from scratch are not progressing as well as was hoped in the glow of the Beijing Olympics and Shanghai 2010 World Expo, China is proceeding to construct low-carbon-footprint architecture and using materials that allow some of its new buildings to achieve the highest LEED standards. It is also developing other Dongtan-like eco-city projects in other parts of China as test cases. If the model is successful in the early phases, China plans to develop more cities as big as or bigger than Dongtan was meant to be. In such an environment, eco-conscious planners, engineers, architects, and designers will be in strong demand, as will clean technology products and services such cities require, including clean energy production, waste reduction and environmental materials.

EFFICIENT CONSTRUCTION

China's market for green buildings and construction materials is growing rapidly because of mandates for China to cut its overall usage of electricity per unit of GDP by 20 percent under the 11th Five-Year Plan and by 16 percent under the 12th FYP. The *jieneng jianpai* themes require decreasing water waste, among other changes. The sum of all these policies was to mandate that all new buildings from 2008 were at least 50 percent more energy efficient. Shanghai went a step further to promote the goal of using 65 percent less energy.

One of the biggest opportunities in this area is construction materials, not necessarily even green construction materials, just *better* materials. China is in love with using concrete. China is in fact the world's largest user of concrete since the construction boom in the middle of the past decade.

This means that almost all urban construction in China is concrete: high-rises, low-rises, even houses—all are built using that material. Concrete is long-lasting and strong, yet has poor insulation qualities. Its production and transportation also come with a large carbon footprint.

The opportunity here is to use more efficient construction methods that take advantage of concrete's favorable properties (durability, strength, and thermal mass—the ability to retain heat or cold), create better admixtures which provide green benefits, and reuse and recycle old buildings rather than knocking them down, as is current practice. Wood is not widely used except in specialty buildings, such as luxury eco-resorts and housing developments.

The interiors of buildings can also be improved significantly, and China is taking steps in this direction, but the going is slow due to the existing stock of buildings.

Generally speaking, office buildings are marginally better at energy efficiency because they usually have a single owner. This landlord has an incentive to invest in the efficiency of the building, to lower overall operating costs, such as heating and cooling. While these buildings may have central air conditioning and heating, they still lack insulation. Glass curtain walls on the outside of office buildings are built from cheap materials that are prone to shatter in the heat, much as they did in Shanghai office buildings—to the public's alarm—several times in 2010 and 2011.

Owner-occupied residential buildings, on the other hand, may suffer from the same collective apathy that China's environment in general suffers from. For example, in much of Shanghai and more generally in all areas south of the Huaihe River–Qingling

Mountains boundary (a somewhat arbitrary north–south geographic divide), insulation and central heating in buildings is practically nonexistent. This is a remnant of the 1950s era government policy to use central heating in northern areas as a cost-saving measure for the then-government-provided social welfare benefit of heating. Buildings in the warmer south, it was thought, did not need central heat. The legacy of this policy, however, is tens of thousands of energy-inefficient buildings in China's south.

When a residential property is sold to a home buyer, it typically does not include any kind of interior finishing—possibly only windows and a front door. Essentially, a buyer takes possession of a concrete box and then finishes the rest with the help of a general contractor. Furthermore, residential buildings south of the Yangtze often lack central air conditioning or heating systems. Even in newer residential buildings, it still may be left out, allowing residents to make their own decisions on air conditioning and heating. When this happens, usually wall-mounted units are placed in every major room and large holes are drilled through the wall to the outside for the air conditioner's uninsulated pipe to the heat-exchanger. Certain places, such as the kitchen or bathroom, are often not climate-controlled at all: cooking dinner can be like working in a sauna, while taking a shower in the winter definitely wakes you up as soon as you stand on the cold tile floors.

Chinese office and residential buildings have, as business case studies like to say, a lot of low-hanging fruit. The companies that provide green lighting, insulated doors and windows, energy-efficient appliances, simple home automation and energy monitoring systems, weatherization and such, will find many opportunities in China's Olympic Decade, as will architects and interior designers who can work under China's sometimes-arcane building codes.

ALTERNATIVE ENERGY GENERATION

In addition to including the shorter-term strategies of saving energy and reducing waste, the 12th Five-Year Plan is proposing longer-term solutions to replace coal and oil as the primary forms of energy in China. If hydroelectric is included, China's clean energy already amounts to more than 8 percent of its total energy needs, but this is far from sufficient when China's economic growth and new energy needs are considered. China wants to take steps to ensure the proportion of non-fossil fuel energy is increased to 11.4 percent at the end of the 12th FYP in 2015.

There is a push for alternatives to coal and oil for energy generation for three reasons.

First, China wants to reduce its dependence on foreign supplies of coal and oil. While China does have the world's third-largest coal reserves, its oil reserves are not large enough to supply its fuel and industrial uses. A cutoff of oil would grind China's economy to a halt as it has little natural reserves of its own, and its strategic petroleum reserve facilities lag far behind those of the United States. China's foreign policy in the past several years has been dominated by its quest to secure resources, of which oil is the most important. Despite what may be termed successes in getting countries in the Middle East, Africa, and other conflict-prone regions to agree to supply China's oil needs, the dependence is still bothersome as the oil must be transported long distances to China by sea or pipeline. China's lack of significant naval power means supplies by sea are difficult to secure. Thus, the desire for a greater measure of energy independence and self-sufficiency is first and foremost.

The second reason is that, by acting quickly, China can become a leader in these new clean technology energy industries. Despite the fact that the original technologies have all been developed abroad, China's domestic companies in solar and wind power, for example, have quickly become formidable competitors. NYSE-listed Suntech Power or Shenzhen-listed Xinjiang Goldwind Science & Technology Company are leading China's way into the solar and wind markets respectively.

The last, and still important, reason for the government to be pushing China toward greater use of alternative energy is the positive impact the technologies have on the environment. For every old and inefficient coal-fired generator China can shut down and replace with a wind farm or solar array, problems such as acid rain and air pollutants get marginally better.

Living with pollution is grudgingly accepted even by China's highly educated white-collar workers as the price of growing prosperity. Their new apartments need air conditioning and heating, their new cars need gas. Everyone realizes that embarking on a green revolution too soon would stymie growth rather than promote it. Haimen's protest against a new coal-generator expansion was an exception; existing cities need the reliable power generation of coal or national gas generators. Shanghai every year comes perilously close to reaching its maximum capacity during summer and winter peaks and must get additional supply from nearby Zhejiang and Jiangsu provinces. Shanghai is limited from deploying clean energy on a wider scale because of its large need for a stable energy supply that only coal, oil or natural gas can deliver. Also, there are limited areas for wind farms or solar arrays that are not already taken by existing development. This is one reason Shanghai built an offshore wind farm near its new Yangshan deep-water port.

It is in China's underdeveloped rural areas that clean energy has a greater possibility of being adopted widely, since some rural and agricultural areas of China are so distant that they already use solar hot water heaters extensively and may have no power at all, allowing them to *leapfrog* to the latest clean technology. The far western Xinjiang Autonomous Region is rich in wind resources and has already built large-scale wind farms. Except for hydroelectric, for which China already has a significant number of installations, solar and wind power are China's biggest clean technology opportunities.

ONE BILLION ROOFS—CHINA'S SOLAR INITIATIVE

Established little over a decade ago, China's solar industry has grown exponentially from practically zero at the turn of the century to become the world's largest in terms of production of solar panels, solar cells, and related solar technology. Along the way, China's solar manufacturers overcame established international rivals from Japan, Germany and the United States.

In fact, China's use of solar energy was already significant— more than 100 million square meters of installed capacity—by 2006, making it the single biggest solar energy user in the world, with about half of the world's total installed capacity. This was not, in fact, photovoltaic (PV) solar panels, which comprise the majority of global usage in everything from street lighting to satellite power. Rather, China's main use of solar energy was the solar thermal water heater. Ubiquitous in China's smaller cities and agricultural communities, solar water heaters are often the only source of hot water for rural communities, and there are already tens of millions of units in use.[12] The use of traditional PV solar cells in China is also growing very quickly, with cities such as Rizhao in Shandong province becoming "solar cities" that both produce and use their own solar products.

Not only because solar is a $300 billion industry globally, but also as part of its renewable energy strategy, China is making solar power a key national priority for production *and* use.

*Challenges to China's Solar Industry*

China's solar industry has three critical structural weaknesses at present. The first is technology—most of it is foreign-developed. The second challenge is criticism of China's industry subsidies, which are beginning to result in trade sanctions. Finally, China's solar industry—much like its wind industry—already suffers from domestic overcapacity—China's solar manufacturers can produce many more panels than China itself needs. Each of these three problems has unique characteristics and different solutions.

First, all of the main patents and technologies in solar energy are foreign developed and controlled, such as the technology to make polycrystalline silicon (PCS), a key and expensive ingredient in both computer chips and solar cells. Furthermore, a new technology being developed—thin-film solar cells—threatens China's dominance in the traditional glass and PCS panel PV cells. It appears that both Nanosolar of the United States and Sharp Electronics of Japan are close to commercializing their separately developed thin-film technology, and it remains to be seen whether China can develop its own competitive version or whether technology-transfer or licensing of the patents will occur.

The second challenge China faces in developing its solar manufacturing industry is criticism from other nations in the World Trade Organization that China's national support for the solar industry is an unfair trade subsidy.

For China, the decision to subsidize and support its emerging industries is not an issue. It *will* support them, one way or another. The question is *how*. Should China subsidize the industry, the user, or the research? Industry subsidies and support was the model practiced by Japan in the latter half of the 20th century when its powerful Ministry of International Trade and Industry (MITI) engaged in picking export winners. Subsidizing the usage through rebates to companies and consumers that "go green" is the practice in Europe and the United States. For example, California has its *Million Solar Roofs* initiative, and a feature of the economic stimulus program of 2009 was President Barack Obama's plan for weatherization rebates. The third choice is to subsidize research and development through university grants or loan guarantees, of which the U.S. government's backing of debt from Solyndra (which went bankrupt in 2011) is one example.

China has often, not just in solar energy, but in other industries as well, elected to go the route of direct support to industry in the form of export subsidies. If the product is exported, tax rebates were given to manufacturers. This encouraged the development of the export-oriented economy. While China removed such subsidies in the boom times of pre-2008, many are back in place in the post-financial crisis stimulus. China also practices the second, though not in solar energy, by giving the state-owned enterprises such as Sinopec and PetroChina a duopoly. Via the state-owned banks, it also implicitly backs funding to both state-owned and private enterprises that qualify as strategic emerging industries. It is for these three reasons the United States and the European Union criticize China's government support for solar energy.

With the failure of Solyndra fresh in the minds of U.S. solar manufacturers, a number of them banded together to make an anti-dumping complaint against Chinese manufacturers in October 2011. It was accepted by the United States International Trade Commission, opening the door to countervailing measures. China's government announced its own investigation against the United States industry, highlighting the fact that Solyndra and other manufacturers were also being subsidized, perhaps illegally, according to the same WTO regulations.

Ironically, some other U.S. manufacturers of solar systems (integrated power units and controls, of which the panels are just one part) actually oppose retaliatory tariffs because they would raise costs for key components, and the American companies' own products would end up being squeezed in the market—or consumers would have to pay higher prices.

Meanwhile, Chinese companies are adapting to the challenges the same way that Japanese companies did when they faced the same challenges to their auto industry in the 1980s and 1990s. Chinese manufacturers are setting up their own facilities in the United States to avoid trade sanctions, and bypassing the U.S. market to sell elsewhere in the world, including developing countries, where solar power is growing quickly.

The third problem of domestic overcapacity is being solved in two ways. First, China is providing subsidies to companies that will set up and operate solar generation facilities in China. The second solution is to encourage Chinese companies to seek new export channels abroad, "Going Out" to seek new market share more aggressively. In early 2012 there was a major news release in the solar sector: one of China's largest solar manufacturers, LDK Solar, announced its intention to purchase a German solar company, Sunways AG, giving LDK a German brand, the German company's technology and direct access to one of the world's largest markets for solar equipment and systems. The price should be astronomical, considering what is really being sold, but actually the Chinese company is going to pay just 24.2 million euros ($31 million) for Sunways.[13]

This may be seen as one of the first steps in consolidation of the solar industry. China will undoubtedly become the global leader, at least in traditional PV modules, perhaps to the chagrin of the countries that actually invented the technology decades ago.

In fact there *was* a window of opportunity where Western companies could have parlayed their earlier start, technological advantages, and better access to PCS when it was in shorter supply. A division of Germany's Siemens created one of the key processes for efficiently manufacturing PV-grade PCS, and for decades the only producers were non-Chinese companies. For a while, a German company, Q-Cells, led the world in PV production.

Despite all these advantages the West had, Chinese manufacturers are now larger than Western counterparts, China has its own PCS producers, and Chinese companies are simply buying the new technology they need through acquisitions—gaining preferential market access at the same time.

The Germans, Americans and Japanese may now be singing, to no avail, *don't let the sun go down on me.* Meanwhile, the *sun also rises* for China, home to the new world's number-one producer of solar PV modules, Suntech Power.

*Case Study: Suntech Power*

Altogether, China accounted for more than half of worldwide PV solar production in 2011. In the past, Chinese manufacturers have relied on price as their strongest competitive advantage. And, especially since China invested in its own PCS production facilities, this advantage remains a defining factor. But with new technologies, including thin-film solar, becoming cheaper, faster, and easier to produce, China's PV manufacturers are also learning to adapt and innovate.

With revenues of $2.7 billion, doubling its pre-financial crisis sales of $1.35 billion in 2007, Suntech Power is now the world's largest solar cell module manufacturer, besting former leaders Sharp of Japan and Germany's Q-Cells. The Wuxi-based company was the first privately owned Chinese company listed on the New York Stock Exchange.

The company's founder and chairman, Shi Zhengrong, once envisioned that his company's sales would reach 100 billion *yuan* ($13.8 billion) by 2012, overtaking both his rivals. Suntech missed the revenue target but still got the prize.

It is hard to imagine how a company established in 2001 in a new industry in China could fly so high in just over a decade. After spending more than 10 years in Australia for his doctorate degree and research in thin-film solar technology, Shi came back to China to start his own company, Suntech Power, manufacturing silicon solar cells and modules. With the support of the Wuxi government and investment from several local enterprises, Suntech was formed with 20 employees.

The company faced financial difficulties in the first few years, as the demand for solar energy was not as great as it is at present. Shi had to purchase secondhand equipment from overseas, which cost only one-third of the new equipment he had purchased earlier. Despite the financial difficulties and the bleak photovoltaic market in the early years, Shi remained convinced of solar energy's future, even when Suntech did not have money to pay wages.

As the solar energy sector began to take off, Suntech's sales shot up from just under $21 million (150 million *yuan*) in 2004 to $111 million (800 million *yuan*) in 2005 and $167 million (1.2 billion *yuan*) in 2006.

Suntech exports most of its production, but with the growing industrial and consumer demand in China for alternative forms of clean energy to supplement its over-reliance on polluting coal, the market potential for solar energy is huge. The main barrier is cost versus other forms of power, especially coal. In China, solar energy costs about 5 *yuan* (80 cents) per kilowatt hour to generate, eight to 10 times the cost of coal-fired electricity. But, with the costs of PCS coming down dramatically due to China's own suppliers coming online, and new technologies such as thin-film solar, solar energy is expected to become competitive with coal. The national target by the Ministry of Industry and Information Technology is to have the cost down to 0.8 *yuan* (13 cents) by 2015 and 0.6 *yuan* (10 cents) by 2020. Whether it involves thin-film or traditional PV, domestic or international, Suntech Power is sure to be an important player in this growing industry.[14]

WIND POWER

China is also a strong proponent of wind power, with 91 wind farms and a total generating capacity of more than 40,000 megawatts. China has achieved this in a remarkably short period of time. From 2008 to 2012, it increased installed capacity by six times, and now exceeds the U.S.'s installed capacity.

Unfortunately, installed capacity does not necessarily equal high generation or usage rates of wind power: though many of China's wind farms are built where the winds are strongest, this happens to be in distant Xinjiang Autonomous Region of China's northwest. Power is most needed, however, on the industrialized eastern coast, far from Xinjiang. China's long-distance grid transmission is too inefficient to get the power to where it is actually needed. As a result, many of China's wind farms are not yet productive and will not be until China's northwestern regions develop their own large cities that can utilize the power.

China's production of wind turbines and blades has also grown quickly because of a 70 percent domestic technology content regulation for its wind farms. One of China's largest wind turbine manufacturers, Xinjiang Goldwind Science & Technology Company, is a beneficiary of that policy. It went public on the Shenzhen stock exchange and bought into a German wind-turbine manufacturer, largely on the strength of China's domestic market demand.

As with the solar industry, China heavily supports and subsidizes the development of the wind industry. Preferable feed-in tariffs were used in an earlier phase of wind industry growth to make wind energy competitive with other sources of energy (a technique also used by Germany). China has also frequently revised its national targets for wind power generation capacity upward during the 11th and 12th FYPs, as installations far surpassed the initial targets. Currently, China plans to have as much as 100,000 megawatts installed capacity by 2020 which, based on current growth rates, would roughly double the installed capacity of its nearest competitor, the United States.[15]

## OTHER CLEAN TECHNOLOGY OPPORTUNITIES

China will soon be the world's number one user of electricity, and it has pledged to keep fossil fuel energy generation below 85 percent. Though China is putting most of its chips on hydroelectric, solar and wind, it is exploring other ways of reducing its reliance on coal and oil. This includes the exploration of nuclear power, so-called clean coal technologies and biofuels. To reduce domestic demand for oil and gas, alternative energy vehicles are also being encouraged.

Though nuclear energy is arguably not *clean* at all when the total value chain from raw materials to production to disposal is considered, China is making use of nuclear energy and, after a short period of reflection following Japan's Fukushima Daiichi meltdown, China's nuclear plans are back on track. In 2012, China and Canada concluded an agreement to allow the sale of significant quantities of Canadian uranium to China, allowing China to diversify its supply away from Central Asian and African countries, where investment costs and political stability respectively are negative factors. China has plans for more than two dozen new nuclear facilities, in addition to the 13 already operating, giving China about 80 gigawatts of capacity by 2020, which will be about 5 percent of its total capacity at that time. Nuclear energy is expected to play a bigger role in the future, with China planning to double its generating capacity every 10 years after 2020.

With China having the third largest reserves of coal globally, making the most of that resource is the reason China's top coal producer, Shenhua Energy, is researching the historical process called coal gasification. This process, widely used before the discovery of oil reserves around the world, converts coal into a gas that can be burned, similar to natural gas. An additional process can convert it into liquid fuels for powering vehicles. Though coal gas has many other uses, its production is not ecologically friendly, so China has not mandated its use except in studying so-called clean coal power generation, which uses a process of coal gasification before burning to generate electricity, rather than directly burning the coal as is the usual and more cost-effective practice. While a very small part of China's research initiatives, it is on the preferred investments list, so China is likely to support such technologies if they become cheaper.

Finally, China has a potential biofuels industry, mostly based on sugarcane from the southern areas, such as tropical Hainan Island, and from rapeseed in other parts of the country. The rapid food inflation that occurred globally in 2007 made the government restrict biofuels projects that use staple food products as a feedstock (e.g., corn-based ethanol) in order to avoid adding to inflationary pressure. But China is encouraging cellulosic ethanol research, since China's farms produce huge quantities of agricultural waste biomass, such as straw and corn husks, that could one day be turned into a source of biofuel.

ALTERNATIVE ENERGY VEHICLES

It is said that world oil supplies could not handle the demand of every Chinese family owning a car. The Chinese government believes the roads couldn't handle it either, as described in the *urbanization supertrend,* with some cities putting high license fees in place to discourage mass use of vehicles.

It is with an understanding of these issues that the Chinese government has made alternative energy vehicles and their components a strategic emerging industry under the 12th Five-Year Plan, figuratively the *roadmap* for the new car industry. At the same time, it began to discourage investment in conventional automobiles, showing its intentions are to create a sustainable industry.

Companies in China, domestic and the Sino-foreign joint ventures, are rushing to develop alternative-fuel vehicles that will be cheaper to run and help reduce the smog that envelops many Chinese cities around rush hour (which is essentially all day in Beijing).

The auto joint venture Shanghai General Motors launched the first Chinese-made hybrid car in 2008, the Buick LaCrosse Eco-Hybrid, a localized update to the LaCrosse model, with new interiors and features designed in China. This remodeling and rebranding turned it from a "grandpa car" in the United States to an executive sedan appealing to China's wealthy businesspeople. GM's new $250 million R&D center focuses on alternative fuel vehicles as a prime research objective—part of the company's strategy to be a leader in hybrid car technology in China.

It appears in 2012 that hybrids are off to a slow start overall. This includes Toyota's Prius which, despite now having a factory in Guangdong Province, has been unable to sell more than a few hundred units per year—and in 2010 sold just a single Prius for all of China. It is unclear which maker will be the first to sell alternative fuel vehicles in significant numbers in China. But China's government is clear about what should be the ultimate goal: it wants fully electric vehicles, developed in China, to be the eventual market leaders. That may seem like a longshot, but there is one businessperson in China who has a dream, and he has even convinced Warren Buffet to believe it, too.

## Case Study: Build Your Dreams

Like the story of Suntech, Chinese manufacturer BYD started from humble origins, very recently, and has risen to near the top of the market in multiple industries. In each industry BYD has entered, it took less than a decade to become an industry leader. It all started in the Special Economic Zone of Shenzhen. There, in 1995, an entrepreneur, Wang Chuanfu, started a business to make batteries.

Odds are good that many consumers have used a BYD product and never noticed. It is one of the world's top manufacturers of batteries for mobile phones. Its entrepreneur excelled in reverse-engineering, taking an existing battery from another manufacturer, breaking it down and figuring out how it all worked. By 2005, growing together with China's OEM mobile phone manufacturers that needed cheap batteries, it was the biggest battery maker in China—and one of the world's top five.

BYD achieved its success like so many other Chinese manufacturers do: it replaced expensive equipment and technology with brute force. Humans would build the batteries by hand by mixing chemicals, laying circuits, folding cases, testing and wrapping. They would live in dormitories on site, eat, breathe and sleep at BYD. China's health and safety laws, as previously mentioned, are not as strict—and China has a lot of labor, so it was not hard for this model to propel BYD and thousands of other manufacturers to the vaunted China price, the lowest price anywhere in the world for an item.

Wang's vision extended to other products that used batteries. Seeking new opportunities, in 2002, BYD bought a small Chinese automobile manufacturer. Though BYD had never built a car, the engineers used the same process they did with batteries: painstakingly reverse-engineering and learning how to build them in the cheapest way possible. Again using little automation and much human labor, BYD introduced its first car in 2003, the Flyer, based on the designs and technology they had purchased from the Chinese manufacturer.

Initially, BYD Auto focused on gas-powered engines and a few no-frills mini passenger car models. They were cheap and they worked, just like the batteries. A few years later, in 2008, its F3 model began outselling foreign and domestic competitors, and was the top seller in China in 2009 and 2010. It even holds the record for the most units sold in a single month in China, more than 30,000 cars. Not bad for a company that didn't even build cars before 2003. But that was not the end of the story.

If BYD's English slogan was "Build Your Dreams," Wang Chuanfu's dream was surely to build an electric car that combined his battery business with the auto business. In 2008, BYD introduced the first Chinese-built hybrid vehicle, but with a twist. Unlike the market-leading Prius, the BYD F3-DM (for dual mode) would be a *plug-in* hybrid. Toyota did not sell a plug-in model until 2012 (only after-market conversion kits were available), and the Chevy Volt had not yet been released. The F3-DM was, in other words, the world's first primarily electric passenger car with the gas engine as a backup.

The kind of speed-to-market and innovation that brought the F3 base model to the top of the sales charts and the F3-DM to be released earlier than its global competitors might have been what attracted the world's most famous investor, Warren Buffet. Buffet's Berkshire Hathaway purchased 10 percent of BYD in 2008 at the depths of the global financial crisis. It seemed to be a prescient buy: within two years the stock had appreciated tenfold, and the original $230 million stake became worth several billion.

Since then, BYD's star has fallen somewhat. It missed its U.S. introduction; it was again accused of copying industrial designs; it missed its China sales targets; it let go 70 percent of its sales staff; and its first all-electric vehicle, the E6, was late to market. By September 2011, the stock fell all the way back to the level it had been at when Buffet bought in and 2011 profits were down 44 percent.

Dreams are not easily forgotten, however. In October 2011, the E6 finally came on the market in China, and in January 2012 the stalwart F3 was still selling more than 12,000 units a month and was the number one domestic-made model. For Wang Chuanfu, only in his mid-40s, there was ample time to build his dream.

~

China's electric car market is not limited to BYD's E6. In fact, as part of the 11th Five-Year Plan (2006–2010) and one of the seven strategic emerging industries under the 12th FYP, support for the development of electric cars goes all the way up to China's top leadership. Huge investments have been made so far, but progress is characterized more by grand announcements rather than actual success stories:

> *Funding:* A 100 billion *yuan* ($15 billion) fund was established to support electric vehicle development.

> *Public transportation:* More than 100 electric super-capacitor buses (charging at bus stops) were deployed for the World Expo 2010, but recharging caused passengers to get impatient.

> *Pilot projects:* In 2011, battery "hot-swapping" start-up Better Place announced a plan to cooperate with a large Chinese utility, and gigantic State Grid Corporation announced China would have 2,300 swapping stations by 2015.

> *Infrastructure:* China's answer to Detroit, the "car town" Anting (part of the Jiading district near Shanghai, known itself as the Shanghai International Auto City), is home to China's largest automaker, SAIC, various automotive sub-contractors, a Sino-foreign auto joint venture and China's Formula One racetrack. The Jiading district gov-

ernment finally started to establish charging stations for an electric vehicle pilot project in 2012.

It seemed China was trying to do everything at once. It was simultaneously trying to build hybrid cars, electric cars, and electric car parts supply chain, battery swapping stations and recharging stations. Dozens of foreign companies and Chinese state-owned enterprises were involved. Nothing was working right, nothing was being coordinated. On top of all that, China's own entrant to the electric car market, the BYD E6, was several years late to market and only went on sale to consumers in late 2011. By mid-2011, all this had caused Premier Wen Jiabao to express doubts and call for a critical look at the plan.

The final arbiter may be the consumer. In January 2012, the all-electric E6 was off to a slow start. Fewer than 100 of the vehicles were sold nationwide. Its hybrid compatriot, the F3-DM, sold a few units less. Even the Prius couldn't break 75 units during the month in which Chinese buy new cars to celebrate Chinese New Year. In 2012, the government was still considering what kind of rebates to offer for clean energy vehicles. Plans include a direct cash subsidy and the benefit of bypassing the expensive license plate auction in Shanghai, but nothing has been finalized, pending the top-level review. This will be one of China's key industries to watch during the Olympic Decade and, if China can get its national strategy back on track, will become a key supplier to global markets for clean energy vehicles.

EFFICIENT AND ECOLOGICAL PRODUCTS

Beyond all of the large-scale opportunities for generating clean energy with solar power or wind, using environmentally sound building practices, deploying electric bus fleets and encouraging the purchase of electric cars, reducing waste and saving energy, there is one last frontier where China is also going green: consumer preferences.

With China already being the source for many low-cost com-modities, attention will now be turned toward making existing products better in an environmental or green way. This could be done by modifying manufacturing processes to be more efficient, changing the products to use less power or resources, or making them easier to reuse and recycle. Under *jieneng jianpai* China is trying all three. The second aspect of this is related to the *consumption growth engine,* where Chinese consumers are becoming a driving force.

Eco-conscious consumers are increasingly looking for reason-ably priced environmental and safe products. The reason is simple. Due to frequent product recalls, investigative reporting, and poisonous chemicals found in everything from baby food to cosmetics, Chinese consumers are starting to pay more attention to product quality and durability, the source of raw materials, organic content and other sustainability factors.

As it concerns China's manufacturers, who may not yet see the Chinese consumer as their main target, large multinational purchasers with a mandate to buy and sell green, such as Wal-Mart and GE, are playing a bigger role in making China go green. Government regulations also play a role, stating that new prod-ucts must have a certain percentage of sustainably produced materials, a higher energy efficiency, or be completely recyclable at the end of product lifetimes, as became the norm in the EU when it implemented new Restriction of Hazardous Substances (RoHS) and Waste Electrical and Electronic Equipment (WEEE) directives, which had wide-ranging implications for Chinese products being sold in that region. Chinese manufacturers are going to use this requirement to *leapfrog* into the role of being some of the most environmentally aware producers on the planet.

## SUMMARY: THE SUSTAINABILITY SUPERTREND

Of all of the opportunities mentioned so far, none are as important from a societal perspective as saving energy and reducing pollution. China's development puts enormous pressure on world resources. It is a relief that the Chinese government is being proactive in solving the dilemma of balancing growth with sustainability. These opportunities promise to be the most socially conscious (and profitable) of the Olympic Decade:

> *Eco-challenges:* China has some of the world's worst pollution—water, land and air—and needs new solutions to these problems.

> *Water:* Nothing is more precious than water. China lacks a sufficient amount of water and is embarking on huge infrastructure projects such as dams, water diversion and reforestation to ensure an adequate supply for China's continued growth.

> *Better buildings:* China is currently the world's largest builder. There is a huge market in China for construction of buildings that are less energy intensive. Eco-cities like Dongtan may use the latest building standards and clean energy.

> *Clean energy:* Solar and wind power are widely used in China, and its manufacturing sector leads global production in the related technologies.

> *Electric cars:* China will lead the way with alternative fuel vehicles such as hybrid, electric and hydrogen cars. But it is uncertain as to which road the industry will take.

> *Consumer products:* As the manufacturer to the world, China's production will need to be updated to be more sustainable. The driving forces are the Chinese consumer and overseas government regulations.

The future of "Red China" is green indeed.

## Chapter 8

# THE AFFLUENCE SUPERTREND

# 繁荣化
*FANRONG HUA*
PROSPERING

China's Olympic Decade is ultimately a story of affluence. The decade, which began in late 2008 with the opening of the Beijing Olympics, was the epitome of Deng Xiaoping's long-ago expression that "Some must get rich first." Some have. The Chinese state is more powerful, Chinese companies are larger, and Chinese people are wealthier than ever before. The *affluence supertrend* refers to all three groups, though the power of the state will be covered in more detail in the third book of this series—*China's Political Supertrends*—and the wealth of the consumers will be covered in the next volume—*China's Demographic Supertrends*. In this chapter, the main focus is on how China's companies—both state-owned and private enterprises—have become rich. For those non-Chinese firms and investors wise enough to get involved or deepen their commitment to China during the Olympic Decade, there is enough prosperity for all. But there are also risks: China may be the biggest bubble the world has ever seen.

China today can plausibly be compared to Japan of the 1980s. Property markets are skyrocketing; the *yuan* is a rising currency—both in terms of buying power and desirability—with the potential to become the world's next reserve currency if it becomes convertible; and China has the fastest accumulation and largest foreign reserves of any net creditor nation ever. From Japan Inc. to China Inc., how true is this comparison?

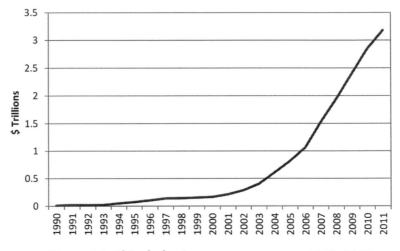

*Figure 16: China's foreign currency reserves, 1990–2011*

As in Japan's economy of the 1980s, there are visible risks to China's economy today—investment bubbles—that threaten to topple the system. Unlike Japan's large middle class, China's population is stratified into *haves* and *have-nots*: the country is staring into the maw of a giant wealth gap. Like Japanese companies of the 1980s, Chinese enterprises are going abroad to buy up assets and competitors. Unlike Japan's firms, most of China's companies going abroad are state-owned enterprises and are backed by state-owned banks, which create even more suspicion and hostility than the Japanese firms once had to deal with, delaying or even halting Chinese acquisitions.

Finally, and most significantly, China's *yuan* currency is managed in a fundamentally different way from Japan's yen, then and now. During the years of the Japanese bubble economy from the 1980s until the bubble collapse in the early 1990s, the yen almost doubled in purchasing power abroad, which is how the Japanese came to own so many Renaissance paintings and large foreign companies. China's currency is not allowed to freely float, and has only appreciated against the U.S. dollar by about 25 percent since 2005, allowing Chinese exports to prosper, but keeping purchasing power down. The *yuan* is likely to appreciate further, but at a pace decided solely by the Chinese government, despite increasing calls from countries such as the United States for China to stop using the *yuan* to undervalue China's exports. Therefore, China is unlikely to experience a "lost decade."

If China is not, then, another Japan Inc. about to collapse, what will happen to it, financially? A number of key questions highlight the challenges and opportunities of China's accumulation of wealth and affluence:

*Foreign reserves:* The persistently undervalued *yuan* has led to a trade surplus—meaning more exports going out than imports coming in, leaving a net accumulation of foreign currency—allowing China to accumulate more than $3.2 trillion of reserves. What is it doing with the money?

*Yuan convertibility:* Though there is growing prosperity in China, the wealth is mostly retained by the state using currency controls. When it comes to China's *yuan,* insiders cannot sell significant quantities and outsiders cannot buy significant quantities, but China's government is increasingly liberalizing the overseas use of the *yuan* through trade and overseas direct investment. When will the *yuan* become a true global currency?

*Stock market health:* China's own stock markets may have been down in 2011, but they are still one of the biggest capital markets in the world for new initial public offerings (IPOs). How is the supply of capital affecting China's growth?

*State-directed global investment:* There are signs that China's wealth is spilling over its borders, through a sovereign wealth fund and state-owned enterprises. What effect will China's affluence have on the rest of the world?

These are the defining questions of China's *affluence supertrend.* Before talking about the opportunities, an understanding of the risks is critical.

## CHINA'S AFFLUENCE CHALLENGES

Still an emerging market economy, China faces a number of challenges in developing stable and world-class financial systems and institutions. The risks range from the institutional—corruption, government misallocation of investment, bad debt and non-performing loans—to the systemic, including inflation risk, financial bubbles and the wealth gap. It is these three major risks that China and the world need to be most concerned with.

### DOMESTIC PRICE INFLATION

With China's consistently high GDP growth and foreign currency controls, it may be said that China is pursuing a kind of neo-Mercantilist trade policy.

Mercantilism is an economic theory that describes how nations, from the 16th century up to about the mid-19th century, promoted national economic growth through strict control of trade. Under mercantilism, Western colonial powers often promoted their own exports while they prevented competitive imports by enacting high tariffs and non-tariff barriers. Trade was often conducted via state-sponsored companies with exclusive charters and territories. The Dutch East India Company was one such firm that even had its own warships.

Under mercantilism, trade was unbalanced. Instead of allowing high-value imports that would balance trade, only low-value raw materials or payment in precious metals was allowed. This led many countries into trade wars, each erecting higher tariffs to protect home markets while becoming increasingly aggressive to protect their interests abroad. In the end, mercantilism was not a workable system and was abandoned for free market theories of Adam Smith and others. Among mercantilism's many flaws—Smith and others pointed out—with no balance of trade, gold and silver tended to accumulate in one place and lose its value.

Modern-day mercantilism seems to be alive and well in China. Although it joined the WTO and ostensibly opened many of its markets, it imports little from the countries it exports to. China uses non-tariff barriers to make foreign products uncompetitive. It restricts the reverse flow of "gold" (i.e., foreign currency) that would balance trade with many of its trading partners. In particular, the United States has had a persistent trade deficit with China for the past two decades, often of more than $200 billion a year. As a result, China had accumulated $3.2 trillion in currency reserves as of March 2012.

An in-depth discussion of inflation and currency management systems is beyond the scope of this book. But, simply speaking, with so much money accumulating inside a closed system such as China's economy, the prosperity of the people is bound to put upward pressure on prices as they seek to spend their increasing wealth on limited goods. In the case of China, this may mean too few apartments or too few listed companies, or even not enough commodities such as pork. Too much money chasing too few goods leads to price inflation, as measured by the consumer price index (CPI).

Three things have prevented uncontrollable inflation—hyperinflation—from happening in China in recent years.

First, since 2005, the *yuan* has been allowed to appreciate gradually, meaning that China's *yuan* can buy more in foreign goods than it could before. However, the purchasing power of the *yuan* in U.S. dollars is still not as high as would be expected as the currency of one of the world's largest economies.

Second, the Chinese population in general does not have a lot of investment opportunities and thus tends to save a lot of money without consumption, resulting in a national savings rate that has been around 50 percent for most of the last decade, compared with a savings rate of essentially zero in the United States until recently.[1] With so much money being saved, instead of consumed or put to more productive uses, inflation pressures may not have been as high as they could have been.

Finally, new opportunities to buy foreign currency have been allowed—such as exchanging money for international travel or buying up to $50,000 in foreign currency per person each year—relieving some of the pressure on the *yuan*.

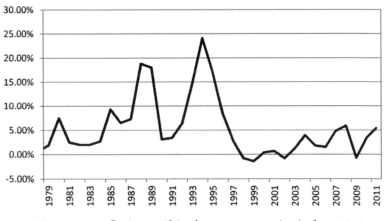

*Figure 17: Inflation - China's consumer price index, 1979–2011*

Even so, these outlets are not enough. Inflation in China has persistently been at rates greater than 4 percent overall, above China's target. Certain components of the CPI, such as fresh vegetables and meat, have tended to rise far more quickly.

*Case Study: The Pig Cycle*

China's CPI *basket of goods,* the items chosen by China's stat-
isticians to represent a typical selection of commodities that
consumers regularly purchase, is almost one-third weighted
toward food. This is much higher than in other countries'
measures and reflects the National Statistics Bureau's understanding of what rural Chinese consumers—the majority—spend
their money on. This, however, makes China's CPI more suscep-
tible to short-term fluctuations based on commodity and,
especially, pork prices.

It all started rather quietly in 2007—with pork prices in the
local wet markets increasing, and people buying more chicken
instead. It had happened before: lacking good market feedback,
government planners and farmers misjudged demand. Farmers
were not slaughtering enough pigs, thereby causing a minor
shortage, prices went up in response, farmers slaughtered and
raised more pigs on this signal, prices fell back to normal or pigs
were even sold at a discount. The pig cycle was almost as constant
a feature of life in China as the yearly rice harvest. Except it
wasn't entirely about misjudging the demand—China suffered a
series of problems that led to a so-called *black swan* event—
something unpredictable.

As a result of the global boom in commodity prices, including
for fertilizers and even basic corn and grains (which were being
used in a biofuels boom), farmers now had to pay more for
animal feed. Then a wave of blue-ear disease hit some pig farms
and entire herds were culled.

For awhile, consumers did without, buying other meats instead. But it is hard to describe how important pork is to the
Chinese diet. It is said that Mao Zedong's favorite dish was *hong
shao rou,* braised fatty pork in red sauce. With the exception of
China's northern or western Muslim areas that tend to prefer
lamb, most of China eats pork in the way Americans eat beef or
Japanese eat fish. Gradually, people started paying the higher
prices for pork.

Then the hoarding began. Aware of the blue-ear disease, regular consumers were seen fighting over what was left of the pork stocks. Some universities announced they would buy enough pork to serve their entire student body for the semester to keep cafeteria prices stable. When all was said and done, pork prices increased more than 48 percent in a single year. Switching over to chicken or beef didn't help much either, those prices were up 39 percent on the year.[2]

~

All of this inflation had the effect of hitting Chinese consumers hard, since they spent so much of their income on food. Little was left for other consumption. The government's plan to stimulate a consumer-based economy languished.

In recent years, China has had a persistent problem with inflation. Whereas most economists would describe a rate of about 2 percent as ideal to "prime the pump" of the economy and encourage people to spend, China's rate was 4.8 percent in 2007 and 5.9 percent in 2008. After a deflationary period in 2009 and moderate inflation of 3.3 percent in 2010, by 2011 inflation for the year was back up to 5.4 percent. These levels of inflation may not seem particularly high compared to the double-digit inflation China experienced in the 1990s, but they are still significant for several reasons.

First, all attempts to tame inflation have apparently failed. After much attention and hand-wringing by the government, it seems very little could be done.

Prior to the crisis, the government tried just about everything to tame inflation. For example, by using its strict regulatory control over the banking industry, China tried increasing official lending rates to discourage borrowing, increasing official deposit interest rates to encourage savings, forcing banks to hold more money in reserve and increasing the amount of foreign currency Chinese residents could buy and hold, in order to try and reduce the quantity of money circulating in the economy. Financially, China tried introducing stiffer penalties for price collusion, levying new taxes on stock market transactions and enacting real estate policies to discourage speculation. All were variously tried with little or no effect. Finally, price controls were reinstated (harkening back to both pre-1978 Communist China and the post-1978 dual pricing system).[3] The government undertook monitoring of key daily use commodities, such as grain, cooking oil, tobacco, salt, meat, milk and the liquefied petroleum gas (LPG) that people run their motor scooters on, automotive gas, diesel and even that most Chinese of foodstuffs, instant noodles. The government hinted at wider-ranging price controls on everything from medical care to tuition, even basic water and electricity. All actions and threats failed.

Having learned these lessons, in the post-financial crisis war on inflation, the government focused its efforts on reducing the money supply by increasing banks' reserve requirements to a record high. This approach has yet to have had a big effect on inflation, and appears to have lost effectiveness as a tool since it cannot get much higher. In the first quarter of 2012, China started lowering the reserve requirement ratio again.

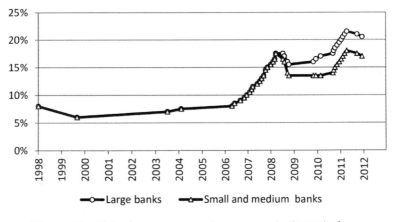

*Figure 18: China's reserve requirement ratio (RRR) changes, 1998–2012*

The government's measure of flooding the system with liquidity during the financial crisis could be said to have been too effective, reflating the stock market and the property market. Or it might be said that government activities to reduce liquidity at least mitigated even higher levels of inflation that could have occurred had no actions been taken in 2011. Either way, high levels of inflation seem part of the *new China normal.*

Second, because of this moderate level of inflation, real interest rates are negative in most years. The real interest rate is the bank deposit rate less the inflation rate. This means saving money in the bank in standard deposit accounts or short-term time-deposits would result in a decrease in the actual purchasing power of the money saved. For example, a one-year time deposit at a Chinese bank in *yuan* in 2011 at 3.5 percent would have a real return of negative 1.9 percent, because inflation for the year was 5.4 percent.

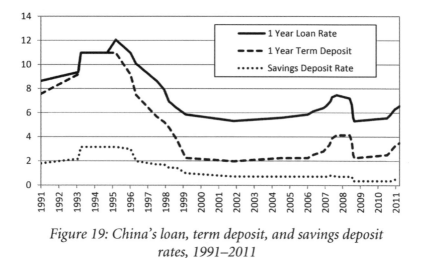

*Figure 19: China's loan, term deposit, and savings deposit rates, 1991–2011*

If Chinese savers took this as a signal to spend on consumption or invest all their money in higher-yield investments, that might stimulate the economy. But many Chinese people feel they must save large amounts of cash for health care and retirement.

While China provides basic amounts of health care and pensions, the systems are already overburdened. The demand for health care and the limited number of hospitals and doctors means there is a literal stampede at some hospitals each morning as patients (or their family members) run to take a number. To get access to a good doctor or have an operation, under-the-table payments are common. The pension system, though comprehensive for every worker paying into the national pension, is far from enough to support future seniors in China's high-cost cities. This problem will be exacerbated by the *urbanization supertrend*, since recent demographic data indicates some of China's city dwellers are living even longer than the overall average: Shanghai's life expectancy is 82.5 years versus 73.5 years nationally.

As a result, many Chinese have high savings rates, not believing in the social insurance system enough to rely upon it for all their needs. So, this combination of low interest rates and high inflation hurts the savers, and transfers private wealth back into the state-owned banking system. When China joined the WTO in 2001, many of its state-owned banks were on the verge of collapse from bad loans. The government transferred all of their toxic assets into state-owned asset management companies, then gave the banks a huge *mandatory* interest rate spread. For example, in 2012, banks charge upward of 6.5 percent for lending and pay the the official non-term deposit rate of 0.5 percent. This has allowed China's state-owned banks, such as Industrial & Commerce Bank of China (ICBC), Bank of China and Agricultural Bank of China, to recover from near collapse, go public and grow to be among the biggest banks in the world in just over a decade.

It is not just individuals who have been suffering from inflation. The Producer Price Index (PPI), measuring wholesale price inflation for materials and other production inputs, reached 6 percent in 2011, which continues its pre-crisis trend.

While CPI and PPI are ways to look at systemic risk in the Chinese economy, sector risk is also present, in the form of stock and property markets that have shown signs of being bubbles.

## CHINA BUBBLES

Whenever economists, pundits and the media in general talk about China's economic bubbles today, they are usually referring to the over-building of residential properties, office space and giant infrastructure projects, such as the nationwide high-speed rail network. In 2007, it was skyrocketing stock market valuations as China claimed the rank of the world's top performing market for two years straight. The markets in China, along with those in most of the world, suffered a major correction. Collapse might be a better word.

Today, China's residential real estate market alone would appear to qualify as the world's largest bubble at present. Should it collapse (a "hard landing" in economic parlance) it would be devastating to China's economy and have ripple effects across the globe in everything from concrete to kitchen appliances. Unlike the response in other countries to recent global bubbles—the global financial crisis, sub-prime mortgage crisis, the dot-com bubble, the Thailand land and stock bubble preceding the Asian Financial Crisis in the late 1990s, or Japan's Bubble Economy of the 1980s—China's state-controlled legal, monetary and fiscal policies may have an exacerbating effect (should the government guess wrong) or a mitigating effect (should it guess right). China bubbles are very risky.

Some people hold the position that the "China model" itself is one giant systemic bubble that is destined to collapse soon, possibly before or just after the leadership changeover in late 2012. If China is presumed to be so weak, this begs the question of the next section.

*Why Hasn't China Collapsed Already?*

Among several economic imbalances, China's currency, the *yuan,* is a common underlying factor. Whether it is inflation, hot money, foreign exchange reserves, or real estate and stock speculation, all can be linked in some way to China's restriction on the free exchange of its currency. In brief, there is too much *yuan* inside China, and not enough ability to take it out of China. Despite the fact that such imbalances could be an indicator of systemic risk, China's currency policy actually has had a bubble-mitigating effect.

China has a managed exchange rate and capital in- and out-flow controls, allowing it to resist speculation and avoid (for the most part) hot money flowing into or out of the economy quickly, as it once entered and then fled Thailand in the Asian Financial Crisis. China's policy insulated it from the worst effects of the contagion. Had China had a more liberal exchange policy, it is likely that even more money would have flowed out of Asia and the crisis would have been prolonged. In addition to China's currency policy, other policies have helped it to avoid systemic collapse thus far.

For example, China wields not only all of the same monetary and fiscal powers to stimulate the economy that the United States and other developed economies do, it also uses regulatory control to effect immediate change with no debate. This allowed China, during the global financial crisis, to flood the system with liquidity, begin massive infrastructure projects in the earthquake-hit Sichuan region, and order the banks to lend out money to state-owned enterprises, all at the same time. China's central control of all three levers—monetary, fiscal and regulatory—allowed it to create one of the largest stimulus packages and start implementing it within the time other countries were debating how big the stimulus should be, much less how it should be spent and where.

Finally, an absence of many types of financial leverage in the Chinese financial system, particularly derivatives such as mortgage-backed securities, means that stock and land price fluctuations are less extreme and China can avoid sudden financial collapses.

In fact, there are only a few things that could upset China's ascendancy to become the biggest economy on earth by 2050, 2030, or 2020 depending on whose estimate is used. Various economists inside and outside China diverge on the details, but there is general agreement that the most likely scenario to derail China's upwards trajectory is inflation.[4]

*Stock Market and Land Bubbles: Dreaming of Prosperity*

2007 was known as the Golden Year of the Pig, according to the Chinese astrological calendar, and for newly born babies (called Golden Pig Babies) it was thought to be auspicious for their future wealth. It was a very good year for China's financial markets as well. Despite nagging concerns about corporate governance, questionable investments, non-transparency and accounting irregularities, China's stocks and major indexes could make one wonder if pigs really could fly. During the year 2007, the peak year before the start of China's Olympic Decade, the China Securities Index (CSI) 300 index (a broad measure similar to the Standard & Poor's index, charting 300 out of China's approximately 1,600 listed firms at the time) led the major global indexes with a 162 percent gain, while the Shanghai stock market closed up 97 percent for the year, reaching a record high of nearly 6,000 points.[5] In all, it was another stellar year for China's markets following 2006, when the indexes more than doubled.

Under the Chinese lunar calendar, February 2008 ushered in the Year of the Rat, and one Chinese *feng shui* master predicted poor performance for the markets. How right he turned out to be.[6] Indeed, even before Lehman Brothers—the first major casualty of the global financial crisis—collapsed in September 2008, China's indexes were already down as much as 50 percent from their highs in October 2007. By the end of 2008, China's markets were the *worst* performing in the world. Shanghai had lost nearly 4,000 points. From world's best to world's worst in just over a year. It is this roller-coaster style that has characterized China's stock markets almost from their reincarnation in 1990.

In fact, there is little surprising about China's markets' quick rise and fall. Chinese people have limited investment alternatives. The three main investment vehicles are stocks, real estate or bank savings. Bank savings, as mentioned, are usually a negative real return. Recently, gold has taken on a new luster as paper gold (exchange-traded funds or ETFs) is easy to buy, but other forms of financial investments are either not common or not possible.

For example, various types of bonds exist, but do not form a significant portion of most investors' portfolios—even seniors' portfolios—because they are seen by many as too conservative, given that stock markets have returned 100 percent or more in recent years. Currency speculation is also possible, but is limited to $50,000 a year per person through official channels with no leverage (not to mention that most people realize that the *yuan* is one of the surest bets to appreciate, making foreign currency unattractive). Certain futures and derivatives are only available to professional high-net-worth investors and institutions, and do not come in as many varieties as yet, having just been introduced in 2011. China's two major stock markets, Shanghai and Shenzhen, have only about 1,600 listed companies *in total*, meaning investors, whether individual or institutional, do not have a lot of choices. Shorting stocks is not possible in the mainland markets for regulatory reasons, making it difficult to hedge or be a contrarian investor, though index futures can be shorted. With so few options available in financial products, the next most popular choice is real estate.

While Deng Xiaoping called for the liberalization of private real estate as early as 1980, the privatization of public land and dwellings took more than a decade to reach wide acceptance. Property values in China began climbing after the private property reforms of the mid-1990s allowed individuals to take ownership of their *danwei (work unit)*-issued residences and buy public housing at market prices. Property prices after 2001 rose more quickly and nearly continuously in China's first-tier cities until about 2005, when real estate prices underwent a correction, resulting from some government moves aimed at cooling the property sector, which was showing signs of a bubble. At that time, newspapers were full of stories of investors who simply walked away from their properties when the mortgage appeared to be higher than the value of the property. Those investors are probably regretting that decision now, as property prices have recovered with a vengeance, sometimes doubling or even tripling their 2005 price levels.

After reaching a plateau and even decreasing somewhat in the global financial crisis, property prices again took off in the 2009 investment stimulus. At that point, numerous state-owned enterprises that had received money from the government stimulus program became real estate developers, pushing land prices up to previously unseen levels.

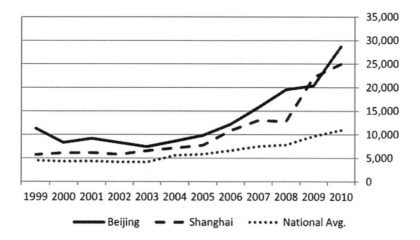

*Figure 20: Luxury real estate price per square meter (yuan)*

For awhile, this seemed to indicate China was back on track, but the first warning sign was when GDP growth was nearly all from investment in 2009. The second warning sign was when, by

2011, property prices in many urban markets had essentially doubled again from their pre-crisis levels.

Popular discontent spurred the government to make some half-hearted moves, but prices still increased. Average consumers could not buy properties. Men remained unmarried, unable to demonstrate to their future in-laws they had the financial wherewithal to own even a condominium. For existing property owners and speculators, it seemed like the boom would never end.

As of 2012, it still had not. Property prices again plateaued, and some new properties in Shanghai and Beijing are even sold at a 20 percent or greater discount (eliciting violent protests from nearby property owners or buyers of a previous block of units, outraged that housing prices might actually go down), but the secondary market was holding firm. In China, many people use real estate as a curb against inflation; in other words treating real estate as an asset that is more like gold than a residence. Many may not even bother renting out their properties or finish the interior decoration, so strong is the feeling of confidence that the real estate market will continue to appreciate.

And it just may. China's urbanization will see tens of millions move into the cities. Urban incomes are increasing in the double-digit percentages every year. Purchasing power may yet catch up to runaway real estate prices. Then again, it may not, and the whole market may collapse like a house of cards.

That said, if China's real estate prices do decline, it will not be because of any U.S.-style sub-prime mortgage crisis: loans in China are not resold to other financial institutions and repackaged. Fixed-rate short-term mortgages are more common; and China's government has moved to restrict property for investments by specifying higher minimum interest rates and down payments for second and third homes within the same family, so the land bubble seems to be coming under control, albeit slowly. Property price declines, it is hoped, will be gradual, and a soft-landing will be achieved.

## THE WEALTH GAP

While China's risk of inflation, its stock market booms and busts, and its real estate price swings are constant dangers to economic and social stability, there is another danger to the economy that also should be considered before any China investment. China's wealth gap, the amount of money the rich—often urban—citizens have versus the amount the poor—often rural—people have, is increasingly wide. What is more, China's poor, if the ratio of the "We are the 99 percent" slogan of the Occupy movements around the world is used, comprise all but 13 million of its 1.34 billion people.

### Gini in the Bottle

To simplify matters, it could be said that the Chinese government has only one domestic policy goal: to make its people rich. Here rich means not just in terms of people's monetary wealth, but also in terms of their health and quality of life. From the time of Deng's reforms the focus had been more on money: GDP growth, FDI and corporate profits. This was especially true in the 1990s with the re-emergence of the stock markets, private property and restructuring of many of the large state-owned enterprises.

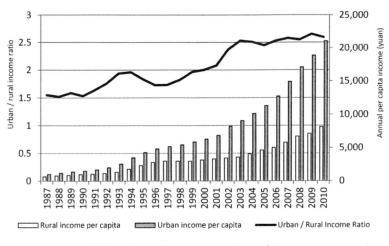

*Figure 21: Urban / rural income ratio and incomes per capita, 1987–2010*

At the start of the new millennium, coinciding with the administration of President Hu Jintao and Premier Wen Jiabao and the start of the 11th Five-Year Plan, introspective questions were asked on whether the rush to affluence had gone too far. Had China focused too much on the monetary wealth, not enough on health, life quality and balanced development?

China has been following a model in which the eastern coastal regions lead development, receiving most of the FDI and profits and doing most of the exporting. In the 1980s and 1990s, affluence of the inland rural areas was an afterthought. However, if China continues the uneven development between the coastal and inland areas, the Gini coefficient—a measure of the distribution of wealth in society—could rise to levels that are thought to indicate the potential for conflict between the haves and the have-nots. In fact, this may already be starting to happen.

According to China's Ministry of Public Security, there have been an increasing number of demonstrations and public acts of protest in the past several years.[7] While sometimes directed at companies, such as land developers, or coal mines that exploit and endanger workers, they are also directed at officials that are thought to cheaply seize property or use their power for personal profit. What is more, the reporting of these incidents—from the anti-government protest in Wukan to the anti-pollution protest in Dalian—is increasing, possibly leading to a feedback loop of more coverage and more demonstrations.

Gini coefficients are only as good as the underlying data from which they are calculated. One now-purged Chinese politician— former Chongqing Party Secretary Bo Xilai—claimed in March 2012 that China's overall Gini was 0.46, similar to the World Bank's estimate of 0.47. Chongqing, which calculates and reports its own Gini figure, had a Gini of 0.42. All of these figures are above the so-called danger level of 0.4, at which point social unrest is thought to become likely. A representative of China's National Bureau of Statistics disputed those numbers, claiming China's Gini was 0.39 in rural areas and 0.33 for urban areas. Even in this case of the National Bureau of Statistics own figures, China's rural Gini index number is still closer to that of the U.S.'s than it is to more middle-class Japan's or Western European countries' Gini numbers. [8] In other words, China's former communes look more like capitalist America than socialist Europe.

While in the United States, wealth accumulation and the gap between rich and poor is an expected outcome of a free market economy, in China, it is more the result of simple unfairness and lack of a mechanism to redistribute wealth adequately. For example, it was only in 2007 that China started to actively collect personal tax from higher income earners. Until the introduction of a pilot project for property taxes was introduced in Chongqing and other large cities, the buying and selling of real estate was taxed at much lower levels than the United States. Capital gains, whether from property or the stock market, are not taxed at all. The lack of a good legal and tax system to redistribute wealth more fairly is one of the problems that, when multiplied by 1.3 billion people, is very tough to solve.

The 12th Five-Year Plan is the most explicit yet at highlighting the disparity and taking concrete steps to correct it. Chongqing, for example, pledged to reduce its Gini coefficient to 0.35 by the end of the 12th FYP. On a national level, urbanization is another one of those steps, as is encouraging foreign companies to invest in western regions of China. Greater social welfare and land reforms for the rural population are others. However, with China still at the lower end of *per capita* income rankings globally, it is necessary that wealth generation must continue, and that is the source of many of the opportunities under the *affluence supertrend*.

## THE AFFLUENCE SUPERTREND CHARACTERISTICS

Where is it good to be in the red? In China, of course, where red is the color of luck, auspiciousness, good fortune. The largest unit of paper currency, the 100 *yuan* note, is red for this reason. So, when the stock ticker goes into the red in Shanghai, do not be surprised if people are pleased. Red arrows and numbers represent gains, while it is green arrows and numbers that upset stockholders. A famous Chinese comedian joked that in 2008 there was so much green on the walls of brokerages that birds flew inside looking for the trees. The characteristics of the *affluence supertrend* are connected to investment and money. Since the start of the Olympic Decade, more companies from China have gone public than from any other country. The average size of the IPOs is also getting larger, raising more capital for expansion, from China's domestic and overseas financial markets.

New China investment funds are started regularly by Western financial institutions to buy and sell stocks in China's markets through the Qualified Foreign Institutional Investors program, under which they are given quotas. Otherwise, individual overseas investors may find it hard to participate in China's stock exchanges because the rules prohibit foreign ownership of the most active common shares listed in *yuan* (called "A-shares").

Foreign investors can purchase a type of preferred share denominated in U.S. dollars (called "B-shares"), but the volatility is significantly higher than for *yuan*-denominated shares. Other foreign investors use Hong Kong's stock exchange as a proxy for investing directly in mainland China's exchanges by buying shares in some of the many Hong Kong-listed mainland Chinese companies ("H-shares"). Finally, foreign investors can always buy Chinese stocks on the NASDAQ, NYSE or other foreign exchanges. However, in regard to the final option, many investors are being newly cautious after 2011, when a U.S. research firm— Muddy Waters, described in this chapter's second case study— started warning investors about Chinese reverse takeover listings on North American exchanges.

For some investors with a higher risk tolerance and greater funding, becoming a venture capitalist or private equity investor in China is an option. As a way of getting in on China's growth at the ground floor, the venture capital industry in China is expanding quickly as foreign capital rushes in. It is finding stiff competition from local firms, however, and a dearth of good investment opportunities within China.

Finally, following the *reverse globalization* turbocharger, Chinese companies and investors are increasingly going overseas themselves, seeking acquisitions, cheap assets and new markets. Even the Chinese government is getting in on the overseas buying trend by creating its own sovereign wealth fund to invest on behalf of the Chinese people.

China has been investing in developing countries—especially in Africa—for much longer. But, since 2008's global financial crisis, China has, in a very short period of time, become one of the world's most important new investors in everything from oil fields to power infrastructure in developed economies— including Australia, Canada, the United Kingdom and Portugal.

Portugal, one of the so-called "PIGS" countries (Portugal, Ireland, Greece and Spain) suffering in the European Union debt crisis, welcomed China's Three Gorges power company (operator of the Three Gorges hydroelectric project) to buy 21 percent of

Portugal's newly privatized electric utility EDP for 2.7 billion euros ($3.5 billion). A few months later, in early 2012, Portugal agreed to sell 25 percent of its national grid operator to China's State Grid Corporation for 387 million euros ($508 million).

The Portugal investments highlight a new trend of Chinese companies and investment funds buying infrastructure, which are often tied to using imported Chinese technology and labor for upgrades and may also come along with promises of additional funding on easy credit terms. The old joke about a gullible person buying the Brooklyn Bridge may not be so far from reality: Chinese companies are already doing fabrication and refurbishment projects for the San Francisco–Oakland Bay Bridge and Alexander Hamilton Bridge in New York. If any cash-strapped municipality has a bridge (or other infrastructure) to sell, the Chinese are possible buyers.

Whether or not these investments will pan out long-term is less important to China than is investing in productive assets rather than financial securities such as bonds. China sees this type of investment as the best way to assist, for example, European Union countries trying to restructure their economies.

By the end of the Olympic Decade, China will be the unquestioned second-most-important capital market in the world, surpassing the importance of Europe and Japan, and will make significant gains against the pre-eminence of the United States dollar as a global reserve currency.

These are the defining characteristics of the *affluence supertrend*.

### The Rise of the Chinese Listed Company

Chinese stock markets have gone through several stages of development. In the early years, there were dramatic price swings, insider trading, pump-and-dump scandals, and few large institutional investors or funds to reduce volatility. Also, there was not enough capital available from so many small investors to support the large billion dollar IPOs China's state-owned enterprises were seeking. There was also a status issue: mainland markets were seen as the Wild East of Asian capitalism. As a result, many state-owned companies and a few private enterprises pursued overseas listings, typically in Hong Kong, where they faced fewer regulatory questions and could get higher valuations, larger amounts of capital and more "face."

When Chinese companies are merely listed in Hong Kong, without having a corporate registration there, their shares are called H-shares. Tsingtao Brewery was the first H-share, back in 1993. ICBC (the world's largest bank by market valuation in 2012) and Bank of China both listed H-shares in Hong Kong, as well as listings on Shanghai's stock exchange, all in 2006.

When a Chinese company sets up a Hong Kong or other overseas-registered subsidiary or joint venture, which is at least 30 percent owned by mainland Chinese (usually state-owned), its listings are referred to as red chips. The prototypical example is China Mobile, one of the most successful red chip companies, thanks to its share of mainland China's mobile communications market—the world's largest. Since a red chip company is technically listed overseas, it cannot list in China under current regulations, but this will soon change. There are 30 such companies in Hong Kong that will likely pursue listings in mainland China.

### Sea Turtles Come Home

These companies, when they return, are called *sea turtles* because they come back to their place of origin. Sea turtle, *haigui,* is the same word that is applied to overseas Chinese people who return home after being educated or working abroad. When used to describe companies, it refers to those which, previously listed outside China, come home to China for a new listing (and more capital). Whether red chip or H-shares, when these companies finally come home they can often raise billions of dollars in capital because of the lack of quality stocks currently on the domestic exchanges.

Once the boom in the Chinese mainland markets had begun in 2006, the need for overseas listings (Hong Kong is considered an overseas market under the *One Country, Two Systems* policy) decreased. In fact, companies that had already listed overseas could raise even more money in the mainland markets at higher price to earnings (P/E) ratios, since an overseas listing was seen as a sign of quality. Everyone knew the biggest and best of China's companies had already gone abroad as national champions in the 1990s and first five years of this century, a time when China's mainland markets were undercapitalized and in a persistent state of malaise from near-continuous scandals. That is why the *haigui* companies would eventually be welcomed home with open arms by investors.

The time for these companies to return home started after 2005 when the mainland's markets started to grow by double—and then triple—digits. With the market conditions finally right, the *haigui* companies could start returning to domestic stock markets for second listings, to take advantage of the demand from inside China for new stocks.

Seven of China's top 10 domestic market IPOs in 2007 were *haigui* companies that had listed previously in Hong Kong. In their mainland listings, they raised new capital totaling 286 billion *yuan* ($39.7 billion), about 66 percent of the total 477 billion *yuan* ($66.3 billion) raised overall in mainland China's stock markets.

*Case Study: The Trillion Dollar Company*

Warren Buffet was once a large investor in PetroChina, China's biggest oil company. PetroChina has investments around the world and employs more than 400,000 people. Through Berkshire Hathaway, Buffet held more than 10 percent of PetroChina's Hong Kong-listed shares at one point. But, in the summer of 2007, he made news by selling off part of the stake in what looked like a very short-term decision contrary to the long-term investment strategy he is known for. By October of the same year he had sold it all.

By all accounts it was a stellar investment decision. Buffet stated Berkshire Hathaway had made a return of about $3.5 billion on an initial investment of about $500 million. However, the timing confused many analysts: he sold off the stake just prior to PetroChina's planned November 2007 Shanghai stock listing. It was to be the triumphant return of one of China's most-prestigious *haigui* companies. The second listing would raise $9 billion in capital.

PetroChina's IPO was also near the time of the historical high that Shanghai's market had reached in October 2007. Surely there could never be a better time to be holding shares in a top Chinese company that was about to make an IPO in the best-performing market on Earth.

Few publicly agreed this was a good decision—it made little sense at the time—but the news that Buffet was selling briefly sent the original Hong Kong-listed stock downward. Then, in the run-up to the mainland IPO, the stock climbed and the IPO was highly oversubscribed, surging 163 percent from the offer price on its opening day. For a few days after the IPO, PetroChina was the world's first *trillion dollar* company, surprising many. It became the biggest company in the world, bigger than both Exxon and Royal Dutch Shell combined. It seemed Buffet had made a rare bad call.

In fact, by most analyses, the valuation made little sense at all. PetroChina was a bloated state-owned firm that had once employed more than a million people. Despite drastically cutting its workforce, closing unprofitable plants, and making profitable investments abroad before the time of high oil prices, it still had only half the profits of Exxon alone. Was a China listing so valuable that it could be worth two of the world's largest firms while having the revenues or profits of neither?

The over-valuation of PetroChina didn't last long. A few weeks after its stellar debut, the stock began a long slide that shaved 50 percent of its value in just three months. So, by February 2008, Buffet was once again looking like an investment genius and had gained newfound respect among Chinese stock market analysts for earlier correctly advising caution about a bubble forming in China's stock markets.

*IPO Fever*

With the world's best performing stock index (the Shanghai Composite) in 2007, perhaps it should not surprise many to know that China was also 2007's IPO capital of the world. In fact, the total amount raised in China by public offerings, $66.3 billion, was larger than all the capital raised in the United States on the NASDAQ, NYSE and AMEX combined. China's figure edged past the U.S.'s $64.6 billion.[9] This was a paradigm shift, that China's capital markets could be that large and of growing importance.

In the years since, China has seen some mega-listings as some of the biggest banks and state-owned industries go public in China. This includes the world's two biggest IPOs to date, for the ICBC in 2006 and Agricultural Bank of China in 2010, each raising about $22 billion. Blockbuster IPOs such as Agricultural Bank were what helped China to again become the world's largest market for IPOs in 2010. China has since repeated the feat in 2011, raising more than 286 billion *yuan* ($45 billion). China seems on track to continue its record for capital formation throughout the remainder of the Olympic Decade.

For state-owned enterprises, China's domestic markets are clearly the right place to raise money due to the guaranteed support they will receive from state-owned banks and regulators. For private enterprises, on the other hand, the picture is somewhat different. Fearing too much dilution of investors' funds and further market declines during the global financial crisis led the Chinese government to slow down the pace of new private-company listings after 2008 and gave preference to state-owned enterprises. Many private enterprises, lacking access to the same equity or even bank financing the state-owned enterprises were getting, turned to overseas listings instead.

In fact, Chinese private enterprises had been receiving strong interest from overseas exchanges since about 2003, but, in 2009, demand for Chinese stocks increased from Western investors eager to get a piece of China's post-financial-crisis miracle recovery.

## Chinese Companies Listing Abroad

Since the start of the Olympic Decade, *new China normal* has been for private enterprises to avoid mainland and even Hong Kong exchanges in favor of the NYSE, NASDAQ and other overseas listings. Part of the reason is the exit strategies for foreign private equity and venture capital funds that may have invested in those firms. For large foreign investors, a listing outside China is preferred in order to cash out more easily. There is also a prestige factor—similar to a decade before with listings in Hong Kong—to list outside of China.

At the start of the Olympic Decade, an increasing number of Chinese companies were following in the footsteps of Suntech Power, Baidu and other mainland companies that had already listed abroad, by choosing to list in the United States rather than China or Hong Kong. The availability of dormant shell companies suitable for reverse takeovers was a factor, as many Chinese companies used this method as an inexpensive way to go public while avoiding undue scrutiny at the same time. However, after a public listing outside of China and the stringent quarterly and yearly reporting requirements, they drew attention from a new type of investor that Chinese companies never had to deal with in their domestic markets: short-sellers.

## Case Study: Seeing Through the Muddy Waters

With all the foreign-listed Chinese IPOs (reverse takeovers mostly, more than 80 on the NASDAQ, NYSE and AMEX alone) and the high-flying performance of many companies after listing on a foreign exchange, some survivors of the dot-com boom and bust may have been getting a sick feeling in their stomachs. Seeing the number of new listings and sizes of Chinese company market capitalizations, one might begin wondering if the underlying business models made sense. As the dotcom-companies were given a premium valuation for being "Internet plays," Chinese listings were often given a pass because they were "China plays"—a bet on the growth of China's economy more than the stock's fundamentals. In 2009, Shanghai's stock market was again the best performing major market globally, growing about 80 percent. That aura would extend to Chinese firms listed overseas. Could there be a dotcom-style bust ahead?

There are two big differences between the China market boom and the dot-com boom worth mentioning:

First, China's mainland markets are driven by large-cap state-owned enterprises, often in industries related to banking and finance, infrastructure, energy and heavy industry. They may be huge, but their size makes them stable and the support of China's central government seems assured. The typical dot-com company was one with few assets and no profits.

Second, China's domestic market growth will sustain many of these companies for years, if not decades, as China develops. Urbanization will still take several decades, and the growth of the Chinese consumer will also be a constant during the Olympic Decade. With the correction in the Chinese markets that took place in 2008, and increasing earnings thanks to domestic growth, P/E ratios are more reasonable than were the often-fictitious dot-com companies' financial projections.

That said, China's *overseas* listed stocks, with the exception of Hong Kong where many H-share and red chip companies can be found—are often high-tech manufacturing or Internet-oriented, which is why they may have often picked an exchange such as the NASDAQ. These companies are often young, many of them with a decade of history or less. Finally, some appeared to be built on business structures (the reverse takeover shell, British Virgin

Islands holding companies, and something called a Variable Interest Entity) that were not always transparent and held the potential for secrets. One firm in particular sought to probe those murky depths: Muddy Waters.

Carson Block, one of the founders of the research firm Muddy Waters, is probably the one person who can be most directly credited (or blamed) for billions of dollars being wiped off of overseas-listed Chinese stocks in 2011. The saga started with a little-known firm named Sino-Forest, a timber trader listed on the Toronto Stock Exchange that had obtained its listing through a reverse takeover. Sino-Forest was accused by Muddy Waters of being a non-transparent firm engaged in a "Madoff"-level institutional fraud. The market response to the report was dramatic. Sino-Forest's stock plummeted, losing nearly 75 percent of its value within a day and a half, and its trading was later halted while the allegations were investigated. In 2012, after conducting an eight-month internal investigation, Sino-Forest's own directors could not rule out that there had been a fraud and said the truth might never be known, but that was little help. The company had lost its CEO and defaulted on bond payments, and had certainly lost the trust of investors, who were still caught in the limbo of the trading suspension.

The Muddy Waters report on Sino-Forest started a wave of investigations of other Chinese companies, short-selling of virtually every Chinese listing, and auditor resignations as one Chinese company after another (most of which had used the reverse takeover method of getting a public listing) lost value. The NASDAQ and other exchanges tightened rules on reverse takeovers, and the Chinese government made it clear the Variable Interest Entities—the corporate structures Chinese companies and foreign investors used to simultaneously avoid foreign ownership restrictions and regulatory oversight—were no longer welcome.

~

While the short-selling undoubtedly affected overseas demand for Chinese stocks, within China itself there was little change. Investors in China still lack other financial products with adequate rates of return, so the stock markets will remain popular inside China for the rest of the Olympic Decade and will rise to and eventually surpass their October 2007 highs by 2018.

Knowing the growth potential of China's markets, professional investors want in, but China's capital inflow controls prevent many types of direct investment in its financial markets. One solution has been to participate at a more fundamental level: the start-up funding of venture capitalists has become extraordinarily popular in China.

## BARBARIANS AT THE GREAT WALL

The history of the venture capitalist (VC) industry in China is rather short. Practically speaking, foreign ownership of Chinese firms was not even legal before the accession of China to the WTO. Even since then, controlling interests are still forbidden in many industries.

American VCs were still suffering from the aftershocks of the dot-com bust in the United States in 2003 when some Chinese companies' NASDAQ listings—such as Chinese Internet portal and game providers NetEase.com and SINA—began to double and triple in price. These early entrants to the NASDAQ were later joined by Chinese search engine and future Google-rival Baidu.com and NYSE-listed Suntech Power and Mindray Medical (a Shenzhen-based manufacturer of medical devices). Chinese stocks began to perform well, motivating venture capitalists and private equity funds to invest more aggressively in China.

Even so, many investment funds only entered China formally as late as 2006 or 2007, when China's markets began to heat up with 100% annual returns. Then the race was on to find the next pre-IPO Chinese firm that would make millions for its venture capital backers.

The pickings, however, have been somewhat slim, and VC firms appear to have gone beyond their typical comfort zones to make large investments in non-standard business models—shirt factories, organic farms, restaurants and hotels. Of course, there were the usual VC staples as well—high-tech and Internet start-ups, such as online video site Youku—but competition for good deals was intense. Also, deal terms have been tough for a number of reasons.

The first problem that venture capitalists encountered on arriving was the amount of competition for good deals. It was a case of too much money going after too few quality firms, and with P/E ratios of Chinese companies in general being very high because of the booming stock markets of 2006 and 2007, pre-IPO valuations were expensive and competitive.

Second, initially many Chinese companies were reluctant or unable to take additional money from VCs. China then, as now, was awash in cash, from state-owned banks giving loans to state-owned enterprises, family members investing their stock market profits in a relative's new manufacturing business, and plenty of family savings. Additional investments for large ownership stakes were unappealing. The opposite problem was that many Chinese ventures were too small, especially the Internet businesses that VCs liked to invest in. Young Chinese entrepreneurs could start online ventures on even more of a shoestring budget—measured in hundreds or perhaps thousands of dollars—than their Silicon Valley peers, which were hardly big enough to attract a VC with millions to invest.

A third reason for VCs finding it hard to get off the ground was entrepreneurs refusal to accept VC money with so many strings attached. Many Chinese firms are true command-and-control organizations, with the founder making all the decisions, and do not like to be beholden to a board of directors or external shareholders. Corporate governance is still catching on, and a sense of building shareholder value may be difficult to foster in many smaller firms where the express goal is to make the founder rich. So, the typical North American VC's focus on growth rather than profits; board seats or even control of the board; shareholding majorities; buyout rights; lock-in periods; and other typical items on any term sheet were unappealing to the typical Chinese *laoban* (boss).

Finally, the legal system and corporate structures for doing business in China are not as transparent as VCs are used to having. For example, contracts with key suppliers or customers may be done verbally based on *guanxi* relationships, while legal structures of a company may be convoluted, near non-existent, or entwined with other companies owned by the founders. Foreign lawyers and auditors are prevented from directly accessing records of Chinese companies; they must act through local licensed intermediary legal and audit firms. If that were not enough, accounting practices may not follow GAAP, and the foreign ownership rules necessitate the creation of a structure— previously mentioned—called a Variable Interest Entity, which is basically a holding company for contracts that govern a relationship with the actual owners and operations of the Chinese business. Thus, for VCs, finding suitable investments takes far more effort; transparency, leverage and security are low; and transaction costs are high.

Despite these barriers and the longer deal cycles, VCs are still making their best efforts in China, and several have had notable successes by participating in companies such as Alibaba, which went public on the Hong Kong stock exchange in 2007, and Focus Media, which is one of China's top advertising networks and listed on the NASDAQ (and is also a company targeted by Muddy Waters in 2011 and 2012).

In fact, the amount of money being invested by VCs and the number of projects are steadily increasing. After relatively flat growth from 2003 to 2005, 2006 and 2007 were huge—seeing investment triple from 2005 to 2007, to $3.25 billion on 440 deals. In 2010, investments hit $5.4 billion, and then doubled again in 2011 to more than $10 billion in more than 1,400 deals, showing that VCs have finally found their footing in China's turbulent markets.

While Western investment funds and venture capitalists pile into China, hoping to find the next Baidu, the start of the Olympic Decade began a new type of investment. This time, however, it was not directed *into* China, as was FDI or VC money. Under the *reverse globalization turbocharger,* Chinese money is going outside of China at an accelerating pace. Chinese companies and investment funds are purchasing stakes in oil fields and coal mines; acquiring competitors and international brands; and seeking better returns on investment than could be found in China. From the perspective of China, this is known as overseas direct investment (ODI). For every other country, it is the *new China normal,* Chinese foreign direct investment.

### CHINESE FOREIGN DIRECT INVESTMENT

The reason *reverse globalization* is a *turbocharger* of the *growth engines* is that it multiplies the impact of what would otherwise be a normal occurrence. In the case of ODI, every developed country does some overseas investment. If nothing else, the stocks and bonds of other countries are purchased in what is known as portfolio investment. However, when these investments come from China, they will be different for two reasons.

First, according to China's own leaders, China is still a developing economy, so it may come as a surprise that it has the same (or even greater) financial strength as the largest *developed* economies. Investments of billions of dollars from a supposedly poor China can cause suspicion in the recipient countries.

This leads to the second point, China's investments are often controversial. They may be government-sponsored. Many times they are designed to extract natural resources. Often they appear to be tied to greater influence for China in world institutions, such as the International Monetary Fund. China previously used its growing financial clout to take more voting rights in the IMF, and it is expected that if the European debt crisis in 2012 continues to worsen, China will insist on additional IMF voting rights for China as a prerequisite for buying more European bonds. For these reasons, Chinese investments may be looked upon with fear, uncertainty and doubt because of the political overtones of many of the investments. Not wanting to look a gift "dragon" in the mouth is the *new China normal* for the Olympic Decade, meaning an increasing acceptance by Western countries of Chinese investments.

## The Dragon Swallows the Elephant

In 2005, Chinese computer manufacturer Lenovo bought IBM's PC business. To date, this is still one of the largest of the few successful acquisitions by a Chinese company of a Western business. At the time, it was thought to be the *snake* swallowing an elephant, which is based on a Chinese proverb: "A man's greed is like a snake that wants to swallow an elephant." Seven years on, it turns out it was not greedy at all. Lenovo became the world's second largest PC manufacturer in 2012, topping rival Dell.

Lenovo actually got three important things by purchasing IBM's computer business: IBM's computer sales and distribution network, top staff from a global multinational and the ThinkPad notebook brand, one of the top-selling notebook brands ever.

As one of the earliest—and still one of the few—Chinese companies to successfully acquire an ongoing foreign business, Lenovo was somewhat ahead of its time. A Chinese company would not achieve the same level of success for six more years, when Chinese automaker Geely acquired the venerable Volvo line and other assets from Ford, for the bargain price of $1.8 billion.

In fact, since 2005, Chinese companies have been very active in acquisitions abroad, but most of the acquisitions are for the kind of companies that never make headlines. If they do, there is probably a national security concern being raised.

China's manufacturers have started to invest overseas for a number of reasons, including gaining a brand name; securing market access and avoiding tariffs; access to technology and patents; and simple business strategy. Much as Japanese companies started to expand abroad in the 1980s and 1990s, especially in the automotive industry, as a way to be closer to their markets and avoid trade imbalance problems, Chinese companies are following suit.

For example, the Chinese appliance manufacturer Haier, established about 25 years ago in the port city of Qingdao as a manufacturer of refrigerators, has more than two dozen facilities overseas in places as varied as Iran and Eastern Europe, and also in the United States, where it makes the ubiquitous "beer fridges" popular with college students. Another appliance manufacturer, Gree Electric, the largest Chinese manufacturer of air conditioners, is setting up a manufacturing facility in the United States in order to better compete with world-leader Carrier and to gain easier access to the North American markets.

It is not just in electronics and clean technology, China's construction machinery companies are also expanding abroad, establishing factories and buying local competitors to gain a foothold in a foreign market. In 2012, China's largest construction equipment manufacturer, Sany Heavy Industries, announced it would acquire a German pump manufacturer. In fact, virtually all Chinese sectors will begin looking for acquisitions abroad now that China's domestic market has become highly competitive. China's government has shown its support for a "Going Out" strategy by all types of companies, which may lead to new growth.

*Countryside Besieging the City...*

A second aspect of overseas strategy that Chinese companies are utilizing is based on an ancient strategy known in Chinese as "the countryside besieging the city."[10] It means surrounding the most valuable areas and biding time to build up strength, then sweeping into the prime territory. Companies such as China's appliance maker Haier and TV manufacturer TCL are already doing this. This is a very long-term strategy but, as any China watcher will tell you, Chinese have a long-term perspective. For this reason, many Chinese companies elect to enter markets in

Eastern Europe, South America or Southeast Asia and bide their time before they are ready for the biggest markets in North America, Western Europe and Japan. Chinese car companies are selling vehicles in South America, learning to work with foreign consumers. Before the end of the Olympic Decade, they will besiege the real target: the huge U.S. auto market.

Chinese companies are already becoming active in overseas mergers and acquisitions either as a way to avoid import restrictions, gain technology or, in many cases, simply gain a brand name. For example, TCL merged with Thompson of the Netherlands in part to gain brand recognition in Europe.

In this way, globalization is turning out to be a boon for the Chinese companies that were previously limited to domestic markets and OEM agreements, and lacked brand power. It is no mistake that many of these activities were led not by the invisible hand, but by the hand of the Chinese government.

## THE CHINESE GOVERNMENT GOES SHOPPING

For most of China's reform period, from 1978 up until the WTO entry in 2001, the only Chinese companies investing abroad were state-owned enterprises and, at that, in a very limited way. China's overseas direct investment was counted in single-digit billions, low-key, and mostly unknown. Then, in 2005, there was the aborted attempt by the China National Offshore Oil Corporation (CNOOC, a state-owned enterprise and China's third largest oil company) to acquire U.S.-based oil company Unocal. The Unocal bid failed, due to intense U.S. political opposition. Noted as reasons were the fact that CNOOC was getting funding for the acquisition from the Chinese state—indicating political motives to some U.S. politicians—and that U.S. companies were barred from making similar acquisitions in China. But various state-owned entities, offshore entities owned by the Chinese government and private enterprises continued to make small attempts at American firms.

In 2007, China's Huawei Technologies (a privately owned telecommunications equipment manufacturer), together with Bain Capital Partners, made a buyout offer for 3Com, the network equipment pioneer that was a technology bellwether during the Internet boom. The deal ended when 3Com voluntarily withdrew its application to the Committee on Foreign Investment in the United States. It had become clear that the national security concerns—3Com's equipment could be found throughout the Internet backbone and technology infrastructure of the U.S. government—would lead to formidable difficulties. Despite the fact that both CNOOC and Huawei failed due to political opposition, those attempts still indicated how rapidly China's companies were growing up.

Due to the intense media attention in the U.S. on the Chinese bids, these two examples were the most visible failures of China's overseas M&A activities. Other countries have opposed Chinese acquisitions on security grounds; for example, Australia rejected two bids for mining assets by Chinese state-owned firms. This reception differed markedly from how Chinese investments were welcomed in Africa or Eastern Europe.

In fact, after the global financial crisis, Western countries have become more amenable to Chinese investment. Chinese companies have quietly bought up Western brands, technology, even entire factories—which they break apart and ship back to China. The acquisitions of Land Rover and Ford's Volvo unit—for less than a third of what Ford paid for the unit in 1999—were just two examples from the automobile industry.

China's biggest investments, however, came from a little-known investment fund that was established at the start of the Olympic Decade.

### Case Study: China Anoints its Investment Sovereign

Facing intense opposition from some countries when Chinese companies tried to buy foreign firms, China took a different approach. In 2007 it established the China Investment Corporation (CIC), a $200 billion sovereign wealth fund.

CIC is known as a *sovereign* wealth fund because of its government-linked ownership. As such, its investment capital has been provided by, and the returns accrue to, the Chinese government. CIC's funding would come from China's foreign currency reserves, allowing the diversification of the reserves—mostly low-yield bonds and cash—into securities and investments with higher returns. The initial size, $200 billion, was quite large, but not exceptional among global sovereign wealth funds, such as those from Abu Dhabi, Norway and Singapore. It would be managed by a team of Chinese financiers, many of whom had experience working for Western investment banks. The Chinese financiers, by their own admission, would take it slow and learn as they went.[11]

This made CIC's first deal all the more surprising. In 2007, it was announced with much fanfare that CIC was buying into then-privately held Blackstone Group, just prior to its IPO. Blackstone is perhaps the firm most symbolic of American capitalism at its pure and brutal extreme. A private equity and leveraged buyout firm, Blackstone specializes in buying other companies, increasing the efficiency by cutting out the fat (whereby fat often means jobs) and then running the firms as cash cows or repackaging them for IPOs or for sale. What could be more Gordon Gekko capitalist than that? And yet here was CIC, a Communist country's sovereign wealth fund, buying in.

CIC had put down $3 billion for a 9 percent stake, a sizeable amount but nowhere near enough for a controlling interest; it didn't even purchase voting-class shares. CIC would essentially be a silent partner, but doubtless thrown into the bargain was a window into the booming Chinese finance industry. When Blackstone had its IPO, perhaps it was just bad timing in the markets, but the Blackstone shares quickly lost value and, at one point on paper, China Inc. was out $1.5 billion. Some Chinese netizens believed conspiracy theories—such as those proposed in China's 2007 bestseller *Currency Wars*—that this was due to a cabal of Western bankers controlling the world economies who were trying to make China lose money. CIC might have been wondering if learning as it went was not such a good idea after all.

Its second major investment, a $5 billion investment in Morgan Stanley for about 10 percent, did not fare much better. Again there was much fanfare—the symbolism of a Chinese Communist government fund buying into one of the originators of modern American capitalism—but it was purchased about a year before the global financial crisis, resulting in another massive loss on paper. Neither Blackstone nor Morgan Stanley have come anywhere close to their pre-crisis valuations, but CIC did increase its stake in Blackstone when the price was lower, billion-dollar cost-averaging, as it were.

Even with the failure of Chinese acquisitions of Unocal and 3Com still fresh, plus the sudden depreciation of its investments in Blackstone and (later) Morgan Stanley, CIC actually ended 2008 as one of the best performing funds in the world. It had kept almost all of its $200 billion in cash, avoiding one of the greatest stock market crashes in history. It is possible this fateful outcome was more due to indecision than anything else, but CIC would soon benefit enormously from its cash-rich position.

As a result, in 2009, it was again one of the world's top performing funds. This time around, it bought a large quantity of undervalued stocks, even in Chinese state-owned enterprises, which recovered strongly in 2009 and 2010. By 2012, CIC had, in fact, learned many lessons. Now a greater than $440 billion investment fund thanks to additional cash infusions from the Chinese government—the most recent in 2012 of $30 billion in order to purchase additional under-valued American and European financial assets—it is the world's second largest fund after Abu Dhabi's.

CIC owns massive amounts of shares in the Chinese state-owned banks. This was partly by fiat—the government granted CIC ownership of the holding company that owns the state's shares in the bank—and partly by design: in the 2011 market downturn, CIC publicly announced it was buying more shares in the banks in an effort to shore up their flagging stock prices.

By 2012, CIC's newest investment strategy had become clear: energy, utilities and infrastructure. In a number of high-profile investments, CIC purchased stakes in oil companies, energy trusts, even part of London's water supply with a stake in utility Thames Water. Also, it brazenly refused the possibility of participating in government bailouts of European banks, with Chinese newspapers describing CIC as "snubbing" German Chancellor Angela Merkel on her visit to China in February 2012 to ask for China's support in a bailout package.

Notwithstanding CIC's mock protestations that it is a "long-term investor" only, and that it would be difficult to invest in European government bonds, its investments in China's own state-owned enterprises will do little to dispel the idea that CIC is anything other than an arm of the Chinese government. It will continue to be looked upon suspiciously by Western democratic capitalist societies, speculating that the Chinese must have some hidden agenda. However, its success at purchasing a number of stakes in energy and infrastructure indicates that it will make significant investments overseas.

If CIC were the only Chinese government or semi-government entity investing abroad, Chinese investments could perhaps be seen less suspiciously. After all, many countries use sovereign wealth funds to manage their foreign currency reserves and petrodollars (money raised by selling oil and other natural resources). China has so much excess wealth that it must use other channels besides its sovereign wealth fund to diversify its foreign currency reserves. While CIC is mainly a silent investor in foreign securities, China sees the post-financial crisis and European Union debt crisis as a golden opportunity to give Chinese companies a leg up as they go outside of China.

For this reason, during the remainder of the Olympic Decade, there are likely to be many more Chinese corporate acquisitions abroad—across all industries. The Chinese government has lined up two of its biggest non-commercial banks—China Development Bank and the Export–Import Bank of China—with infusions from China's $3.2 billion foreign reserves to aid Chinese companies with financing. It is hard not to see this as government-sponsored and government-funded, which will make such acquisitions a tough call during any national vetting process. And yet, inasmuch as Japanese investments were once similarly opposed—and eventually embraced—so, too, will Chinese investments, especially when jobs are at stake.

As yet, there is no reason to panic in the same way Western economies were once panicked by too much Japanese foreign direct investment. From 1978 to the end of 2011, China's cumulative non-financial outbound foreign investments totaled about $322 billion, compared with its accepting about $1.2 *trillion* in inbound foreign investment over the same time period, meaning than foreign ownership of companies and assets in China is about four times that of Chinese companies' holdings abroad.

While some Chinese banks are active in property loans in New York, they are far from buying up architectural landmarks, such as the Japanese did in 1989 by buying Rockefeller Center and Radio City Music Hall. China's overseas investments are still overwhelmingly going to Hong Kong (for return trips to the mainland China on better terms), to nearby Asia countries (for business) and to Africa (for resources). Chinese direct investments in North American and European markets are comparatively small, although several major Western economies have begun to embrace Chinese direct investment.

The United Kingdom has made its intention to welcome Chinese investment crystal clear, by making the Thames Water investment happen and by making numerous statements and trade missions to China to attract investment, especially for its aging infrastructure.

Canada is another country newly amenable to money from China. After rejecting a deepening of ties with China for many years of Prime Minister Stephen Harper's government, Canada, in 2011 and 2012, has shown an increased willingness to accept

Chinese investments in its oil sands and other natural resource sectors.

~

The trends outlined in this final *supertrends* chapter are indicative of how China's geopolitical role in international finance will develop. Several of these themes will resurface in the third volume of this series, *China's Political Supertrends.*

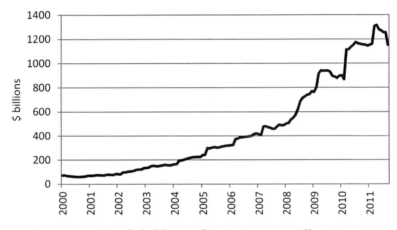

*Figure 22: China's holdings of U.S. Treasury Bills, 2000–2011*

First, China is holding increasing amounts of foreign currency reserves in the form of national bonds. It had already become the U.S.'s largest foreign holder of Treasury Bills—taking over the long-held status of number one creditor from the Japanese—and will continue to be so for many years to come. In early 2012, after six months of decreasing its holdings of shorter-term bonds through attrition as the T-bills matured, China started buying again. At the time, it had $1.16 trillion of China's $3.2 trillion foreign reserves in U.S. Treasuries. Hoping China will diversify its foreign reserves, Germany and other European Union nations desire, even expect, China to participate in bond purchases and bailouts—helping out one of its largest customers, as it were.

At the same time, China has become increasingly vocal in its opposition to a dollar-denominated global reserve system. Putting words into action, it has established bilateral currency swap agreements with many trading partners since 2008, making the *yuan* more useful for trade and increasing its international clout.

This trend started, like many others, at the beginning of the Olympic Decade, in 2008. As of 2012, 17 agreements have been signed for tens of billions of U.S. dollar equivalent currencies each, with countries including Argentina (one of the first), Thailand, Malaysia, Singapore, Indonesia, New Zealand, Hong Kong, South Korea, Japan and, most recently, Australia in Asia; the United Arab Emirates, Pakistan, Kazakhstan, Belarus and Uzbekistan in the Middle East and West Asia; and in Europe, Iceland and, most recently, Turkey.

By making currency swap agreements with many of its (often natural resource) trading partners, China negates the need for an intermediary currency, such as the dollar, to balance national accounts. It is a win-win situation for both parties to the agreements: China increases the international status of the *yuan* and the partner countries get an appreciating currency in their reserve accounts. This, however, is just the first step in replacing the dollar, and, at a total of just several hundred billion dollars—a minor amount compared with the trillions of dollars in currency swaps traded every year—it is a small step.

The second, larger, step is to reduce the dollar's role as the preferred currency of trade settlement. To this end, in March 2012 China began allowing a majority of its exporting companies to accept trade settlement directly in *yuan*. To the extent that Chinese companies are able to negotiate for this term, the dollar and other major trading currencies will be replaced by the *yuan* and the dollar's status as an international reserve currency will be diminished.

Finally, China is resisting global pressure—but especially from the U.S. and the EU—to allow the *yuan* to appreciate. The saga of China's global rise will continue in the form of a 21st century currency war pitting the dollar against the *yuan*, much as the U.S. dollar once metaphorically fought with the British pound for supremacy in the 20th century. Which currency will win this new currency war is far from certain, but the first skirmishes are already taking place and will escalate significantly by the end of China's Olympic Decade.

## SUMMARY: THE NEW AFFLUENCE SUPERTREND

China's increasing affluence and influence are significant in the current global climate of financial uncertainty. China is getting richer, via accumulated foreign reserves, an appreciating currency and growing consumer wealth from the real estate and stock markets.

> *Risks:* China's biggest risks—the things that could potentially stymie or even reverse its meteoric rise—are inflation, land and financial bubbles and the wealth gap. Paying attention to these is critical in any analysis of China's financial and social stability.

> *Chinese companies rising:* Thanks to the Hong Kong and New York stock exchanges, many of China's largest state-owned enterprises went public abroad, then later led the Chinese domestic stock market boom when they returned for domestic listings.

> *Investment in China:* Many Western investors want a piece of China's growth, leading VCs, investment funds, and people like Warren Buffet to invest in stakes in domestic Chinese companies.

> *Chinese ODI:* The *new China normal* is not FDI *into* China, it is Chinese investment *overseas.* Chinese companies are making acquisitions abroad, and the Chinese government invests via the CIC.

It is China's influence and its newfound assertiveness that, when combined with its affluence, will truly make China a global superpower by the end of the Olympic Decade.

# PART THREE: CONCLUSIONS

# 结论

## Chapter 9

# HOW TO USE THE GROWTH ENGINES, TURBOCHARGERS, ROADMAP AND SUPERTRENDS

The only constant in China is change. This phrase, though now a cliché, still rings true. Dr. James Yuann and I created the concept of the *supertrends* in the early part of 2007. At that time we wrote that, even though there had already been many years of high growth—the culmination of the so-called 30 glorious years since 1978—there were still countless more opportunities at the dawn of China's Olympic Decade. We coined the phrase *"China's Olympic Decade"* (from August 8, 2008 to August 7, 2018) to encapsulate our vision for China's next 10 years.

At the time I was full of optimism after living and working in China for five years, having seeing the positive changes that had taken place even in that short period of time. I had been studying China since the early 1990s, and was surprised at how quickly it had developed. My optimism in China's future, though slightly shaken by the global financial crisis, was not misplaced. China's growth will continue throughout the remainder of the Olympic Decade, making it one of the surest trends of all.

When I have a chance to interact with readers, I am often asked whether I think that the best opportunities in China have already passed. People ask, is it still a good time to do business, invest, or work in China? As my co-author and I wrote then in *Supertrends of Future China*, and I will write again now, opportunities here are like a bunch of 100 *yuan* notes on the ground: they are everywhere and yet quickly picked up. China's economy could be said to have money scattered on every street in every town and city. But, while everyone knows conceptually that such opportunities exist, the difference is whether you can be the one to pick it up before somebody else does.

The second-most frequent question I am asked is, how can one use the concepts in the book to make decisions about business, investing or a career? I would like to share some of my thoughts on this question now, with an important caveat. With the understanding that every reader's situation is unique, I will not attempt to delve too deeply into these answers. Ultimately, this book's analysis of the *growth engines, turbochargers, roadmap* and *supertrends* is best interpreted through one's own background, environment and requirements.

## WHEN IS THE BEST TIME TO DO BUSINESS, TO INVEST, OR TO WORK IN CHINA?

The answer is still, and always, an emphatic *now*.

This book establishes the *growth engines, turbochargers, roadmap* and *supertrends* that propel China forward. They are not short-term trends; they are the defining characteristics of China's Olympic Decade and may be a defining part of what will likely be the China *century*. The global center of gravity is shifting to Asia and, sooner or later, will be focused on China. This book has shown why and how to be there, but what and when is up to you.

FOR EXECUTIVES AND BUSINESSPEOPLE

China's *growth engines* are *exporting, foreign direct investment* and *consumption*. The *growth engine* that should most interest businesspeople is the new *consumption growth engine*.

While there are still opportunities in exporting, those are becoming more difficult as China's labor costs increase and Chinese domestic competitors get more sophisticated. Foreign direct investment is still welcome in some industries, but China is more selective now, and investments may need to be in research, or placed in China's less developed regions. Furthermore, many industries are still highly regulated and closed to some types of foreign investment; for example, energy and finance, where MNCs, if allowed at all, must be in joint ventures with Chinese partners. Even so, 30 percent of global CEOs ranked China as their top growth market for 2012, according to a survey by PricewaterhouseCoopers.

Using the *consumption growth engine* means targeting Chinese consumers for the next wave of growth. Instead of simply producing in China, companies should be selling there as well. A growing trend is that as China's *yuan* gets stronger, a foreign enterprise may be able to import products produced in its domestic market for sale in China.

The *turbochargers* are *reverse globalization, leapfrogging* and *Chinese determination*. The *turbochargers* have *an* impact on businesspeople.

*Reverse globalization* means finding the next products, services or concepts from China that are going to shake the world. Think of what it meant to be a Toyota dealer in the U.S. in the 1960s: poor quality vehicles that nobody wanted. Fast-forward to the 1970s and the oil price shocks; suddenly everyone wanted smaller fuel-efficient cars. BYD, Geely and Chery are today's Toyota, Honda and Suzuki. There are opportunities in exporting Chinese services as well: the demand for Chinese-speaking staff is enormous, whether they are nannies, translators, teachers or lawyers. Being part of China's growing service industry exports and outsourcing industry today is like being part of India's software outsourcing industry in the 1990s.

*Leapfrogging* means looking for the technology, culture and ideas in China that are jumping over Western models. Numerous examples can be found in China, from new mobile phone communication hardware to the fast-paced adoption of *weibo*— China's answer to Twitter. China's Internet, more than any other in the world, is a mobile Internet. China leaped over dial-up and even high-speed ADSL and now offers citywide wireless networks and complete coverage across the country. China may even skip the emphasis on building traditional combustion-powered-engine automobiles, in favor of hybrids and electrics. It has already jumped to a high-speed rail network more comprehensive (and faster) than that of Japan and Europe.

*Chinese determination* is likely to be found in your Chinese competitors and, if you are lucky, in your Chinese employees. That feeling is a powerful and unpredictable force, an emotional *turbocharger*. For example, care must be taken to use *Sinification* to design products and services to be more suitable for sale in China and acknowledge China's importance to your company, but such localization should not be overdone. Chinese consumers hate to see their national symbols disparaged as so many advertisers have unintentionally done. At the same time, being extra careful about quality and service is important too, as Chinese consumers are more demanding than ever.

When it comes to the *supertrends,* these will vary depending on your industry. But some of China's biggest opportunities of the Olympic Decade and beyond can be found within them. Using a process I call Supertrends Strategy Management, new ideas, new products and new services can be developed in markets where competition is slow or undeveloped.

Some of the industries where one or more *turbochargers,* the *roadmap* and a *supertrend* are aligned are where the greatest business growth opportunities can be found.

For example, China's government has cleared the path for foreign investments under the *sustainability supertrend* that produces environmental technology as described in the Five-Year Plan and Preferred Investments *roadmap*. Furthermore, the *sustainability supertrend* is turbocharged by *reverse globalization:* China's solar industry is now second to none in terms of production, and it will begin to define standards used by the rest of the world because of the *consumption growth engine*. Chinese companies and consumers have woken up to the need for a healthier, safer and cleaner environment. Together with China's national strategy of energy self-sufficiency, this opportunity cannot be understated.

FOR INVESTORS

Here I define investors as either individuals or institutions that desire to invest in China via the financial markets. In other words, people or funds that aim to profit from China's rise but do not need to operate a business of some kind in China. One may purchase the overseas-listed stocks of Chinese companies, buy one of the many China funds provided by Western financial institutions under special investment quotas, or even buy stocks of Western companies doing business in China and poised for greater growth.

Let me preface this section with the usual proviso that I am not offering investment advice nor advocating the buying or selling of individual stocks or financial instruments. Such decisions, of course, should be made with a full understanding of risks and returns, and be made in accordance with one's own investment profile. Investments in mainland Chinese stocks in China versus H-shares or red chips in Hong Kong, versus overseas-listed Chinese companies can be dramatically different. Investing in China and Chinese companies is largely closed to non-Chinese investors, and complicated by the *yuan's* non-convertibility.

That said, the *growth engines, turbochargers, roadmap* and *supertrends* offer many ideas for forming investment strategies keyed to China's future growth potential.

When it comes to the *growth engines*, these become indicators of a good investment, in particular the *consumption growth engine*. Companies that target Chinese consumers may benefit from the development of China's growing middle- and affluent classes. By the same token, Western companies that are still making quality *foreign direct investments* into China may be seen as more proactive or committed to China strategies and stand to benefit more from China's growth than companies that do not. The *exporting growth engine* is a positive indicator for Chinese companies that are expanding overseas under their own brands.

The *turbochargers* are, as with the previous section for businesspeople, indicators of a more powerful *growth engine* or *supertrend* effect. The *reverse globalization turbocharger* may mean looking for companies and ideas that originate in China and are just starting to become popular abroad. Little Sheep Hotpot was clearly attractive to Yum! Brands not only for its Chinese presence but its growing overseas success.

A company that is *leapfrogging* its competitors may be able to disrupt a larger incumbent's business model. For example, China Mobile is the test bed for China's newest mobile communication technology. While TD-SCDMA has not caught on, perhaps TD-LTE (a so-called 4G high-speed technology) will.

The *Chinese determination turbocharger* is also an interesting indicator. Many Chinese companies are young, established within the last decade or two. They are often helmed by strong personalities, many of whom went through hardships to build their companies under extremely risky conditions. They are *determined* to succeed. Entrepreneurs such as Suntech's Shi Zhengrong, Huawei's Ren Zhengfei, or BYD's Wang Chuanfu are examples of this. Their leadership hand is inspirational to their employees, but their companies are sometimes overly dependent on them.

Finally, the *supertrends* can indicate the places where China's highest growth can be found, especially when they overlap with the *roadmap* or *turbochargers*. A *supertrend* may form the basis for a sector-based investment strategy—such as China's solar industry for the *sustainability supertrend,* or China's heavy machinery industry for the *urbanization supertrend.*

For example, a company featured prominently in *Supertrends of Future China* in 2008 was Chinese search engine Baidu. Then struggling to monetize its service compared with industry leader Google, it was also plagued with copyright infringement claims. Its stock had done well since launching on the NASDAQ in 2005, but it was strongly underperforming Google. Baidu was, in fact, much better positioned in China than Google to take advantage of the *consumption growth engine.* China's Internet users were then starting to increase by 70 million or more each year. Baidu's founder Robin Li, a *haigui* returnee Chinese, was prototypical of the new Chinese entrepreneur: smart, young and overseas educated. In other words, Li was a person who was able to bring home a new business model and use *Sinification* to make it a hit with Chinese users. Baidu had more features Chinese users wanted. Baidu was operating as a social media pioneer under the *Inter-networking supertrend* (described in the second volume of the *China Supertrends* series, *China's Demographic Supertrends*), a combination of the Internet and the Chinese concept of *guanxi.* By 2012, its stock had appreciated nearly five times from its 2008 levels.

The key to what I call Supertrends Investing is modeling how the concepts in this book can align together to form an investment strategy that is based on China's growth.

FOR INDIVIDUALS

In my presentations to groups inside and outside China, one question individuals often ask is, *should I work in China?* The question is asked by young and old, Chinese and foreign nationality, students and seasoned professionals. I have also written frequently on this topic and spoken to hundreds of readers seeking knowledge about how to align their career with China's growth. The *China supertrends* provide an answer.

Again, a proviso, only *you* know what is best for your career and what will make you happy. For me, my career in China has been rewarding in every way and I highly recommend working in China to most people I speak to. Aligning your career to the concepts in the book involves a series of steps.

First, a realization must be made that China is drastically different from the conceptions and stereotypes often held abroad. Several political commercials during the 2012 Republican presidential primaries used anti-China sentiments. One, against Jon Huntsman, a former U.S. ambassador to China, showed him speaking Chinese, questioned whether he had "American values" and even portrayed him as Chairman Mao. Another advertisement by a U.S. Senate candidate in Michigan showed an American-Chinese actress speaking broken English riding a bicycle through rice paddies with farmers in the background.

There is no better way to understand how different China is from these common misperceptions than to visit and see for yourself. It is critical to have the right mindset and expectations about China before making a major career move.

Second, China in the first decade of this century was welcoming to foreign expatriate managers and not especially picky about things like Mandarin-speaking ability. Today, many MNCs are localizing their workforces to the point that even managers of MNCs are usually local hires. This has several implications: finding a job from outside of China is difficult; an ability to speak Mandarin and understand local culture is preferred, if not crucial; and managerial positions are harder to come by and highly competitive due to the greater number of qualified Chinese applicants as well as the increased desirability of a posting in China.

Finally, aligning one's education and career path to the *supertrends* must be done carefully. The Olympic Decade will end in 2018 but educational or career decisions can last a lifetime. A strong self-understanding of your goals and how they might fit with the growth of China can be attained only after much research and planning.

So, what exactly is a *China supertrends career?* The *growth engines* indicate changing priorities in the Chinese economy, but they are too broad for specific career planning purposes. Instead, the *growth engines* can be general indicators. For example, one might plan one's career around the *consumption growth engine* by learning how to communicate in Mandarin. This would make one more effective as a marketer at understanding the needs of Chinese consumers, or perhaps as a provider of better service to the millions of Chinese tourists who will travel abroad by the end of the Olympic Decade.

*Turbochargers*, likewise, are indicators of the *speed* of development of a career option, but may not be useful in deciding which career choice is best. For example, *reverse globalization* tells you that the tourists mentioned in the previous paragraph will increase quickly in the remainder of the Olympic Decade. This means that, if you want to learn Mandarin, taking an intensive six-month course with six hours of study a day in immersion in China will give you the best chance of success.

The *roadmap* and *supertrends* themselves offer some of the best ideas for career development. In particular, the Preferred Industries list is an indicator of which specific areas China wants to develop. If your existing skill can be applied to an industry in the *preferred* category, China might invite you to be a "Foreign Expert," able to collect subsidies and bonuses for agreeing to live and work in China. China's strategic emerging industries are long-term, so the chances are good that education in this area will be a highly sought employment factor. There are no guarantees, but China's strategic industries will be around five, even 10 years from now, given the billions of dollars being invested in them today.

The *supertrends* themselves offer the greatest wealth of employment opportunities. For example, city planners, engineers and architects might find work under China's *urbanization supertrend* working on one of the many new eco-city projects. The *new manufacturing supertrend* requires expertise in areas such as health, safety and environment, Six Sigma, Total Quality

Management, and so on. The *sustainability supertrend* requires technologists, scientists and engineers specializing in clean technology. China's clean technology manufacturers need foreign salespeople to cover all the overseas markets that are buying China's solar and wind energy equipment. The *affluence supertrend* will need more non-Chinese executives and managers who can operate overseas as China's companies go abroad. For these executives, being able to speak Mandarin and understand the Chinese culture will allow them to communicate effectively with the China headquarters. For people who are not looking at a corporate job, there are other options for working in China.

While entrepreneurship in China is frequently highly competitive, China is a land of entrepreneurs and home to the attitude that *if there is a will, there is a way.* Many returnee Chinese (such as Baidu's Robin Li) have never looked back to their adopted overseas homes, finding extraordinary success in their homeland. Non-Chinese have been successful as well, in almost every industry that is open to foreign ownership. Some run popular restaurants; others have established Internet startups that have even gone public on the NASDAQ.

For new graduates, there are plenty of suitable jobs as well, including internships at some of the world's top companies. These assignments are now highly sought after. Other typical entry-level jobs are plentiful in China, including working as an English teacher in the English as a Second Language industry. China's children are increasingly learning English from an early age, a topic that will be covered in *China's Demographic Supertrends.* However, jobs at the entry-level in MNCs and Chinese companies are increasingly being staffed by some of the millions of new Chinese graduates China produces each year. They work at salary levels ($300–$500 a month) that are far lower than what Western university graduates could expect in their home countries.

I remain optimistic that any person with the desire, the passion and the ability will be able to find a place in China's growing economy.

## FINAL THOUGHTS

In this book you read how the Chinese economy has become rich via the *exporting* and *foreign direct investment growth engines*. Now it is going to get even richer through *consumption*. The first two *growth engines* are not going away during the Olympic Decade, nor will this mark the end of "cheap China," as CNN proclaimed in February 2012. There is simply a restructuring of China's economy and a disruption of established business models. Businesses with an eye on China's growth, even those with increasing costs, will find a way to continue operating there.

This book introduced the first four *supertrends*—the *economic supertrends*. These are the *supertrends* that have the greatest impact on China's economy and, by extension, the global economy. China has today already become the "world's largest" in many ways: it has the largest labor force, it has the most exports, and it even leads the world in consumer goods such as the annual purchase of cars, and the number of mobile phones and Internet users. With growth rates in all of these areas far in excess of most Western countries, it has also already become the world's most *important* economy.

The second book in this series will introduce the *demographic supertrends*, three cultural and societal forces that are going to change not just China, but also the world. China's massive 1.3 billion population has a great impact on everything from the global supply of raw materials, to what media the world is watching, to the number of Chinese students in foreign universities, to travel and health care. Like the *economic supertrends*, the *demographic supertrends* will bring many challenges and opportunities.

The final volume is *China's Political Supertrends*. To be published after the changeover of China's top political leaders (and their policies) in late 2012, this book will cover the final three *supertrends* and show how China's new power is influencing geopolitics. *China's Political Supertrends* will shake the world.

The Olympic Decade, which started August 8, 2008 and will not be over until August 7, 2018, is bringing more changes to China's economy, society and political environment.

If you would like to be notified of when the second and third books in the series are released, please visit the book's official website below and sign up.

Also, special online features are included only on the website, including:

> The China Supertrends Photography Project, a collaborative effort to document the changing face of China's economic, demographic and political situation.

> Video, audio and slideshow presentations for the content in the books.

> Chart data so you can see all the numbers behind the diagrams and make your own charts using the downloadable data sets.

> Free sample chapters from the upcoming two volumes *China's Demographic Supertrends* and *China's Political Supertrends*.

> A Q&A forum for readers to interact with each other and me to discuss issues in the news related to the *supertrends*, questions about the books and general discussion of China-related topics.

> Event listings for upcoming speaking engagements in your area.

> Online listing of endnote entries, PDFs referenced in the book.

> Articles posted on the China Supertrends blog, which include links of interest, new charts and translations of Chinese social media content related to the themes.

All this and more about can be found at the official website:

www.ChinaSupertrends.com

You are invited to join me there to catch the *China Super-trends.*

Jason Inch
March 2012

# NOTES

Regarding these notes, where possible an online reference for articles and research has been provided for easy retrieval by readers. While every effort is made to verify the links prior to publication, some links may change.

Where a widely known fact has been reported in media outlets and is used within the text, a source is generally not provided. Comments or corrections are welcome and may be submitted through the book's website.

A broad range of sources and data from both organizations inside and outside of China has been referenced.

For example, when it comes to academic papers, research from Chinese researchers (based in China), Chinese researchers (overseas), and non-Chinese researchers has been used. Institutional sources cover data from both internal Chinese organizations, such as China's National Development and Reform Commission, and external organizations, such as the World Bank, IMF, CIA Fact Book, WTO and other organizations. Private companies, including think tanks and consulting companies, such as the Peterson Institute, McKinsey, BCG and others are also used. For general statistics, such as GDP, trade and FDI, China's own data are used, typically from the National Bureau of Statistics, Ministry of Finance and Ministry of Commerce. Where possible, a source for the original data set has been cited. Where that data, research or other information was originally in Mandarin, a use of that data or reference in an English-language media report or translation has been provided instead.

Due to the persistent problems of data reliability, underestimates, overestimates, restatements and lack of transparency, readers are reminded that the data in this book are for reference only and should be verified prior to your own use.

## PREFACE

[1] As in the 2006 book by James Kynge, *China Shakes the World: A Titan's Rise and Troubled Future,* the original reference, perhaps lost in translation, attributed to Napoleon who is thought to have compared China to a sleeping giant that, once awakened, would shake the world.
[2] China's national media paid more attention to total gold medals rather than aggregate gold, silver and bronze medals, to imply it was the unofficial winner of the Olympics, a *tour de force* in every way.
[3] Throughout the book, the standard and most recognized translations of common Chinese terms, works and proper names will be used (e.g., Sun Tzu's *Art of War* instead of *sunzi bingfa* or Chiang Kai-shek instead of *Jiang Jieshi*), with the exception of presenting names and other proper nouns in their standardized *pinyin* alphabetic representation according to the current practices (e.g., *Beijing* or *Mao Zedong* rather than Peking or Mao Tse-tung). Chinese words written in *pinyin* will be italicized with the exception of proper names. The use of *pinyin* is the increasingly common practice in Chinese and global media.
[4] In *On China,* Kissinger also makes an interesting comparison of strategy in *weiqi,* the Chinese game of Go, with the strategy of *shi* based on an article by David Lai in "Learning from the Stones: A Go Approach to Mastering China's Strategic Concept, Shi." 2004
[5] Wen reportedly first said in a November 2003 interview with the Washington Post, "Any small problem multiplied by 1.3 billion will end up being a very big problem, and a very big aggregate divided by 1.3 billion will come to a very tiny figure…" Thereafter this became a common talking point, covered in numerous locations, one of which is here: http://english.people.com.cn/200403/04/eng20040304_136505.shtml
[6] *Yuan* is actually the word for the unitary denomination of currency (e.g., 6 *yuan renminbi).* The other units are *yi* (100 million*), wan* (ten thousand), *qian* (one thousand), *bai* (one hundred), *yuan* (one), *mao* (0.1), and fen (0.01), *Renminbi* (RMB), then, is the "People's Currency," so a correct usage would be to say "30 million *yuan renminbi,"* i.e., "30 million units of People's Currency." On foreign currency markets, the Chinese currency is known as the Chinese Yuan (CNY) as in "CNY 30 million." For readability and consistency, herein *yuan* will be used to represent both *renminbi* and CNY, and any amounts where the original number was in *yuan* will be listed with their U.S. dollar conversions as "30 million *yuan* ($4.8 million)." All monetary figures will be converted at the prevailing rate in January 2012 of 6.3 *yuan*/$ except where noted and except where used in historical data. U.S. Dollars will be used for all other numbers as well as statistics commonly reported in dollars, e.g., GDP

## INTRODUCTION

[1] *On China,* Henry Kissinger, 2011: Chapter 9.

[2] A title that has been more recently been conferred on Japan due to its post-bubble economy's "lost decade."

[3] The report, On the Development of Chinese Talent in 2006 conducted by the Chinese Academy of Social Sciences, said that a million students had gone abroad between 1978 to 2006.

[4] The slogan, "Some must get rich first" was attributed to Deng many times starting about 1978, at the time of the first economic reforms, sometimes in reference to places, sometimes in reference to people. It is variously translated into English based on the translator, as is another common expression attributed to Deng, "To get rich is glorious."

[5] In the 1970s Chinese couples averaged six children before the one-child policy, a rate which has been reduced to an average of 1.8 children per couple at present. There are a number of circumstances in China where multiple children are allowed: Rural families whose first child is a girl, is disabled, or who pay a fine can have a second child. Urban dwellers can have multiple children if a fine is paid or, more recently, if both parents came from single-child families themselves. These multiple effects have probably created a mini-baby boom starting in 2007 as the eligible children reached marriageable age right about then and people aimed for Olympic Babies (having a child born in 2008) all at the same time.

[6] Counterfeit parts have been found everywhere, including within the U.S. defense industry. In just one example in 2011, fake parts were found in a Boeing aircraft, see "China Counterfeit Parts in U.S. Military Boeing, L3 Aircraft," Bloomberg, Tony Capaccio, Nov. 8, 2011: http://www.businessweek.com/news/2011-11-18/china-counterfeit-parts-in-u-s-military-boeing-l3-aircraft.html

[7] Before the 2009 campaign began, many high-profile cases of bribery were only uncovered when it was politically expedient, as in the case of Shanghai's former mayor Chen Guangyu. The more-recent anti-corruption campaign launched by Hu has been more practical and far-reaching. See: "Billions Uncovered in Campaign Against China's 'Covert Coffers'," Wall Street Journal Asia, Brian Spegele, Jan. 18, 2012: http://blogs.wsj.com/chinarealtime/2012/01/18/billions-uncovered-in-campaign-against-covert-coffers/?mod=WSJBlog

[8] The World Bank's Chief Economist, Justin Lin, an esteemed academic from China, once calculated that as early as 2030 China's GDP could be 2.5 times the size of the U.S.'s and its per capita income half that of the U.S.'s, compared to about 1/20th now, in the May 2008 Chinese-edition of Harvard Business Review, as referenced in China Daily, May 3 2008, "GDP could be 2.5 times that of the U.S. by 2030": http://www.chinadaily.com.cn/china/2008-05/03/content_6657813.htm

[9] According to a story in *The Economist,* May 1st 2008, "An aberrant abacus," print edition.

[10] For more information about China's GDP, GDP per capita and other economic statistics, see the National Bureau of Statistics website at http://www.stats.gov.cn/english/ and the China Statistical Yearbook published by the NBS.

[11] With exception of three years when growth of GDP was 5.2 percent or less, China has maintained 7 percent or greater growth (sometimes as high as 15 percent) for the last 30 years.

[12] Shanghai is reported to be the city most affected in China by land subsidence, according to the Chinese Ministry of Land and Resources, reported via Xinhua, February 10, 2007, "Chinese Cities Suffer Land Subsidence":
http://china.org.cn/english/news/199613.htm

## CHAPTER ONE

[1] The so-called "China price" was written about in a book of the same name by Alexandra Harney (*The China Price: The True Cost of Chinese Competitive Advantage,* 2009) and "the end of cheap China" is also the name of a book (*The End of Cheap China,* 2012) by Shaun Rein.

[2] Data from the China Customs and CIA World Factbook:
http://www.e-to-china.com/2012/0207/99876.html
and
https://www.cia.gov/library/publications/the-world-factbook/rankorder/2078rank.html

[3] In part to appease U.S. trade negotiators and reduce the amount of the trade imbalance, China cut or abolished a number of export rebate programs in 2007, and reduce the number of low-tech labor-intensive products it sells to the United States via export limits. This article from Bloomberg summarizes some of the changes, July 25, 2007, "China to Limit Exports of Labor-Intensive Products":
http://www.bloomberg.com/apps/news?pid=20601080&refer=Asia&sid=a9c64IDUkhpo

[4] NAFTA was once thought of as a strong three-way partnership between the United States, Canada and Mexico, wherein Mexico played the part of the factory. The three countries were one another's largest trading partners. Now, Mexico has lost its cost advantage to China, and China has surpassed it as the U.S.'s second -largest trading partner. In 2008, Democratic presidential candidates Barack Obama and Hillary Clinton were openly criticizing the NAFTA agreement on the basis of lost jobs.

[5] Niall Ferguson. The Ascent of Money: A Financial History of the World (Kindle Locations 4576-4577). Penguin. Kindle Edition.

[6] The latest information on China's tax incentives and mitigating policies at the time of writing are summarized at the China website of PricewaterhouseCoopers here:
http://www.pwccn.com/home/eng/chinatax_news_mar2008_2.html

A summary of China's new unified corporate tax, effective from 2008, and the associated policies to reduce the shock to foreign companies that were previously attracted by low tax rates, can be found via China Daily, December 30 2007, "Policies to cushion impact of new corporate income tax law":
http://www.chinadaily.com.cn/china/2007-12/30/content_6360500.htm

[7] Bloomberg.com, January 11, 2011, "Foreign Direct Investment in China in 2010 Rises to Record $105.7 Billion ":
http://www.bloomberg.com/news/2011-01-18/foreign-direct-investment-in-china-in-2010-rises-to-record-105-7-billion.html

[8] The reform and opening up policy, the *gaige kaifang* ( 改革开放), is actually not a single all-encompassing policy but a series of related steps that, taken together, are referred to as such. In fact, many of the policies were not the sole actions of Deng but were based on earlier calls for reform, notably by Zhou Enlai before his death in 1976. Deng's support for the general idea of reform was one of the reasons he had been purged by Mao. When Deng came back into power in 1978, he again threw his support behind the ideas of reform and opening up and, this time, was successful.

[9] Whether these are NTBs, retaliation against certain countries or companies, or actual quality problems, China has actually caught hundreds of foreign imported products that do not meet its stringent quality standards. Pure spring water is perhaps the most counter-intuitive product that would be caught by such regulations. Cosmetics are another frequent target: even some of the top luxury cosmetic brands have been caught by China's quality watchdogs.

[10] As reported by China's National Development and Reform Commission, referring to the period between the opening of China in 1978 to 2007, on the government's official website, May 6, 2008, "Official: most of world's top companies invest in China":
http://english.gov.cn/2008-05/06/content_962250.htm

[11] Or $83 billion total, if financial portfolio investments in real estate, stocks and so on are included. The amount of portfolio investment as a component of the total is relatively low because China still restricts many kinds of foreign investment in mainland stocks and real estate. Therefore, unlike in many developed countries that allow access to their capital markets, most foreign investments in China are non-portfolio investments and are used for things such as building factories, or providing operating capital for joint or wholly owned ventures.

[12] WOFE, the acronym for wholly owned foreign enterprises, is popularly pronounced "woofy," though the official term from the Chinese government is WFOE—meaning a wholly foreign-owned enterprise—possibly because "woofy" sounds undignified. Few know how to pronounce WFOE anyway, which perhaps not entirely unintentionally includes the word "foe."

[13] For another look at the same story, *Mr. China* is written by Tim Clissold, a former employee of Perkowski's.

[14] The World Bank report, titled "China Governance, Investment Climate, and Harmonious Society: Competitiveness Enhancements for 120 Cities in China" October 8, 2006, can be found at:
http://siteresources.worldbank.org/INTCHINA/Resources/318862-1121421293578/120cities_en.pdf
Also, see a related report, also from the World Bank, "China 2030: Building a Modern, Harmonious, and Creative High-Income Society" February 27, 2012:
http://www-wds.worldbank.org/external/default/WDSContentServer/WDSP/IB/2012/0 2/28/000356161_20120228001303/Rendered/PDF/671790WP0P127500Chi na020300complete.pdf
[15] The Atlantic online, November 2009, "The Nine Nations of China":
http://www.theatlantic.com/magazine/archive/2009/11/the-nine-nations-of-china/7769/
[16] See research from China Center for Economic Research. Justin Yifu Lin, February 2004, "Is China's Growth Real and Sustainable?":
http://www.asianperspective.org/articles/v28n3-a.pdf
Also, "Consumer Durables Ownership [in China] 1990 - 2002":
http://www.chinability.com/Durables.htm
[17] To be sure, Rovio is not the only company making video games that are popular in China, and many other mobile apps, such as Fruit Ninja, have achieved prodigious amounts of downloads, but Rovio is unique in two ways. It is embracing China with localized offerings for China, and it is going to deploy a multi-channel strategy of partnerships, marketing campaigns and retail. See: "Angry Birds' Peter Vesterbacka: If Disney Were Alive Today, He Would Be Making Games For The iPhone," TechCrunch.com, Alexia Tsotsis, Nov. 5, 2011:
http://techcrunch.com/2011/11/05/angry-birds-creator-if-disney-were-alive-today-he-would-be-making-games-for-the-iphone/
Also, "Rovio Plans to Open 200 Angry Birds Merchandise Stores in China," MICGadget.com, Star Chang, June 27, 2011:
http://micgadget.com/13323/rovio-plans-to-open-200-angry-birds-merchandise-stores-in-china/
[18] Data source, China's National Bureau of Statistics. More information can be found about China's second-, third- and fourth-tier city business expansion in the following articles: China Daily, via Xinhuanet, June 29, 2007, "Real estate focus turns to China's secondary cities":
http://news.xinhuanet.com/english/2007-06/29/content_6306920.htm

## CHAPTER TWO

[1] For more information, see "Culture to be pillar industry," China Daily, February 17, 2012:
http://www.chinaipr.gov.cn/newsarticle/news/government/201202/1279682_1.html

[2] During the Cultural Revolution (1966–1976), Mao attempted to eradicate old culture, old customs, old habits, and old ideas—with disastrous results. Academics were ostracized, youth sent to the countryside for re-education in order to understand the working class, and numerous symbols, structures and items of historical significance were destroyed.

[3] Also see the GLOBE Project:
http://business.nmsu.edu/programs-centers/globe/

[4] See the Confucius Institute Online for more information:
http://english.chinese.cn

[5] A discussion of the Mandate of Heaven—the Emperor's God-given assent to govern, which could be lost and gained resulting in the fall and rise of new rulers or Dynasties—will be covered in *China's Political Supertrends*. For an excellent discussion of the Mandate of Heaven, see Henry Kissinger's *On China*.

[6] The Great Leap Forward was a disastrous policy of speeded-up industrialization to catch up with the West. Implemented around 1958, it required farmers to be more efficient—beyond their capability, in fact—resulting in bizarre practices, such as establishing backyard mills for making steel, dumping fertilizer into large pits with piles of seeds and killing sparrows by clanking cookware until the scared birds died from exhaustion, in an effort to increase crop yields. The consequences of this policy were mass starvation. The Cultural Revolution (1966–1976) is described in this chapter's Endnote 5. A discussion of both these events will be covered in *China's Demographic Supertrends*, and *China's Political Supertrends*. Curious readers can see Richard McGreggor's *The Party*, for a recent discussion on the Great Leap Forward. For a film adaptation of the atmosphere during the Cultural Revolution, Chen Kaige's *Farewell My Concubine* and Zhang Yimou's *To Live* both have segments covering the period.

## CHAPTER THREE

[1] Showing amazing support and coordination between government and industry, the iron industry cut production by 29 million tons, above its target by 7 million tons, which the steel industry missed its target yet still cut a 15 million tons. The National Planning Office and Ministry of Finance assisted by providing incentives and support to the affected provinces to offset lost tax revenue and employ displaced workers.

[2] In 2007, state media reported China closed 553 coal generators, according to Xinhua, January 2 2008, "China exceeds target in closing 43 percent small coal-fired plants":
http://www.ccchina.gov.cn/en/NewsInfo.asp?NewsId=10367
In 2008, the country continued its campaign, shutting 83 smaller coal generators in the first quarter, according to Chinese state media, April 25 2008, "Gov't shuts 83 small coal-fired power plants":
http://www.china.org.cn/environment/policies_announcements/2008-04/25/content_15015693.htm

[3] The feed-in tariff rates in a country as large as China are complex and at times contradictorily reported in China's media. One point on which all media agree in 2012 is that solar tariffs have been introduced to encourage more building of solar energy installations. At the same time, wind power has been deprecated for being overbuilt during the last five years. Consequently, its previous preferential feed-in tariff has been reduced or eliminated.

## CHAPTER FOUR

[1] The concept of a *supertrend,* as with the *growth engines* and *turbochargers,* will also appear in the following two volumes of this series, *China's Demographic Supertrends* and *China's Political Supertrends.* The term *supertrend* was picked with respect to John Naisbitt, who coined the term *megatrend* in his widely read 1982 book *Megatrends* and, a year after the original *Supertrends of Future China* was published in 2008, published *China's Megatrends,* co-authored with his wife Doris, in 2009.
[2] Numerous such studies have been done by industry specialists, reporters, and academics. The study we used is titled *Who Captures Value in a Global Innovation System?: The case of Apple's iPod,* from the University of California, Irvine—Greg Linden, Kenneth L. Kraemer and Jason Dedrick, and can be found at:
http://escholarship.org/uc/item/1770046n
An updated study, concerning the iPhone and iPad, by the same authors was published in 2011, with similar conclusions: most of the value and benefit is to the U.S. economy and not to Chinese economy. See:
http://pcic.merage.uci.edu/papers/2011/Value_iPad_iPhone.pdf
[3] Statistics from China's State Intellectual Property Office:
http://english.sipo.gov.cn/statistics/2011/12/
[4] If there is no basis for calculation of a compensatory award due to lack of information or some other issue, a maximum discretionary award of 500,000 *yuan* ($79,000) per case (rather than per infringement as is often used in the U.S.) is allowed.
[5] There is no official figure for the amount of new jobs that need to be created, but typical Chinese government announcements in the last several years for urban jobs needed are between 8–10 million a year, while an additional 10–14 million yearly are needed for rural residents. These estimates are based on the number of new graduates from universities and high schools, the number of expected layoffs from inefficient state-owned enterprises, modest population growth, the amount of migrants moving to the cities (i.e. urbanization rate) etc. See: Speech by Chinese Ambassador to the United Kingdom Fu Ying's speech to the Royal Society of the Arts, November 23, 2007:
http://www.fmprc.gov.cn/ce/ceuk/eng/sghd/t383809.htm

Also, notes on Hu Jintao's meeting with United States President Bush, also by Fu Ying in a March 2008 speech to the University of Kent: http://www.fmprc.gov.cn/ce/ceuk/eng/sghd/t416383.htm
[6] Accurate information about the number of migrant workers is, of course, hard to come by as many of them are unregistered and do not want to be found. Guangdong province, which includes major manufacturing cities such as Guangzhou, Shenzhen, and Dongguan, is estimated to have more than 26 million migrant workers, according to the Guangdong Provincial Department of Labor and Social Security.
[7] An interesting demographic trend is that if it weren't for all the younger migrants who have moved to Shanghai and had children in the last decade, there might not have been enough workers for the service industry as registered Shanghainese skew older than migrants. The aging of China's urban population will be discussed further in the *China's Demographic Supertrends*.
[8] A NASA study released in March 2008 shows clear evidence by satellite imaging of how particulate pollution spreads from China to other parts of the world via air currents in as little as ten days, according to Geology.com, March 2008, "Satellite Measures Pollution From East Asia to North America": http://geology.com/nasa/monitoring-pollution-by-satellite.shtml

CHAPTER FIVE

[1] American Chamber of Commerce in Shanghai 2010–2011 China Business Report
[2] Naturally, wages had gone up in nominal terms, but during those 30 years inflation was also quite high. Real wages are those after taking out the effect of inflation.
[3] A Gallup poll of Chinese households in 2005 said "half of all [China's roughly 400 million] households owned a VCD player," a figure including both traditional VCD and the newer SVCD models, as reported in "Chinese families double their incomes in 10 years," China Daily, January 12, 2005: http://www.chinadaily.com.cn/english/doc/2005-01/12/content_408150.htm
[4] Parts of this case study adapted from "Optical Storage In China: A Study in Strategic Industrial Policy," Greg Linden, September 2003 For additional information on the VCD and SVCD standards, as well as their adoption in Asia, see "Video CD," Wikipedia: http://en.wikipedia.org/wiki/Video_CD and also "Super Video CD," Wikipedia: http://en.wikipedia.org/wiki/Super_Video_CD
[5] The licensing fee initially required by Sony, Philips and other rights-holders was considered too high ($15–20) by many Chinese DVD manufacturers. Many simply did not pay. They sold their hardware exclusively in

China and in places where the rights-holders were unlikely to sue. However, as the prices for DVD hardware came down to the sub-$100 level and below, the fees were negotiated down to a level the Chinese manufacturers would agree to pay, under $5 per player.

[6] See "Homegrown CBHD discs outsell Blu-ray by 3-1 margin in China," Ars Technica, August 2009:
http://arstechnica.com/business/news/2009/08/homegrown-cbhd-discs-outsell-blu-ray-by-3-1-margin-in-china.ars

[7] For more information about CH-DVD, see the Wikipedia entry:
http://en.wikipedia.org/wiki/China_Blue_High-definition_Disc
press release from Tsinghua University's Optical Memory National Engineering Research Center (Mandarin version) on ZDNet China:
http://stor-age.zdnet.com.cn/stor-age/2007/0907/495410.shtml
Also, a story based on a translation here:
http://www.tech2.com/india/news/optical-drives/china-develops-new-hddvd-format/15671/0

[8] See "China rolls out low-cost Maglev trains," China Development Gateway, January 21, 2012:
http://en.chinagate.cn/2012-01/21/content_24459000.htm

[9] See "Emerging Markets Driving Commodity Prices Increase In 2011," Gourmet Coffee Lovers, Dan Harrington, April 2, 2011:
http://www.gourmetcoffeelovers.com/emerging-markets-driving-commodity-prices-increase-in-2011/

[10] There are conflicting reports of whether China was, in 2011, the world's biggest market for luxury goods or number two. Where reports do not list China as number one, they all agree that China will be number one within two to three years at most. See "China becomes world's second-largest luxury market," People's Daily Online, May 26, 2011:
http://english.peopledaily.com.cn/90001/90776/90882/7372293.html
For China's growth to number one, see:
http://www.clsa.com/about-clsa/media-centre/2011-media-releases/china-to-become-the-worlds-largest-market-for-luxury-goods.php
and
http://www.wantchinatimes.com/news-subclass-cnt.aspx?id=20110403000004&cid=1102
China has already become the world's number one market for luxury goods as of 2012:
http://news.xinhuanet.com/english/china/2012-01/21/c_131372046.htm

[11] BIOS—the *basic input/output system*—is found on the CPU chips that form part of the hardware of a computer's motherboard. In order to make a clone of the IBM PC that was fully compatible (so all software would run on it and third-party hardware could connect to it), the hardware and the BIOS had to be in the same configuration as an IBM PC—an IPR violation if manufactured in this way without licensing. By redesigning the BIOS from the ground up to allow the same functions as an IBM PC's BIOS (albeit in a different way, in order to avoid IPR violations itself), other

manufacturers' PCs could run all the same software on a variety of hardware but avoid paying licensing to IBM. IBM wrongly believed that all the value of a PC was in the hardware and famously allowed Microsoft to license MS-DOS to anybody that wanted it, giving birth to the WINTEL—Windows / Intel—partnership that came to define a PC as virtually indistinct from an IBM PC, i.e, a clone.

[12] Parts of this case study came from the following sources:
Regarding the M3 and M6 MP3 players:
http://en.wikipedia.org/wiki/Meizu_M3_Music_Card
And:
http://en.wikipedia.org/wiki/Meizu_M6_miniPlayer
Regarding Meizu's smartphones, the first model was originally called Mini One, and profiled in a Popular Science article, August 7 2007, "China's iClone":
http://www.popsci.com/iclone
Other sources:
http://www.electronista.com/articles/10/10/09/apple.stops.meizu.over.m8.cloning.dispute/
http://www.electronista.com/articles/10/10/10/apples.jobs.explains.meizu.shut.down/
http://www.meizume.com/general-meizu-m8/12293-steve-jobs-own-words.html
http://www.electronista.com/articles/10/11/14/firm.wants.apples.chinese.iphone.patents.invalid/
http://en.meizu.com/products/mx-specifications.html

[13] How enterprises can qualify as high-tech industries and R&D centers is something of a complicated process, and the system is manipulated by many companies that would otherwise not be considered high-tech or R&D elsewhere in the world in order to gain the tax credits. For example, token researchers might be hired but there is no legitimate effort at R&D. For readers interested in the tax credits specifically, a summary and more information can be found at China Briefing:
http://www.china-briefing.com/news/2011/12/12/china-to-offer-incentives-to-its-high-tech-cultural-industries.html

[14] The story is long and somewhat convoluted, arising as it does in a virtual world, but has nevertheless attracted much real world publicity. Anshe Chung Studio's published a press release announcing Graef's millionaire status:
http://www.anshechung.com/include/press/press_release251106.html
The company and entrepreneur were profiled in BusinessWeek:
http://www.businessweek.com/magazine/content/06_18/b3982001.htm
They were also profiled on earlier at CNN, "The Virtual Rockefeller":
http://money.cnn.com/magazines/business2/business2_archive/2005/12/01/8364581/index.htm?cnn=yes

[15] The facility, which had been discussed for many years, broke ground on May 15th 2007, according to the Tianjin Free Trade Zone website, May 29,

2007, "Tianjin Assembly Line of Airbus A320 Series Airplane goes into operation on 15th May":
http://www2.tjftz.gov.cn/system/2007/05/29/010011906.shtml

## CHAPTER SIX

[1] Wu and Yang were married; the wife and husband may have different surnames in China. The wife generally keeps her own maiden family name, according to general custom.
[2] More information about the "nail house" can be found on numerous media sites, it was front-page news in many Chinese publications for its precedent-setting events. One summary from the Asia Times:
http://www.atimes.com/atimes/China_Business/IC31Cb01.html
[3] See "Beijing plans new residence permit," February 2, 2012:
http://english.sina.com/china/2012/0201/436559.html
[4] It is all a rather complicated system, with the full rules being listed in the following article:
"Beijing's new traffic rules surprise some drivers," China Daily, Luo Yujie, January 5, 2011:
http://www.chinadaily.com.cn/bizchina/2011-01/05/content_11798638.htm
[5] More information on the Three Gorges Project can be found at the official website:
http://www.ctgpc.com/
Or, the Wikipedia entry for Three Gorges Dam:
http://en.wikipedia.org/wiki/Three_Gorges_Dam
[6] The travel occurs mostly as a result of China's 240 million migrant workers, who all want to go home for the holidays. The travel is often long and hard, as profiled in the *Last Train Home,* a documentary about China's migrant workers as seen through a single family's trials to become more prosperous. Bad weather, as happened in 2008 when a major blizzard disrupted the train network and electrical grid, can create havoc for millions of people. Ticket scalpers are another constant source of trouble for the travelers, though in 2012 the Railway Ministry introduced a real name ticket system in an effort to reduce the effects of scalping. Data from China's State Council Information Office.
[7] Global Times, October 27, 2011, "China's high-speed black hole"
[8] Daily Telegraph, Malcolm Moore, July 11, 2011, "Chinese motorway collapses after just two days":
http://www.telegraph.co.uk/news/worldnews/asia/china/8629905/Chinese-motorway-collapses-after-just-two-days.html

## CHAPTER SEVEN

[1] China accelerated its use of coal generation in 2006 and 2007, introducing dozens of new coal power plants a year even while shuttering some of the older, less efficient ones.
China's energy generation by source and other statistics can be found at the U.S. Department of Energy's China page:
http://www.eia.gov/countries/country-data.cfm?fips=CH
[2] More information on the Yangtze white dolphin, the *Baiji*, can be found at its Wikipedia page:
http://en.wikipedia.org/wiki/Baiji
[3] China has the world's third largest reserves of coal after the United States and Russia. It is the world's largest producer and consumer due to its coal-intensive power generation policy. For more information see, the Wikipedia pages on Major Coal Producing Regions:
http://en.wikipedia.org/wiki/Major_coal_producing_regions#China
World Coal Reserves page:
http://en.wikipedia.org/wiki/Coal#World_coal_reserves
[4] According to the Beijing Olympics official website, January 27, 2007, "Beijing strives for reducing energy consumption":
http://en.beijing2008.cn/35/33/article214013335.shtml
[5] Regarding increase in blue sky days, see Xinhua, May 2, 2008, "Beijing reports more 'blue sky' days in first four months":
http://news.xinhuanet.com/english/2008-05/02/content_8090524.htm
[6] For more information about the planned pollution controls to be used during the Olympics, see New York Times, January 24, 2008, "Smoggy Beijing Plans to Cut Traffic by Half for Olympics, Paper Says":
http://www.nytimes.com/2008/01/24/world/asia/24beijing.html
And via Xinhua, March 6, 2008, "Beijing still Mulling Timing of Vehicle-cut Measure":
http://english.cri.cn/3100/2008/03/06/189@330744.htm
[7] Some of the companies on the list included cement firms, mining companies, and chemical producers. The list was made public in China's 21st Century Herald newspaper, via Sina.com.cn (Mandarin), February 26, 2008:
http://news.sina.com.cn/c/2008-02-26/092015020772.shtml
English translation of the above article can be found at China Digital Times:
http://chinadigitaltimes.net/2008/02/green-securities-act-blocks-10-polluting-public-companies/
[8] The case of Wuxi and Tai Lake is the exception rather than the rule when it comes to the government getting tough, but it is a very concrete example that things can change. For years Wuxi had hosted polluting factories and drew its economic livelihood from them, but the pollution was just too much. More details can be found from China's state-run media:
http://www.china.org.cn/english/environment/227180.htm
Details of the pollution blacklist can be found at:
http://www.china.org.cn/archive/2007-07/31/content_1219199.htm

[9] Information from various government sources, including Ministry of Environmental Protection.
And, Wikipedia, "Water resources of the People's Republic of China": http://en.wikipedia.org/wiki/Water_resources_of_China
[10] For more about China's north/south water imbalance, see People's Daily, March 10, 2001, "Northern China is One of World's Most Water Deficient Areas":
http://english.people.com.cn/english/200103/10/eng20010310_64651.html
Information about China's drying rivers can be found at Newsweek, April 15, 2007, "Where China's Rivers Run Dry":
http://www.thedailybeast.com/newsweek/2007/04/15/where-china-s-rivers-run-dry.html
[11] The current plight of the Yellow River is dire, two recent reports have noted: National Geographic, May 2008, "Bitter Waters: Can China save the Yellow—its Mother River?":
http://ngm.nationalgeographic.com/2008/05/china/yellow-river/larmer-text
Also, see New York Times, November 19, 2006, "A Troubled River Mirrors China's Path to Modernity":
http://www.nytimes.com/2006/11/19/world/asia/19yellowriver.html?_r=1&oref=slogin
[12] In fact, China's National Development and Reform Commission says the national target is 150 million square meters by 2010, and by 2020 should hit 300 million square meters, providing hot water to hundreds of millions of people, according to official Chinese website.
[13] Bloomberg, Stephan Nicola, January 3, 2012, "LDK Solar Enters German Market":
http://www.bloomberg.com/news/2012-01-02/ldk-solar-enters-german-market-adds-technology-with-sunways-bid.html
[14] Information about Suntech Power via is official website:
http://am.suntech-power.com/en/about.html
[15] On increasing the national target for wind power generation to 100,000 MW by 2020, see Shanghai Daily via Xinhuanet.com, April 28, 2008, "Fanning wind power capacity":
http://news.xinhuanet.com/english/2008-04/28/content_8065702.htm

CHAPTER EIGHT

[1] The U.S.'s savings rate is essentially zero or below zero because it imports more than it produces. The figure for China's consumers' savings rate is widely reported, though varies depending on the source, but generally always greater than 50 percent.
[2] Figures vary depending on the source, the Chinese National Bureau of Statistics has the 2007 increase in pork price as high as 48.3 percent, while other sources were lower. One thing is certain, China's overall inflation

increase was due in large part to increases in food and agricultural commodities.
From Xinhua:
http://news.xinhuanet.com/english/2008-01/30/content_7527600.htm
[3] To assist the transition from a single fixed government price to free
market pricing in the 1980s, the *dual pricing system* was put into place for
many commodities. Under the system, the government had an official price
for goods it would purchase under a mandatory quota, and there was a
second, floating, market price which could be used for excess production
above the quota. A farmer, for example, could choose to sell their entire
production to the government at the fixed price, or sell just the quota to the
government and then sell the rest at the (usually higher) market price, since
many commodities were still in shortage in the 1980s.
[4] Economists and China watchers may be divided as to what is China's
biggest threat currently, but the government is unanimous: The Chinese
Premier, Wen Jiabao, following the announcement of China's 2008 first
quarter economic performance, said in a statement that inflation was
China's biggest threat, and the Deputy Premier Wang Qishan labeled
inflation the biggest economic problem in China and reaffirmed that the
government would maintain a tight monetary policy, according to an
article in the International Herald Tribune, May 9, 2008, "Producer Prices
on the Rise":
http://www.nytimes.com/2008/05/09/business/worldbusiness/09iht-
yuan.1.12728237.html
Economists are divided on whether the inflation is monetary or supply-side
in nature. Food commodity prices have increased rapidly, while efforts to
reign in China's money supply have been insufficient as of early 2008.
[5] Though the Shanghai Composite Index closed off its highs reached in
October 2007, it still closed out the year up 97 percent, according to
Reuters, December 28, 2007, "China stocks end year up 97 pct, uptrend to
slow":
http://www.reuters.com/article/rbssFinancialServicesAndRealEstateNews/i
dUSSHA20340620071228
[6] Tony Tan, a former broker turned *feng shui* master, correctly predicted
the 2007 bull run, and predicted poor performance in the China stock
markets in 2008 at least until April. Coincidentally, China's markets made a
recovery in late April off their lows, whether due to the government
intervention or the *feng shui* forces in the year of the Rat, nobody can really
say. By November 2008, however, all markets were in chaos.
[7] As discussed in the article in Financial Times by Pei Minxin, November 7,
2005, "China Is Paying the Price of Rising Social Unrest":
http://www.carnegieendowment.org/publications/index.cfm?fa=view&id=1
7677&prog=zch
[8] According to the United Nations' Human Development Program report
on *Inequality in Income or Expenditure*, China's Gini index is .469, while the
U.S.'s is .408. These values are relatively close. In Japan, a country that has a

much larger middle class (i.e. less of a wealth gap) the Gini index is only .249. More information can be found at the UN site: http://hdrstats.undp.org/indicators/147.html

[9] Figures in this and the preceding paragraph were calculated at 2007 rates, when there was a slightly weaker *yuan* rate, so an exchange rate of 7.2 *yuan* per dollar was used to convert the numbers in this paragraph into U.S. dollars for purpose of comparison with that year's figure for funds raised in the United States. Also, complications were introduced in calculating the figures from the use of HK$ by some analysts. However, the point that China is near or greater than the United States in terms of public offerings remains valid. For example, Asia Times reports "According to data provided by PricewaterhouseCoopers, the value of IPOs in Shanghai and Shenzhen topped HK$496 billion ($63.5 billion) in 2007 while the United States market raised a total of HK$492 billion. The London Stock Exchange was third, raising HK$387 billion; Hong Kong was fourth with HK$295 billion last year." This means China's IPOs raised more than did United States IPOs.

[10] In Chinese, 农村包围城市, *nongcun baowei chengshi.*

[11] For more information about the global activities and sizes of sovereign wealth funds, see the Sovereign Wealth Fund Institute: http://swfinstitute.org/

Also, more information about China Investment Corporation can be found from a *60 Minutes* report, April 6, 2008, "China Investment An Open Book?": http://www.cbsnews.com/stories/2008/04/04/60minutes/main3993933.shtml

# INDEX